THE CHALLENGE OF OUR TIMES

THE CHALLENGE OF OUR TIMES

Contemporary Trends in Science and Human Affairs
as Seen by Twenty Professors at the
University of Wisconsin

Edited by
FARRINGTON DANIELS
and
THOMAS M. SMITH

KENNIKAT PRESS
Port Washington, N. Y./London

THE CHALLENGE OF OUR TIMES

Copyright 1953 by Farrington Daniels
Reissued in 1971 by Kennikat Press by arrangement
Library of Congress Catalog Card No: 70-118510
ISBN 0-8046-1405-9

Manufactured by Taylor Publishing Company   Dallas, Texas

ESSAY AND GENERAL LITERATURE INDEX REPRINT SERIES

THE CHALLENGE OF OUR TIMES

based on the course

Contemporary Trends in Modern Civilization

at the

University of Wisconsin

by

Eugene P. Boardman
Marshall Clagett
Noble Clark
James F. Crow
Farrington Daniels
Chester V. Easum
A. Campbell Garnett
Fred Harvey Harrington
Charles W. M. Hart

Ralph K. Huitt
C. Leonard Huskins
Mark H. Ingraham
Theodore Morgan
Ralph O. Nafziger
Michael B. Petrovich
Llewellyn Pfankuchen
William B. Sarles
Abbott Payson Usher

Richard Hartshorne

Edited by

Farrington Daniels
and
Thomas M. Smith

INTRODUCTION TO THE REISSUE OF 1971

Nearly two decades ago twenty professors at the University of Wisconsin sought to analyze the world's social and political problems and responsibilities of leadership which the United States inherited. This book sought to show that "it is within our power to guide the future for the benefit of all the people".

Two decades have made improvements but the major challenges still remain. These years have shown excellent support by the government of many areas of basic scientific research and an unprecedented support of its application in such matters as human health and the exploration of outer space. Science is still exerting a powerful influence on our economic, social, and political development. This book attempts to "explain the nature of science", using atomic energy as a specific example, "to point out the role of science in developing technology and to cite the problems that new technology brings into being and the ideas that are offered for their solution". In 1970 this wisdom is even more needed to meet the challenge of today's problems of war, race, population and pollution in which the general public now takes an intense interest and demands solutions.

In 1953 this book pointed out the trouble spots in Southeast Asia, the unequal distribution of wealth among nations, and the struggles between communism and democracy; but progress in meeting these challenges has been slow.

The book cited the important principle that the rights and opportunities of minorities must be guaranteed by the majority just as those of the majority must be respected by the minorities. We have seen the serious difficulties that arise when this principle is violated.

The book emphasized the problem of the rapid expansion of the world's population beyond the capability of the world's resources, a problem now universally recognized with its allied problem of our over-crowded cities. There are still challenges to meet.

The need of freedom in research and education and communications, freedom in politics, in economic development and in international relations which the book stressed is still vital.

The greatest threat which the world faced two decades ago and still faces is that of atomic warfare. Two surprise atomic bombs, the only two in existence, ended the Japanese war. Now that other nations have atomic capability, a single bomb would unleash a holocaust that might annihilate the human race. We can solve most of our problems if we have time, but if atomic warfare starts, *there will be no time. We must act now. We have been tragically slow to recognize that war is obsolete.*

The last two decades, thus far, have been a period of economic success in the United States, and standards of living have risen in many countries, particularly in the nations which were given technological and financial aid after the devastation of the war in the 1940's.

The younger generation has not found prosperity itself sufficient, and is impatient with the slow progress that is being made in the solutions of the world's problems. This revolt of youth is a matter of new concern, unpredicted in the 1950's. It gives a new urge, and possibly a new hope, toward meeting the challenge of our times.

The editors are grateful to Kennikat Press for reissuing this book of the early 1950's and making the thoughts of these university scholars available to the general public of the present time. The editors believe that the social, political and economic analyses and treatment of modern science for the layman given in this book, together with the historical perspectives and central theme, remain as pertinent and as provocative as ever.

They hope that the challenge of directing our future will still be met with the courses of constructive action which it sets forth.

May 25, 1970   *F. D.*
                                                                    T. M. S.

FOREWORD

It is now within our power to guide the future for the benefit of all people. This is the challenge of our times

Analyses of the world's social and political problems and the responsibilities of leadership which the United States has inherited are here described by historians, sociologists, political scientists, philosophers, and others. Each part of the picture is presented by a man who has devoted years of study to it. To show the power of science, for example, the editors have chosen atomic energy as a case history and, in non-technical language, have traced its dramatic development and its political impact. Science and technology are so changing our political and economic relations that growing pains are inevitable. The resources of the world are not distributed equally among the continents, nor are these resources utilized with equal effectiveness by different peoples. Differences of resources and effectiveness lead to rivalry and jealousy among peoples now brought close together by improvements in transportation and communication. Although physically we are essentially one world, in our cultural, political, and economic relations we are still composed of many conflicting units.

Tomorrow's world will be fashioned from today's as today's was fashioned from yesterday's. The editors hope these glimpses will help us to understand our world and challenge us to aid the directing of our future.

Permission has kindly been granted by the publishers to reproduce from: Bulletin of the American Association of University Professors, Feb., 1940; and Walter Lippmann, "The Indispensable Opposition," Atlantic Monthly, Aug., 1939.

The editors acknowledge gratefully the help of Mrs. Marshall Clagett, Mrs. Olive Bell Daniels, and Miss Patricia Struck.

F. D.
T. M. S.

PREFACE

This book is written in the faith that it is possible to make clear to the intelligent reader--be he specialist or not--the basic aspects of certain problems that grow out of technology. It arose from the effort of members of the University of Wisconsin faculty who joined in teaching a course in Contemporary Trends. This course was suggested to the faculty by a curriculum committee, whose chairman was Professor Farrington Daniels, editor and coauthor of this book. The committee proposed that a course in science and social problems be opened to students in their senior year in every college of the University.

The course was inaugurated in 1941. Although it has changed from year to year (since changes are the very essence of its nature), it nevertheless has held throughout to the theme of explaining the nature of science, its role in developing technology, the problems that technology brings into being, and the ideas that are being offered for their solution. During the preceding five years Professor Daniels has been chairman of the committee which gives this course.

If we were to list the "ten plagues" of the modern world, we would certainly include among them the apparent inability of intelligent people to communicate with one another. Not only is it true that one scientist frequently cannot tell another what he is doing, but scientists as a group are not aware of just how scientific knowledge becomes technology and how technology not only solves but creates problems in the social world. Too frequently, the investigator who lacks the knowledge and imagination to envisage the results of his investigations is also without a sense of responsibility. The social scientist, moreover, must struggle with the problems created by science. Yet he is too often unaware of how science and its work develop. The average intelligent citizen is often uninformed of either the scientific process or its social implications. This lack of information is frequently the result of the unwillingness of the specialist to write in terms intelligible to others.

While this book is the outcome of the course in Contemporary Trends, it is not the publication of a group of lectures. True, many of these chapters are based upon lectures, but they are offered here with the reader rather than the listener in mind. It is hoped that the book will be both absorbing and clear, for the same men with the same subject matter not only hold the attention of a large class at the University of Wisconsin, but create for the School of the Air of the State Radio Station one of its most appreciated series.

We are proud that this record of one of the University's successful ventures is now given to the general public.

Mark H. Ingraham

June, 1953
Madison, Wisconsin

CONTENTS

Foreword ii
Preface .... Mark H. Ingraham
      Dean of the College of Letters
          and Science iii

PART ONE
SCIENCE IS EVERYBODY'S BUSINESS

Chapter

1. FISSION, FUSION, AND SUNLIGHT 1
   Farrington Daniels
   Department of Chemistry

2. EXPLORING THE ATOM 9
   Farrington Daniels

3. EXPLODING THE ATOM 17
   Farrington Daniels

4. SCIENCE HAS A LONG HISTORY 28
   Marshall Clagett
   Department of the History of Science

5. THE INSIDE OF RESEARCH 39
   Farrington Daniels

6. PUTTING SCIENCE TO WORK 49
   Farrington Daniels

7. CONTROLLING THE BOMB 59
   Farrington Daniels

8. CONTROLLING SCIENCE IN THE
   UNITED STATES 71
   William B. Sarles
   Department of Bacteriology

9. CONTROLLING SCIENCE IN
   RUSSIA 81
   C. Leonard Huskins
   Department of Botany

PART TWO
NATIONS IN TURMOIL

10. MAN MOLDS THE WORLD 103
    Abbott Payson Usher
    Departments of Economics and History

11. MOUTHS TO FEED 116
    Noble Clark
    Associate Director, Agricultural
    Experiment Station
    James F. Crow
    Department of Genetics

12. WORLD PATTERNS IN POLITICS
    AND GEOGRAPHY 128
    Richard Hartshorne
    Department of Geography

13. RUSSIA AND THE COMMUNIST
    WAY OF LIFE 148
    Michael B. Petrovich
    Department of History

14. THE WAY WE THINK IN THE
    DEMOCRATIC WEST 163
    Llewellyn Pfankuchen
    Department of Political Science

15. TROUBLE IN EUROPE 178
    Chester V. Easum
    Department of History

16. ASIA EMERGES 188
    Eugene P. Boardman
    Department of History

17. COLONIAL PEOPLES IN
    TRANSITION 199
    Charles W. M. Hart
    Department of Sociology and
    Anthropology

PART THREE
OUR WORLD COMMUNITY

18. COLLECTIVE SECURITY — PATH
    TO PEACE 217
    Llewellyn Pfankuchen

19. WORLD GOVERNMENT 230
    Llewellyn Pfankuchen

20. WHY TRADE? 242
    Theodore Morgan
    Department of Economics

PART FOUR
WHAT THE UNITED STATES CAN DO

21. THE UNITED STATES —
    PRODUCTIVE GIANT 251
    Theodore Morgan

22. DEPRESSION AND INFLATION 259
    Theodore Morgan

23. HELPING THE WORLD 275
    Theodore Morgan

24. OUR FOREIGN POLICY:
TOWARD A BETTER WORLD 285
Fred Harvey Harrington
Department of History

PART FIVE
WHAT WE CAN DO

25. MAKING SENSE OUT OF
POLITICS AND PRESSURE GROUPS. 301
Ralph K. Huitt
Department of Political Science

26. MAKING SENSE OUT OF
PROPAGANDA 310
Ralph O. Nafziger
Director, School of Journalism

27. INTELLECTUAL FREEDOM — ITS
SOCIAL USE 321
Mark H. Ingraham
Dean, College of Letters and Science

28. "LIFE, LIBERTY, AND THE
PURSUIT OF HAPPINESS" 335
A. Campbell Garnett
Department of Philosophy

APPENDIXES

SUGGESTED SUPPLEMENTARY READING .. 349

ABOUT THE AUTHORS 351

INDEX 357

PART ONE

Science is Everybody's Business

Our civilization is unique in its tremendous demand for energy--for the coal and the oil and the hydroelectric power that we take for granted, but which are not everywhere plentiful. Domestic and foreign affairs, political and economic issues are centered around this demand. In this chapter a scientist pictures the great untapped resources that lie tantalizingly just beyond the frontiers of current research.

CHAPTER 1

FISSION, FUSION, AND SUNLIGHT

Farrington Daniels
Department of Chemistry

Our modern civilization is unique in its tremendous demand for energy. Not only do we require it continually-- in the food we eat--to stay alive, but we consume great amounts of it to run the engines we have built. All this energy, regardless of the form it takes as food or fuel, comes originally from the sun. Sunlight makes possible the growing of the plants that supply our food. Sunlight of past ages made possible the forests that were converted into coal, and the tiny organisms which left the oil that we use in our automobiles.

Since we are so truly dependent upon sunlight, we may well ask if we are now making the best use of the solar energy that floods in upon us. What are the ways in which that energy is conserved in food and fuel, and how is it used? What possible new sources of energy exist for the distant future when our coal and oil will be gone?

In trying to answer these questions it will help if we realize that all life processes and the operation of most of our engines depend upon the energy released when carbon-containing materials combine with the oxygen of the air. All of this carbon-containing food comes from the growth of plants, whether we eat the plants directly or feed them first to animals so that the food is converted into meat. The plants, of course, require sunlight, and we can say that one square foot of land in the United States receives an average of about one large calorie of heat per minute from the sun--as much heat as comes from burning half of a wooden match.

Each acre of land receives about 20 million large calories of energy from the sun per day. Since there are two billion acres of land in the United States and about 150 million people, there are thirteen acres of land per person. Each person in the United States then has a theoretical daily heritage of 13 x 20 million or 260 million large calories of solar energy. This heat is many times our present energy requirement per person, for the average American eats daily the equivalent of about 3,000 large calories. The average individual in the world as a whole uses about 2,500 large calories. People who are doing heavy manual labor require more. Hibernating animals that sleep through the winter require less. If we eat more than 3,000 large calories daily, we suffer from overweight and possibly, later on, from high blood pressure. If we are active and eat much less than 2,000 large calories over long periods of time, we suffer in health and disposition. In an agricultural community the people are largely self-sufficient in obtaining their food supply. If they have a surplus they can sell the food in the cities. At the time of the American Revolution it took many persons living in the rural districts to produce the food required by one person living in the city. At the present time in the United States, only one farmer is necessary to provide food for six urban residents. Scientific farming and the use of power machinery in the factory and on the farm have been important in expanding our economy and raising our standard of living.

The energy requirements of our machines vastly exceed the energy requirements of our bodies. If we divide the total energy equivalent of our daily production of coal, oil, and gas in the United States by our total population, we arrive at a figure of 150 thousand large calories per person per day. In other words, we in the United States feed our machines fifty times as much as we feed ourselves. This ratio is far greater than in many other parts of the world. In fact, on an over-all average, the world's machines consume only ten times as much energy as do the world's people.

Our demand for large amounts of energy to run our machines gives us our high standards of production and transportation, but it is just this sort of demand that is responsible today for much international tension. This is why areas possessing large petroleum reserves, for example, are "trouble spots"--for in both military and economic competition, the nations that control large sources of energy have a distinct advantage.

If energy is so precious, how can we obtain more of it? How can we store it? We cannot eat sunshine, we cannot carry it around with us, and we cannot store it as sunshine. The best use we can make of it at the present is to help nature grow plants. This involves the process of photosynthesis.

In photosynthesis, carbon dioxide is combined with water in the presence of the green chlorophyll which exists in all living plants. Sunlight supplies the energy for this remarkable reaction, which produces sugars and other organic materials. Scientific researches in the laboratory show that under the most favorable conditions approximately 30 per cent of the light absorbed by growing plants can be stored. Under ordinary existing conditions, the storage of sunlight in growing plants is much less than this. If a farmer burns up all the plant material harvested from one acre of an average corn crop he will obtain as heat one tenth of one per cent of all the solar energy received on that acre during the whole year.

Energy amounting to one tenth of a per cent may seem very inefficient in comparison with the 30 per cent actually stored in the laboratory under the best conditions. But we must remember that the growing season in most of the United States is confined to about four months of the year and that half of the sun's energy is in heat rays which are not absorbed at all by the green plants. Moreover, in ordinary agriculture the sunlight is too bright and the carbon dioxide concentration in air is too low for good results. Considering all these facts, it is evident that the farmer, at an efficiency of one tenth of a per cent, actually does a very effective job in storing the energy of the sun and converting it into food supplies.

This average conversion of one tenth of one per cent of the annual energy of the sun seems to hold approximately for many different agricultural crops including grains, hay, and even scientifically forested trees. The growth of algae in many lakes also yields an efficiency of about a tenth of one per cent of the annual solar energy. Hybrid corn on rich, fertilized soil can store several tenths of a per cent of the sun's annual energy. Sugar cane in Hawaii, growing all the year around, gives a still higher conversion of solar energy.

In the United States, except for wood and cotton, most of the products of photosynthesis are used for food directly, as grains, fruits, and vegetables, or indirectly, as meat. When the plants are fed to animals, a large loss of energy occurs. The energy value of meat is less than one tenth of the energy value of the food that has been consumed by the animals in providing the meat. The animals themselves have to retain the major part of the food for their own living and motion. This is the reason why, in overpopulated areas where food shortage is serious, the people cannot afford to eat much meat and are forced onto a vegetarian diet in which a greater amount of solar energy reaches human consumption.

We have seen that our engines and industrial operations in the United States require fifty times as much energy as we require in the form of food for ourselves. Very little of our energy fuel comes from wood produced by present-day photosynthesis. Practically all of it comes from fossil fuels: coal, oil, and gas which were produced by plant material originating from photosynthesis millions of years ago. These have been conveniently preserved for us in the ground, waiting for us to mine them or pipe them at our convenience.

But this bountiful supply of energy will not last indefinitely. It is probable that our natural gas will be pretty largely gone in 20 years, our petroleum in 200 years, and our coal in 2,000 years. Chemists can easily convert gas into gasoline, or petroleum and coal into gas, or even coal into gasoline--but these operations do not prevent the final exhaustion of our fuels. Many students of this subject believe that these are optimistic estimates and that actually the shortages will come much sooner than indicated here.

When our fuel from past photosynthesis is exhausted and our rate of photosynthesis on agricultural land is not sufficient to maintain the standard of civilization we desire, what will we do? The answer lies in reasonable control of the world's population increase and in scientific research into new sources of energy. Research into the utilization of solar energy has been too long delayed. Although the heating of houses by solar energy has already been started, it can be expanded considerably. The growth of algae in plastic bags on waste land is beginning to receive attention. The direct utilization of sunlight to produce mechanical power through heat engines is possible, but the economics of the solar engine do not seem feasible. Too many focusing mirrors and other mechanical accessories are necessary.

Although we have seen that our requirements in heat can theoretically be realized through our current supply of solar energy, it is unfortunately true that we can use only a very small fraction of this heat for producing work. There is a theoretical limit to the conversion of heat into work which depends on the difference in temperature.

The situation is like that of water power--we have lots of water in the ocean, but we must provide a difference in level to operate a water wheel. In the same way, we must provide a difference in temperature through which heat can pass, to do work. The gentle heat of sunlight cannot be easily converted into useful work because the temperature is too low. Mirrors and lenses can provide the higher temperature by focusing the heat on boilers in solar engines, but an acre of mirrors requires too high a capital investment. In other words, such an enterprise has too low a priority in our use of manpower and materials. Another difficulty lies in the fact that the engines could not operate at night. New developments in storage batteries or their equivalents are badly needed.

Nevertheless, it has been calculated that theoretically it would be possible to produce electrical energy at the rate of 50 horsepower per acre continuously in Arizona and 30 horsepower in New York State. Perhaps we will be driven to this type of utilization of solar energy in the distant future or perhaps someone will come up with an entirely new approach. Solar engines under present economic circumstances do not appear promising. Direct conversion of solar energy into electrical energy is theoretically possible, and photochemical production of energy-rich products is definitely possible. Intensive, long-range research on the utilization of solar energy should be started at once.

Energy from a new and mighty source began to be available December 2, 1942. Energy produced by splitting the atom of heavy elements like uranium--the process called fission--then became a reality.

This beginning of the atomic age is portrayed in the accompanying illustration. Wartime research was carried out in great secrecy under the football stands at the University of Chicago. Scientists had been working feverishly, calculating, designing, purifying uranium and graphite and developing control and safety devices. They wondered, would it be possible to start a self-sustaining atomic chain reaction that would evolve large quantities of energy continuously--under full control?

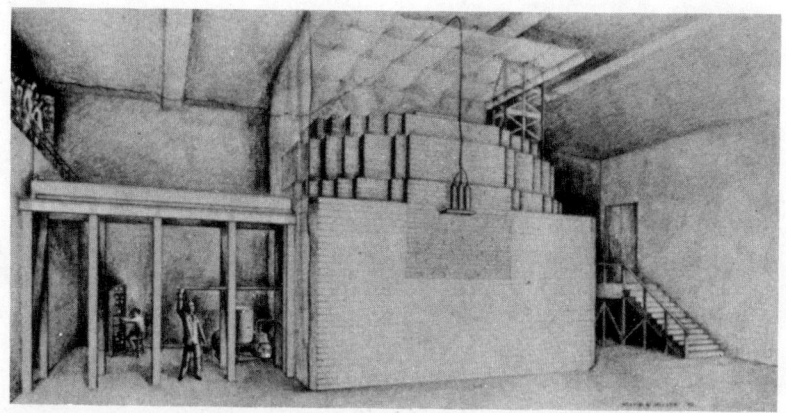

December 2, 1942--the beginning of the atomic age. On this date the control rod was withdrawn far enough to put the first atomic reactor into operation.

Finally, in December the stage was set and the dignitaries responsible for the development of new and powerful weapons were in the gallery. Each man asked himself, "Will the meters in the background show that man can use atomic energy as his ancestors found they could use fire?" As the control rod was withdrawn from the pile, the pointers on the meters moved. The atomic age had come into being.

There is something symbolic about this picture. The young scientist in the foreground can pull out the control rod a fraction of an inch and obtain enough energy to light a flashlight. He can pull it out a little farther and obtain enough energy to light the building, a little farther and obtain enough energy to provide power and light for a city. Or, he can pull it out still farther and create a catastrophe. Man has it in his complete power to use this new force of nature in any way that he may choose, for good or for evil. The essential problem is not the control of the atom, but man's control of himself.

We shall see in the next chapter how the splitting, or fission, of uranium gives off enormous quantities of energy because matter is converted to energy.

The enormous energy within the sun comes from a similar atomic change in which matter is lost by being converted to energy, but in this case the light elements like hydrogen combine to form somewhat heavier elements in a process called fusion. Is there any chance that man can really mimic the sun and bring about fusion as well as fission? If so, he will obtain a vast new source of energy. The hydrogen atoms are much more abundant and cheaper than the heavy uranium atoms used for fission, but they undergo fusion in the sun because the sun has the inconceivably high temperature of 20 million degrees centigrade. The highest temperature we attain in ordinary experiments on earth is usually about three or four thousand degrees. Fortunately, the sun carries on this reaction for us under control at a safe distance so that only the gentle warmth of sunshine reaches the earth. We cannot get to the sun to obtain dangerous quantities of concentrated energy to be misused for destructive purposes.

But wait--we have now learned how to obtain very high temperatures through atomic fission, as hot as the sun in fact. Perhaps we can use this as a match to ignite the larger energy of fusion. It is difficult but not impossible.

How have these remarkable developments of science come about? What is this scientific method that has proved such a remarkable tool in molding the world to man's needs? Can the same methods be used also to help in other areas of human activity? The atomic age has created new problems in science, industry, and politics. It leads to an important phase of our civilization that merits our attention in the several chapters which follow.

How has the scientist succeeded in harnessing the atom? When the story began, more than fifty years ago, he had no such practical goal in mind.

CHAPTER 2

EXPLORING THE ATOM

Farrington Daniels

Man has long been thinking about the nature of materials around him such as water, air, stones, and gold. Within the last two or three centuries he has learned that most materials can be separated into chemical compounds which are always alike. As a result of patient laboratory experiments, he has come to know that all these compounds are made up of less than a hundred elements, such as hydrogen, oxygen, and carbon, which combine according to definite patterns. A hundred years ago it was supposed that these elements were made of atoms which were hard and round and could not be subdivided into anything smaller.

Then, about half a century ago, radioactivity was discovered. This set scientists of all nations to work exploring further into the atom, devising new apparatus with which to make accurate measurements, correlating data, drawing conclusions, and checking these conclusions with carefully designed experiments. They were impelled by their scientific curiosity, and they published their results so that other scientists with different backgrounds and other points of view could build onto the rapidly growing knowledge of the structure of the atom.

That is, they used the powerful methods of science to produce one of man's most remarkable achievements, the harnessing of atomic energy. This great force has raised a host of social and political problems, even while promising better living to all. In this chapter we take up briefly some of the historical and technical facts with which informed citizens should be familiar.

* * * * *

We begin our story with the last two decades of the nineteenth century when an English physicist, J. J. Thompson, experimenting with the passage of electricity through gases at low pressures, connected two wires to a source of high-voltage electricity, and they emitted light after the fashion of present-day neon signs. When he pumped out more gas the light dimmed and disappeared, but parts of the glass tube became bright, as in our fluorescent lamps.

Studying the rays that produced these fluorescent spots, he found them to go in straight lines and to be easily deflected by a magnet. The tiny particles composing these rays were deflected in such a direction as to show that they were negatively charged, and at such an angle as to show that each particle weighed 1/1800 as much as the atom of the lightest known element, hydrogen. Here was the first evidence that atoms are complex. Here was the electron, a negatively charged particle, recognized as the fundamental unit of electricity. The electron led at once to a better understanding of many physical and chemical phenomena.

In 1895 a German physicist, Roentgen, found that when a beam of electrons generated in an electrical discharge tube hit a metallic target, a peculiar invisible ray was given off which passed through opaque objects and blackened a photographic plate. This was the discovery of X-rays.

A year later another physicist, the Frenchman Becquerel, reasoned that because uranium salts emit visible light when exposed to sunlight, they might give off invisible X-rays also. He placed a photographic plate in a light-tight envelope, laid a key on top of it, placed some uranium salts over the key, and exposed them to the sun. When he developed the plate he found the shadow of the key. Light capable of penetrating the black envelope had been produced. His hypothesis seemed to be correct. But in checking this experiment he found on one cloudy day that the shadow of the key was obtained anyway. Sunlight wasn't necessary! What was the cause? Further experiments led him to conclude that the uranium salts had spontaneously provided penetrating rays. This was the discovery of radioactivity.

Now Professor and Madame Curie took up the research at Becquerel's suggestion and found that an impurity in the uranium emitted much more of this radiation than uranium itself. After many painstaking purifications of the mineral from which uranium came, the Curies succeeded in 1897 in getting materials of much greater activity and soon they isolated a new element and named it radium. It gave off light and heat spontaneously and continuously; and it produced radioactivity. This again was something new.

By the turn of the century scientists in many countries were studying this radioactivity. They soon identified three different types of rays: gamma rays, which are like X-rays; beta particles, which are the same as electrons; and alpha particles, which are four times as heavy as the hydrogen atom. They all come off with tremendous velocities approaching that of light. Alpha particles are stopped by a thin sheet of paper, beta rays are a hundred times more penetrating, and gamma rays are a hundred times more penetrating than the beta rays.

The intensity of radioactivity can be measured by photographic plates or by meters that measure the amount of electricity passing through a gas exposed to radioactivity. A "Geiger counter" is a particularly sensitive type of meter.

In 1911 an English physicist named Rutherford carried out a significant experiment in which he bombarded a target of thin gold leaf with alpha particles from radium. Calculations showed that the energy of the alpha particle was so great that it should go right on through the gold as a rifle bullet goes through tissue paper. He was astounded, however, to find that occasionally a particle would be reflected backward from the gold target. A bold new assumption was now necessary: namely that most of the material of each atom in the target must be concentrated in an extremely small nucleus. This was the start of the nuclear theory of the atom.

This idea led a Danish physicist, Bohr, to a useful mathematical theory that each atom has a small central nucleus with electrons going around it in elliptical orbits, as the planets go around the sun. The number of negative electrons going around the nucleus of a given atom is equal to the number of positive electrical charges on its nucleus.

About this time in England, X-ray techniques were perfected which made it possible to determine the number of electrical charges on the nucleus of an atom of any given chemical element.

It was realized that the number of these charges determines the chemical properties of the element. Long before this, in 1869, a Russian chemist, Mendeleev, had arranged all the then-known chemical elements in order of increasing weight and found that there was a recurrence of properties in every eighth element. Thus, the third lightest element (lithium), the eleventh lightest (sodium), and the nineteenth (potassium) proved to be metals which were very much alike. All the elements could be arranged in eight successive groups having similar physical and chemical properties. The periodic arrangement of an increasing number of the nuclei enables one to predict the properties of a given element.

In the second decade of the present century a new complication arose. Scientists in England and in the United States found that although all the atoms of a chemical element have the same electrical charge on the nucleus and the same chemical properties, they do not necessarily all have the same weight. For when a beam of charged molecules is passed through a magnetic field, some of the molecules are deflected more than others. From this arose the concept of isotopes--varieties of the same element having nearly the same chemical properties but differing in weight.

Our understanding of the atom was advanced greatly in 1932 by the experimental discovery of the neutron by Chadwick in England. The neutron is one of the two great building blocks of which the nuclei of the atoms of all the chemical elements are composed. The other building block is the proton, which is the atomic nucleus of the lightest element--hydrogen. Both the proton and the neutron have practically the same weight--almost the same as that of the hydrogen atom. The difference is that the proton has one positive electrical charge and the neutron has none. The number of protons in the nucleus of an atom determines, then, the number of electrical charges, the position in the periodic table of elements, and thus the chemical properties of the element. The total number of protons and neutrons combined, however, determines the weight of the element. For example, hydrogen has one proton in its nucleus but there are three isotopes of hydrogen--hydrogen 1 has no neutron; hydrogen 2 has one neutron giving a total weight of two (one proton + one neutron); hydrogen 3 has two neutrons, giving a total weight of three.

The elements that occur in nature contain definite proportions of their different isotopes, all going through the same chemical reactions together. In hydrogen, for example, there are 5,000 atoms of the isotope weighing one for every atom of the isotope weighing two.

Some of these proton-neutron combinations are stable. Others are unstable, and they rearrange themselves to give new elements. In so doing, they emit beta or gamma rays. For example, the isotope of carbon that weighs 14 is unstable and decomposes very slowly into nitrogen. It takes 5,000 years for half of this carbon 14 to turn into nitrogen. This is called the "half-life" of carbon 14. Each isotope has its own term of half-life, which may vary from fractions of seconds to millions of years.

Until recently we laughed at the ancient alchemists who tried unsuccessfully to turn lead into gold. Before the discovery of radioactivity, we firmly believed that chemical elements could not be changed into other elements. Radioactivity showed, however, that uranium in its natural state decayed spontaneously into a number of elements such as radium and eventually became lead. This challenge led men to try once again in the laboratory to convert one element into another. This time they had a vast supply of fundamental knowledge which had not been available to the alchemists.

The first success came in 1919 when Rutherford made hydrogen from nitrogen. He showed that alpha particles from radium, smashing into nitrogen atoms, sometimes knocked out a fragment which traveled so far that it could be nothing other than a lightweight hydrogen nucleus.

New and powerful high-voltage machines were developed in the 1930's, chiefly in the United States and England, and were used successfully for smashing atoms and converting one element into another. In these atom smashers positively charged protons are accelerated by millions of volts until they acquire sufficient energy to penetrate an atom and reach the nucleus, thereby adding to it one electrical charge and an extra weight of one. This new nucleus usually is unstable and decomposes further; thus new elements are formed.

In 1932 in France, Joliot-Curie and his wife, instead of using protons, generated neutrons by exposing the element beryllium to alpha particles from radium. The neutron is electrically uncharged and it can easily pass through the outer electrons and penetrate to the nucleus of atoms. They shot their neutrons into such common elements as sodium and iron and succeeded in converting these targets into other elements that proved to be unstable and underwent radioactive decay into still other elements.

Fermi, in Italy, and others exposed all the elements to bombardment with neutrons. By 1935 most of the chemical elements had been converted in this way into new isotopes, many of which were radioactive. Men were learning more and more about atomic energy, but they could produce it only at tremendous cost.

Another important aspect of nuclear reactions was predicted first by Einstein in 1906. According to two fundamental principles of science--the conservation of energy and the conservation of matter--neither energy nor matter could be created or destroyed. But Einstein, in one of the world's most brilliant mathematical studies, pointed out theoretically that energy and matter are of the same fundamental nature and that one can be converted into the other. Einstein's famous equation is:

$$E = mc^2$$

Energy (E) equals mass (m) multiplied by the square of the velocity of light (c)

The square of the velocity of light is an enormously large number (9 followed by twenty zeros) and so it was concluded that the disappearance of just a little matter would result in the evolution of enormous quantities of energy. Here was the explanation for the energy of radioactivity and for the tremendous energy of the sun and the stars.

If one compares the exact weights of all the atoms and neutrons or protons involved in a nuclear change with the weight of all the atoms and neutrons and protons which are produced, he will find that there has been an actual loss of weight. While this represents a loss of less than one tenth of one per cent of the original weight, it means, nevertheless, the evolution of stupendous amounts of energy.

What possibilities this presented! There was much speculation about how such energy could be obtained, but most people believed that to get this energy out of matter, enormous quantities of energy would have to be utilized to start the release of atomic energy. No responsible scientist dared to predict in 1938 that within less than a decade atomic energy would be an important factor in human affairs.

And then came fission. Hahn and Strassmann in Germany bombarded many elements with neutrons and studied the new elements produced. When they experimented with the element uranium they obtained a curious effect which they could not at first believe. The new elements produced from uranium by neutrons were lighter elements such as iodine, which weighed about half as much as uranium. Why? In January, 1939, Lise Meitner helped to supply the answer: uranium atoms had split--that is, fissioned--into two nearly equal fragments. The staggering implications of atomic fission by a chain reaction are described in the following chapter. Never before had scientists so quickly blazed such a trail of exploration--from X-rays to fission in 44 years.

By 1940 certain physicists suspected the atom could be put to work to help win a war. This chapter tells in simple terms what happened in the next five years: building the atomic bomb.

CHAPTER 3

EXPLODING THE ATOM

Farrington Daniels

In the preceding chapter we have seen how scientists in less than half a century accumulated fundamental knowledge about the nucleus of the atom. It took teamwork by physicists, mathematicians, and chemists in many different lands. They were impelled only by the urge of scientists to unravel the mysterious laws of nature. This period of free fundamental research came to an abrupt climax with the discovery of fission early in 1939.

At this time Niels Bohr of Denmark was going to Washington to give a lecture on the structure of atomic nuclei. He passed on Lise Meitner's explanation of Hahn and Strassmann's experiments to his friends in the United States. The startling, new hypothesis electrified the nuclear physicists into action. They retreated hastily into their laboratories and in an incredibly short period of weeks came out with corroborating evidence. They realized that the fission of uranium might well release enormous quantities of nuclear energy and give a military explosive of a greater order of magnitude than ever had been achieved with gunpowder or TNT.

Meanwhile, Hitler had invaded Europe, and many noted scholars had fled to freedom in this country and become American citizens. Einstein, Fermi, Szilard, Wigner, and others were passionately committed to preserving the democratic freedoms. They feared that German scientists and engineers might produce a nuclear explosive soon and win the war in Europe. Aided by a letter from Einstein, scientists appealed to President Roosevelt, who immediately authorized scientific research on the feasibility of an atomic bomb. He used special funds, and the National Research Council of civilian scientists went to work on the problem. They hoped that if a bomb were possible and were first produced by the United States, an early end of the war might be achieved and countless lives saved. Tremendous effort was put into the venture. It cost some two billion dollars, together with valuable priorities on scarce materials and still more scarce scientists and engineers. A new agency took charge, the so-called "Manhattan District" of the Engineer Corps of the United States Army, under the leadership of Major General Leslie R. Groves.

The scientists truly hoped that an atomic bomb could not be made and that neither Germany nor the United States could produce one, but by 1942 they realized that the super weapon was possible. They imposed voluntary censorship on themselves. They stopped publishing in the scientific journals, contrary to the habit of scientists, who further their knowledge by sharing their findings with all interested. Then complete secrecy was imposed. Only after the war was it discovered that two scientists, who happened to be British subjects, had betrayed the project.

The whole venture remained secret until President Truman, on August 9, 1945, announced that the city of Hiroshima had been destroyed by a single bomb. Three weeks later the war was over.

What had gone on in the laboratories for the secret three and a half years since fission had been established?

From laboratory experiments and mathematical computation it became known that one pound of uranium upon fission would give off heat equivalent to that given off by a train load of 1,500 tons of coal. It was also found that the process of fission was self-propagating, that is, on the average, for every neutron going into a mass of uranium 235, additional neutrons are released. These are absorbed by other uranium atoms, which in turn are split, and so on in a chain reaction. The classic experiment of December 2, 1942, when the first pile went into operation, proved that this nuclear chain reaction was possible.

Could this chain reaction by completed instantaneously for military purposes and could it also be completed in the slower evolution of heat for peaceful applications of atomic power? The experiment showed that it could.

It was soon found that only uranium 235 (the uranium isotope that weighs 235 times as much as hydrogen) undergoes fission. The other isotope of uranium, 238, absorbs neutrons but does not undergo fission. In fact, it stops the nuclear chain and quenches the explosion. Common uranium contains a large excess of uranium 238. How could it be separated out? At Columbia University, Harold C. Urey started on the principle of separation-by-diffusion, and the Carbon and Carbide Company quickly put this method into large-scale production. Since the desired uranium 235 is slightly lighter in weight it will diffuse a little faster through tiny holes than the uranium 238--just as a small boy can get through a crowd faster than a man.

There were many problems in this diffusion process to solve, such as the production of a stable gaseous compound of uranium, and the finding of an inert material which would form the walls and passages and not be subject to chemical corrosion. At best the separation was only very slight and the gaseous material had to be diffused over and over again until an appreciable amount of uranium 235 was collected.

A huge plant was built in the nearly uninhabited Oak Ridges of Tennessee--a town of 70,000 people was erected nearby almost overnight. Finally, early in 1945 the enormous project was completed. Miles of pipes and gas pumps worked automatically. The building was four stories high, a block wide, and a mile long. Another plant is now being built in Paducah, Kentucky, and another one in Ohio, along improved technical lines.

But the diffusion process was not the only one possible. Under war pressure it was decided to go forward with three processes simultaneously. Nuclear physicists and chemists were assembled at the University of Chicago in the so-called Metallurgical Laboratory under the able direction of Arthur H. Compton. Seaborg and Glenndenin had shown that the abundant isotope, uranium 238, is converted by neutrons into a new man-made element, plutonium 239. It was found that plutonium undergoes fission when struck by a neutron just as uranium 235 does. It was proposed then to have uranium 235 undergo fission under controlled conditions and to use the extra neutrons produced to change the uranium 238 into plutonium.

This proposal opened up an important possibility which was eagerly seized. It is much easier to separate chemical elements from each other than it is to separate isotopes, because the chemical properties of the elements differ whereas the chemical properties of the isotopes are practically the same. In this case, since nothing was known about the chemistry of the new element, plutonium, fundamental research on the properties of plutonium and its compounds had to be carried out. Moreover, in 1942, there was not enough plutonium in the world to be seen with the naked eye. The chemical operations were followed by means of careful measurements of radioactivity. Furthermore, there was great danger in handling the materials since the fission process produced a large number of radioactive elements, and the radioactivity was millions of times greater than had ever been encountered before. New methods of working by remote control had to be devised.

The contract for the plutonium process was handled by the Du Pont Company. A very large plant and community were designed and built at Hanford, Washington. The plant was operating in late 1944 and material for bombs was available in mid-1945. Probably no engineering operation and chemical processing has ever been scaled up so fast, in spite of unknown factors and great hazards, from microchemical laboratory experiments to hundred million dollar production plants. The process was extraordinarily efficient from the beginning.

The two processes, the diffusion at Oak Ridge and the plutonium at Hanford, started at the same time. They were carried out by different teams of scientists, engineers and industries and both came successfully into operation in about three and a half years.

These miracles of engineering were made possible by the vigorous hard work of the country's scientists and by the existence of a large backlog of fundamental scientific knowledge published in the scientific journals of the world and available to all. They were made possible also by the efficient organization and accumulated know-how of our big industrial companies which built and operated these plants under contract with the government. Their experience in solving construction problems, procuring materials, and making practical applications of science on a gigantic scale was a major national asset. The complete and unselfish co-operation between scientists, engineers, industrial managers, and Army officers was also responsible in large measure for the success of the atomic energy project.

Meanwhile, on the remote mesa in New Mexico, the laboratories at Los Alamos, directed by J. Robert Oppenheimer, were engaged in research on the bomb and detonated the first experimental one, fusing five acres of desert sand to glass.

This completed the research. The Army employed the bomb and ended the war.

When the war was over the responsibility for the atomic energy program was given over by the Army to the newly created civilian Atomic Energy Commission. It was hoped that our chief efforts would be directed toward peaceful applications of atomic knowledge, for the helpful use of isotopes in scientific research, and for creating atomic engines to generate electricity. But as we shall see in the next chapter, the aggressive tactics of the Communists, the failure of Russia to agree to the control of atomic weapons, and the fear of a third world war, led to continued emphasis on production of atomic bombs.

Nevertheless, government laboratories for research were greatly strengthened: at Oak Ridge, where isotopes are produced; at the Argonne National Laboratory near Chicago, where emphasis is placed on nuclear reactors; at the Brookhaven National Laboratory on Long Island, where experimental research is stressed; at Los Alamos, New Mexico, where research on weapons is carried out; at Berkeley, California, where machines have been developed for splitting atoms with charged particles at extremely high voltages; and at the new station in Idaho, where new reactors for generating atomic power are tested.

Nuclear reactors, or "atomic piles", offer the greatest hope for making practical use of exploding atoms. The first reactor is pictured in chapter one. The Oak Ridge reactor, similar to it, is about 40 feet square and 30 feet high. It involves several general principles. First, a sufficient quantity of uranium is required. Less than the so-called "critical size" will allow so many neutrons to escape before they can be absorbed by surrounding uranium atoms that there are not enough neutrons to continue the nuclear chain.

Second, metallic uranium rods, which constitute the atomic fuel, are placed in channels made in large graphite blocks and are kept cool by air blown through the channels. The graphite slows down the neutrons so that they will be more readily absorbed in the uranium. Control rods of neutron-absorbing material, such as boron, are moved back and forth in the channels to give the desired rate of energy production.

Finally, six feet of concrete or its equivalent is placed around the pile as a shield to prevent exposure of the operating personnel to neutrons and to gamma rays, which, like X-rays, are dangerous.

About 200 various isotopes are produced as a by-product in the Oak Ridge pile and distributed at nominal cost by the Atomic Energy Commission. They are used in a great variety of scientific researches. Radioactive isotopes have been spoken of as the greatest new scientific tool since the microscope. They provide the scientist with a means of tagging the atoms he is studying so that he may discover where they go in chemical changes and biological processes.

For example, in studying the mechanism of plant growth it is very helpful to know what chemical compounds are first produced in the plant by the carbon dioxide which is absorbed. A little radioactive carbon dioxide is mixed with ordinary carbon dioxide and a sensitive Geiger counter can follow its progress through the plant.

In comparing the efficiency of different lubricating oils in reducing the wear of pistons in automobile engines, the old way was to operate engines for several days until enough metal was ground off by friction to be measured in the oil. Now the pistons can be made of radioactive iron and after they have been operated only a few minutes the amount of iron worn away can be measured by the amount of radioactivity.

In medicine, it is known that iodine is taken up by the body selectively and concentrated in the thyroid gland. When the thyroid gland becomes enlarged, causing the abnormal condition of goiter, the patient is given the proper amount of radioactive iodine. This goes to the thryoid gland, destroys part of the excess tissue by its radioactivity, and cures the goiter. The radioactivity remains for perhaps a week. Many hundreds of cures have been effected in this way.

Again, there had been speculation regarding the rate at which molecules in animal tissue or bone are replenished. Does a given atom of phosphorus stay in a bone for a minute, a month or a decade before its place is taken by another atom of phosphorus? Radioactive phosphorus was fed to rats at suitable intervals of time and the bones were checked for radioactivity. It was found that the bones are always in a state of flux, new atoms replacing old ones continuously so that a given tagged atom of phosphorus remains in the bone for only about two weeks.

These examples are typical of the important uses of isotopes obtained from the Atomic Energy Commission.

Another important peaceful application of atomic energy is in the production of industrial electricity. This development is just beginning. We will have to wait several years for its full development.

There are several nuclear reactors operating in Chicago, Oak Ridge, Los Alamos, Brookhaven, Canada, England, France, and Russia, all producing neutrons and generating heat. The great reactors at Hanford are evolving enormous quantities of heat. But until the close of 1951 no use was being made of the heat evolved in nuclear reactors. It seems foolish to use valuable electric power to pump part of the Columbia River through the Hanford reactors to cool them when theoretically the heat evolved could be used to produce electric power. Yet there is a real difficulty: the materials used in their construction does not permit them to be operated at a temperature high enough to run an efficient engine and generator.

To run generators it will be necessary to operate atomic furnaces at higher temperatures, but higher temperatures create engineering problems of heat-resistant materials. Under wartime pressure the engineers left these problems for a later time. They had the immediate problems of finding materials that would withstand the new conditions of neutrons and radioactivity. After the war several different designs for the solution of higher-temperature problems were offered. Some designs utilized ceramic materials in their construction, some utilized new and difficult-to-get metals of high purity. Since all furnaces get too hot without a flow of cooling material through them, different cooling materials were proposed--air, water, gases under pressure, and certain liquid metals. One of these cold fluids is pumped into an atomic furnace and emerges heated. If hot enough it then runs a standard steam engine or gas turbine.

The first plans stressed economic operation and were not concerned with the size of the furnace. Unfortunately, as the international situation deteriorated, greater emphasis had to be placed on military objectives, and the earlier plans were crowded out in favor of atomic engines for submarines, in which small size is all important and cost is relatively unimportant.

In large atomic power plants it is possible to use natural uranium. In small plants it is necessary to use uranium 235, separated by diffusion; or plutonium, made from uranium 238; or uranium 233, made from the element thorium, which is somewhat more common than uranium. The process of creating either plutonium from ordinary uranium or uranium 233 from ordinary thorium is carried out in what is known as breeder piles. The interesting breeding process may be likened to an imaginary coal furnace where it would be possible to convert cheap stones placed around the outside of the furnace into new pieces of coal for the furnace. When this coal was consumed, the converted stones could be used and more stones placed around the furnace to be turned into fuel. This is the sort of process that goes on in breeder piles.

The economics of atomic power is not clear. The costs cannot be known until experimental units have been built and operated. For example, if the atomic fuel has to be removed frequently and treated chemically, the costs may be prohibitive. On the other hand, if the reprocessing is infrequent, the costs may be acceptable. The fuel cost is about a fifth part of the total cost of generating electricity. Electrical equipment, dynamos, switch boards, transmission lines, and many other costs remain the same regardless of the fuel source. While atomic furnaces with their safeguards and remote control apparatus require higher capital investment than coal furnaces, any saving would have to be in the cheaper fuel. The United States pays three and a half dollars for a pound of uranium in low-grade ores. It costs several times as much as this to extract it and purify it and make it into suitable forms for atomic furnaces. But theoretically, one pound of uranium or plutonium is equivalent to 1,500 tons of coal, which would cost in the neighborhood of ten thousand dollars.

Probably atomic power will be used first in submarines. There are also four large industrial companies looking into the possibility of economically generating industrial power. They might also produce plutonium as a by-product which they would sell to the government.

Atomic power might well be used in isolated areas where large amounts of electrical power are needed for mining or irrigation but where both fuel and transportation are lacking. Or it might be used in those countries, such as India and Brazil, which have large deposits of thorium and little coal or water power, yet seek to increase their industrial productivity.

Atomic fuel is essentially weightless fuel. Compare the pound of uranium the size of a walnut with the train load of coal. This essential weightlessness has led to wild speculations concerning its uses in autos, planes, trains, ships, and rockets. It is not likely that automobiles will be powered with uranium. A small amount of uranium will do nothing. The critical amount of uranium 235 would be prohibitive in price. Besides, the engine would require six feet of concrete around it for a radioactive shield. Small airplanes are equally out of the question. Much research is going into the use of atomic fuel in large airplanes, where tons of shielding for the operators can replace tons of gasoline which would no longer be necessary. Trains might be a border-line case. Large ships should offer no great technical difficulties. If a rocket is used without a crew, even the shielding may become unnecessary. It is true that theoretically a mass of uranium could give, on fission, enough energy to escape from the gravitational prison of the earth and carry with it into space a million times its own weight. But other obstacles exist, such as the inability, when it is outside the earth's atmosphere, of cooling the atomic engine.

One more question will be asked by any thoughtful dreamer of future sources of industrial power. Is there enough uranium and thorium in the world to be important? According to prewar estimates, the known deposits of uranium were only enough to provide electrical power in the United States for a few years. But prewar uranium was considered an unimportant element with few uses. Now that it has become one of the most important strategic materials, prospectors are hunting feverishly for it all over the earth, and we believe that much is being found. The Belgian Congo in Africa was and is by far the largest source of high-grade uranium; Northwest Canada was second, and the Colorado plateau, third. Uranium in very low concentrations is found widely distributed in many areas of the world. With the new urgency, new methods are being developed for mining economically lower and lower grade ores. Large supplies of uranium will come as a by-product from gold ores in South Africa. Moreover the large phosphate deposits in the United States which are used for fertilizer contain small amounts of uranium and intensive research is being directed toward the practical recovery from this large tonnage of low grade ore.

Most atomic scientists believe that atomic energy eventually will become an important source of industrial power, but much research and development is still required. The challenge to scientists, engineers and industrialists is great. A successful economic solution should help to relieve international tensions that hinge on the present scramble for limited reserves of coal and oil throughout the world. Unfortunately, much of the world's effort in atomic energy is going into stock piles of atomic bombs. But we should remember that when satisfactory international agreements are made and peace comes, we can turn our swords into plowshares and use the very material in the bombs for the productive and constructive generation of industrial electricity.

The preceding chapters have shown how scientists mastered the atom. This chapter explains the origins of the powerful method of science in which speculations are tested by carefully planned experiments.

CHAPTER 4

SCIENCE HAS A LONG HISTORY

Marshall Clagett
Department of the History of Science

Today most of us feel the influence that science has on our daily life. We are taught to marvel at its most recent achievements and applications, and we are somehow left with the impression that science is something essentially contemporary that devours and destroys its past. But while we are constantly looking for the "latest" in scientific discovery, we ought to pause for a moment to see how old scientific activity really is, to find out what are its roots in the past, how much of its past is incorporated in its present form and organization. Such an examination is justified not only in terms of the general cultural interest, but on the very practical ground that we can learn much about contemporary science, its basic methods and attitudes, if we inquire into its origins.

Before beginning this brief inquiry it will be profitable to ask, "What do we understand by science?". The plain answer is that the scope and techniques of science are so varied that it is almost impossible to find complete agreement on a definition.

Actually, most of us know something of the general nature of science. We know that science hopes to achieve an understanding and explanation of nature. To achieve that understanding and explanation, a series of tools and techniques has been developed, and we must regard these tools as an essential part of science. Thus we can characterize science on the one hand by the knowledge or understanding of nature that constitutes the content of scientific knowledge, and on the other hand by the many tools and techniques developed to achieve that understanding. In tools and techniques we include such things as logic, mathematics, and the procedures of experimental research.

We cannot hope, of course, to say much about the growth of substantial knowledge in one brief chapter. But we can perhaps say enough about the development of the tools and techniques of science to grasp something of the essential character of scientific activity in the past and the present.

So we ask the question, "How far back into man's history can we trace systematic attempts to arrive at an orderly comprehension of nature?" In one sense we can go back to the early reaches of man's life in prehistoric time. Already at that time he distilled his experience of nature in the hand tools he fashioned. And who cannot feel the intimate knowledge of nature expressed in the naturalistic stone-age cave paintings of northern Spain and southern France? Man was a naturalist even before he became a farmer or a politician.

For the written evidences of man's early efforts to understand nature we must search the earliest of his civilizations in the Near East, particularly in the Nile Valley and in Mesopotamia. The proto-scientists of these areas took the first steps towards systematic science in mathematics, in astronomy and in surgery. The scientific efforts in these provinces of learning were, on the whole, grossly empirical in nature; that is, they employed trial-and-error methods without due attention to theoretical explanation. The painfully complicated and inept methods of multiplying and adding used by the Egyptians illustrates this tendency.

The objectives of the early science of Egypt and Mesopotamia were largely social. Pure science was scarcely distinguishable from applied. Political and economic needs demanded calendars which were to jibe with the seasons, and the development of these calendars stimulated observational efforts in astronomy. Similarly, problems of architectural and civil engineering brought the Egyptians a facile and practical geometry.

Empirical as this early science was, steps were sometimes taken to organize data in a systematic way. The oldest known medical treatise dates ultimately from about 2500 B.C. and does a masterly job of describing and organizing certain types of wounds and their treatment. And despite the magical regard for the universe in Egypt and Mesopotamia, these surgical cases completely escaped such magical influences.

There were occasional attempts in this pre-Greek period to predict phenomena on the basis of scientifically organized data and by the use of mathematics. Such was the case in Babylonian astronomy, where methods of long- and short-range prediction about the movements of heavenly bodies were devised. A mathematical astronomy thus was born in Mesopotamia, but we must await the development of Greek astronomy for it to mature.

When we turn next to ancient Greece, we see the vague and occasionally scientific tendencies of early mathematics and astronomy crystallizing into organized knowledge. This organized learning we can recognize as something closely akin to modern scientific enterprise. Greek science arose from early speculative philosophy in the sixth century B.C. Three centuries later, in the third century B.C., it achieved full maturity in the deathless works of Archimedes, Euclid, Aristarchus, Eratosthenes, Appolonius, and many others. The third century B.C. is as crucial in the early development of science as the seventeenth and nineteenth centuries A.D. are for its later development.

The first point to notice about Greek science is its rather complete freedom from the mythological point of view that dominated the speculative efforts of early man. This freedom expressed itself in a naturalistic critical spirit: it was truly a remarkable step in the history of science when a medical author writing a treatise on epilepsy, a disease called by the Greeks the "sacred disease," began his treatise with the observation, "I am about to discuss the disease called sacred. It is not, in my opinion, any more sacred than any other disease, but has a natural cause, and its supposed divine origin is due to man's inexperience and to his wonder at its peculiar character."

Another distinctive feature of Greek science was the emergence of the basic concept of a "generalized" science as distinct from a set of empirical rules. The Egyptians, in their mathematical writings, had given specific problems such as the finding of the area of a _particular_ field with particular dimensions. But the theoretical and abstract geometry that lay behind these observations remained unexpressed and latent. Now, with the Greeks, it was the theoretical and abstract geometry that became the object of attention. For example, starting with fundamental definitions, axioms and postulates, they arrived at the _general_ solution for the area of _any_ triangle.

Closely connected with this rise of a generalized theoretical and abstract science, and with the rise of the naturalistic critical spirit that we have noted, was the evolution of a discipline of reasoning: logic. Together with its kindred discipline of mathematics, logic is a fundamental instrument of science. Observed data, even were they assembled by the most careful experimental means, would mean little if we had no rules for testing the truth and falsity of arguments.

By the time of Aristotle, in the fourth century B.C., the Greeks had organized logic as a powerful discipline. We know they used logic with great skill in their mathematics. The Greek mathematician made himself the master of _deduction_ (the drawing of necessary inferences from given premises). The Greek scientist understood less adequately <u>inductive</u> logic (the drawing of probable conclusions from many particulars in such a way that the relative probability of a conclusion depends on the completeness of the set of particulars).

Although the Greek scientist's discussion of the relationship between arguments and experience was somewhat unsatisfactory, in practice he often exhibited an almost intuitive understanding of the proper relation of a scientific theory to observed data. The whole of Greek astronomy can be viewed as one mathematical system fashioned after another to account for the movement of heavenly bodies. We can also mention, as an example of the careful use of the data of experience, Aristotle's patient collection and discussion of zoological data to explain the generation, growth, structure, and habits of animals.

The Greek scientist did not limit his contacts with experience to passive observations. He often <u>experimented</u> in the modern sense of this word, carefully controlling certain natural phenomena so that they would reveal the answers to specific questions put by man to nature. For example, Greek optics were based on experimentation, on the careful observation and recording of the paths of reflected and refracted light rays.

If, then, there was considerable experimental activity we might well ask in what way Greek science fell short of modern science. The answer is that the greater success of modern science lies in the maturity and universality of its use of mathematical-experimental techniques. There is no question that a Greek mathematical-experimental science existed in beginning form in optics and in applied mechanics. Nor is there any question that a mathematical-observational science was present in Greek astronomy. But the techniques of these sciences were often primitive and were not yet commonly considered the necessary method in all phases of natural inquiry.

The next question that strikes us as important in tracing the history of science is, "How did the early Greek mathematical and experimental techniques grow into the modern methods?" The first factor of importance is that Greek science and learning has had a continuous and corporate history. The great body of Greek learning was translated into Arabic in the ninth and tenth centuries and then again from Greek and Arabic into Latin in the twelfth and thirteenth centuries. This body of laws provided the content of medieval university studies. For two or three hundred years the medieval scholars pored over it. It then became the indispensable base on which early modern science was built.

The acceptance of this essential continuity in the development of Western thought does not belittle the scientific activity of the seventeenth century, the century of Galileo, Boyle, Hook, Leibniz, and Newton. Rather it serves to clarify that knowledge, to show how in part it arose from the interplay, modification, and rearrangement of older stock ideas as they were fashioned into an essentially new system.

In the seventeenth century there occurred an extraordinary burst of scientific activity whose direction and elaboration in the next two centuries transformed the essential nature and outlook of Western man. The seventeenth century perhaps is the most significant hundred years in the history of science.

It is more and more clear to the historian of science that the geniuses of the seventeenth century were prepared in their work by the prior activity of numerous scientists and philosophers. We can detect in the high and late middle ages several currents of activity that were to converge and produce that extraordinary acceleration of scientific activity that identifies the seventeenth century.

We can point first to the increasing dependence on experience as a criterion of truth or probability in the late medieval university discussions of physical problems. From at least the thirteenth century experimental activity increased in optics, statics, magnetics, anatomy, and other fields. There was a rising naturalism evident in zoological and botanical illustration. It coincided with the rising naturalism of the late medieval and Renaissance painting.

These currents of experience, experiment, and naturalism were no doubt nourished by changes in social and economic organization--changes toward a more highly developed money economy. It should not be surprising if the increasing evidence of empiricism in economic activity had some influence on intellectual currents, although exact connections between the two are elusive.

The extension of a quantitative approach to physical problems was equally important. This approach was particularly evident in the thirteenth century when the great works of Greek mathematics and mechanics were being mastered and used by original and clever mathematicians like Jordanus de Nemore and Gerard of Brussels. This quantitative approach was extended to other mechanical problems in the fourteenth century at the Universities of Oxford and Paris. It spread rapidly to the Italian universities, there to persist until the time of Galileo. This quantitative approach, stimulated originally by a knowledge of Euclid and to some extent Archimedes, was nourished further in the sixteenth century by the even wider spread and use of the works of Archimedes.

At the same time that these techniques which were to characterize seventeenth century science were slowly developing, a philosophical base for the new science was being prepared. The Aristotelean philosophy with its concept of a finite cosmos, of matter and form, of substance and accident was giving way to an atomic philosophy with its unbounded universe. There appears to have been some intimate connection between the rise of a mechanics interested in measuring matter in movement and a philosophy which reduced everything to matter in movement.

We have continually characterized modern science and its prototypes as mathematical and experimental. Both these aspects of modern science should be kept in mind.

We cannot explain Galileo's success in laying the foundations of modern mechanics by saying merely that he experimented. As important as experimentation was for Galileo, his "geometrizing" of the problems of mechanics was of even greater significance. We have suggested already that we first owe to the Greeks the method of mathematical abstraction in physical problems, or if you will, the selection and mathematical manipulation of idealized quantities. The thirteenth century investigators recognized the power of this method and they used it with some success but Galileo employed it with far greater skill in the seventeenth century than did any of his medieval predecessors. However, even his mathematical techniques fell far short of those of his most important successor, Sir Isaac Newton.

It is, then, the skillful use of mathematical abstraction--and indeed the recognition of its paramount importance--that sets Galileo off from a Francis Bacon, the former a successful mechanician, the latter an advanced empiricist. This use of abstraction must set out from experience and must ultimately be able to return to experience if successful physical investigation is to follow.

Speaking technically, the most successful modern physical theories start from idealized postulates and expand to a systematic explanation by deducing specific examples from these general postulates. Theories must then relate the specific deductive conclusions to experience by as many independent routes as possible. It was to the great glory of the physicists of the seventeenth century that they recognized the importance of the mathematical-deductive procedure as well as the relationship that scientific theory must have with experience. We cannot pretend in this chapter to describe how Newton, for example, in his <u>Mathematical Principles of Natural Philosophy</u> used this mathematical-experimental technique to erect a far-reaching mechanical system on the basis of two fundamental ideas--inertia and gravity. Nor can we tell the story in any detail of now Newtonian mechanics grew in power and diversity until the end of the nineteenth century, when it began to suffer important citicisms that led to the recent creation of relativity physics and quantum mechanics.

But while we cannot tell these substantial facts, we can notice certain other achievements of seventeenth century science that have foreshadowed significant modern results. For example, the importance of measurement in the method of the seventeenth century scientist stimulated in remarkable fashion the development of new precision instruments. To the late sixteenth and the whole seventeenth century we owe the invention of the telescope, the microscope, the barometer, the thermometer, precision calipers, the pendulum clock, and numerous other instruments.

It is also to the seventeenth century that we owe that characteristic scientific institution--the scientific academy. Originating in Italy, the idea of the scientific society or academy spread in the second half of the seventeenth century to England, where the Royal Society was founded, and to France, where the Academie Royale was initiated. These societies gained extensive local and foreign memberships and functioned as clearing houses for the important scientific information of the day. They began to publish scientific journals and started the tradition which plays a paramount role in modern science: the free and widespread exchange of ideas. The most successful and persistent of the seventeenth century journals was the Philosophical Transactions of the Royal Society.

As we pass from the seventeenth century into the eighteenth, we see the quantitative technique, first developed in mechanics, being successfully applied to other areas of scientific thought. Chemistry became more quantitative and experimental under the influence of Black and his successors in England and, later, Lavoisier in France. The achievements of the latter in the last quarter of the century prepared a chemical revolution only slightly less significant than that of Newton for mechanics.

The scientific organization begun in the seventeenth century continued and spread in the eighteenth--more societies, more journals, more public museums, gardens, and zoos. In addition, co-operative scientific enterprises were undertaken, such as expeditions to study and describe eclipses.

The eighteenth century was the century in which the influence of Newtonian science was felt in many nonscientific quarters. The technique of scientific popularization was perfected, and much more was done to create the popular legendary view of the scientist as the "true" herald of progress and the learned opponent of superstition.

Scarcely less important than the seventeenth century in determining the essential character of modern science was the nineteenth century. All phases of nature were subjected to careful mathematical and experimental techniques Even geology, which during most of the eighteenth century was the product of the wildest speculation, became in the nineteenth century highly observational and on occasion experimental.

The enormous growth of specialization was perhaps the most impressive result of the century's activity. Where there was a single science of chemistry at the beginning of the century numerous specialized branches existed at the end of the century: inorganic chemistry, organic chemistry, physical chemistry, and others.

Similarly, scientific organizations multiplied. Separate societies for the separate sciences were formed. The societies of all kinds tended to become even more international than in the past. The number of specialized journals multiplied.

With the increasing specialization came important improvements in technique. The modern university laboratory is largely a creation of the nineteenth century. New instruments of all kinds extended and deepened the scientist's research possibilities. The camera allowed him to make permanent records of detail. The spectroscope opened up the very constitution of the stars that had been confidently predicted to be forever out of the reach of detailed analysis.

With the phenomenal growth of all aspects of science in the nineteenth century, the enormous practical possibilities of applying the fruits of science were recognized. The whole electrical industry that underlies almost every feature of twentieth century life is little more than a century old. It stems from apparently useless experiments with electric batteries in a laboratory at the end of the eighteenth and the beginning of the nineteenth century. Synthetic textiles--rayon, nylon, orlon--have a similar history.

In spite of this extraordinary growth of science in recent centuries we can still see the roots of man's early scientific efforts. While today we may apply a non-Euclidian geometry or some new algebra for our interpretation and explanation of nature, we are doing essentially the same thing that Ptolemy was doing when he applied spherical geometry to interpret the movements of the heavens. We are still trying to explain the phenomena by mathematical construction. Without an Aristotle and Ptolemy as predecessors a Newton is inconceivable, and without a Newton an Einstein is inconceivable. Science truly has a long and continuous history.

From the picture of science that the previous chapters have given us, we can now gain a better idea of what goes on in the inside of research. This chapter spotlights some of the outstanding techniques.

CHAPTER 5

THE INSIDE OF RESEARCH

Farrington Daniels

The scientific method is one of man's most powerful tools. Scientific observations were made and recorded in early civilizations, and theories were ably propounded by the Greeks, but it remained for modern Western civilization to put observation and theory together and to plan experiments in an effective technique which has come to be known as the scientific method. It involves four stages: observation, correlation of observations, theorizing and predicting, and finally checking and rechecking of the theory by experiments. This method is widely used, consciously or unconsciously, by scientists and by many others in the solution of everyday problems.

Most people are familiar with the accomplishments of science. They read of airplanes that fly faster than the speed of sound, of rockets that penetrate 100 miles into the stratosphere, of atom smashers that operate at a hundred million volts. They hear of machines that will weigh to a billionth of an ounce or that will carry out in a tenth of a second a calculation that would require 100 years of human mathematicians. These achievements and these gadgets make the headlines, but they are not the essentials of science. The center of science is the scholar who thinks and works in certain ways.

We have followed the story of atomic energy and noted the successes of the scientists. It is easy to be overimpressed by these successes. Many of the men who contributed to this development were Nobel Prize winners, but we should remember that for every scientist who makes the headlines, there are hundreds who work quietly and persistently in spite of frustrations. Each may contribute some bit of scientific knowledge and publish it, until finally the work of many together shows some new pattern of truth. Often it appears as if the successful scientist had put them together, a miscellany of many men's work, and completed a picture puzzle.

In working out his problems the scientist makes important use of measurement. Improvements in the precision and range of measurements often lead to new development in science. The lens, the microscope, the ultramicroscope, and the electron microscope, each in turn has opened up new worlds to measure. Each has enabled the scholar to peer deeper into the finer structures of matter. Each new decimal point achieved in greater accuracy also reveals new relations and opens up a wealth of new material to the experimenter.

We should distinguish between different kinds of measurements. While the number of pigs in a pen is definite, the accuracy with which we can measure the length of an iron bar depends on the mechanical aids available. Our description of this length in terms useful to others requires reference to a standard yardstick. We have a standard weight and a standard temperature scale. We have a standard rat for biological studies. Whenever our standards are ill-defined, our science is inexact.

Next in importance to measurement comes calculation. Calculation is necessary for correlating results and formulating and testing theories. Arithmetic and algebra are replaced by calculus and advanced mathematics as the quantitative relations become more complicated; and now new mechanical and electronic computing machines are taking us far beyond the limitations of human computing, both in speed and complexity.

Graphical methods are of great value in bringing out the relations in a scientific investigation. Everyone is familiar with those graphs in which business sales are plotted vertically and the months and years are plotted horizontally. There are many researches in which one variable, such as pressure, is plotted vertically and another variable, such as temperature, is plotted horizontally. The scientist often tries to find some way of plotting which will give straight lines. When there are three different factors involved in a given phenomenon, it is sometimes convenient to make space models in three dimensions.

When the scientist makes calculations he often is compelled to put numerical values on the errors of measurement. Successive measurements of the same quantity may differ and when they do, it is common practice to take the average value. But how significant is this average? This is difficult to determine. Particularly in the biological and social sciences it is very difficult to evaluate the magnitude of the errors. New methods of statistical analysis are very helpful here, so that what once was largely guesswork now approaches a more exact science.

The importance of pure mathematics to the scientific method can scarcely be exaggerated. By reason of its very abstractness, mathematics is effective. Because it is free from specific limitations, it can be used in solving a host of problems of great variety. As fast as the mathematicians develop new abstract relations and means of calculating them, the physicists, chemists, biologists, and engineers follow quickly with their practical applications.

In chemistry and physics the scientists have a comparatively easy time, because they can manipulate their materials in the laboratory and can devise any experiments they wish within the limits of the range and accuracy of their apparatus. In their calculations they can rely on the laws of probability because in their measurements even the smallest amount of material still contains billions and billions of molecules--numbers so large that the statistical laws of average apply with exactness.

The botanists and the agriculturalists have a more difficult task. As a general rule they have to be content with a lesser degree of accuracy because there are more variables involved and greater variations in the behavior of individual plants and cells. The biologist is further limited because he has to consider the comfort of a co-operating animal. Astronomers and geologists have to take most things as they find them, for they can't order a volcanic eruption or an eclipse of the sun to suit the convenience of their experimental program.

Human affairs are even less manageable. We are practically helpless in planning our experiments and can rely only on our ingenuity in taking quick and intelligent advantage of situations that are occurring naturally. Only rarely do we get voluneers to accept the imposition of disease--as did the heroes of yellow fever--to provide experimental facts for study so that others may be saved. We don't initiate an epidemic or create a financial depression or start a war just to provide laboratory material for scientific study. But when these calamities do occur, it is the work of the historian, social scientist and statesman to study them scientifically to try to find out their causes and, if may be, their cure. Here the methods of science, being difficult to apply, have been little used. Many feel that greater use might give greater results.

Modern science is so specialized and has such a large body of technical knowledge in each of its specialized fields and such a huge vocabulary of technical terms that it is often difficult to explain to the layman.

A research project at the Argonne National Laboratory on radiation sickness may perhaps serve to illustrate some of the principles of scientific research. It was known that exposure to very intense radioactivity produces illness and, in extreme cases, death. But the mechanism of this damage to the living organism was not fully understood. It was this mechanism that needed to be studied. The scientists reasoned something like this: "The first question to ask ourselves is, 'Is this a matter of direct physical damage or is it a matter of chemical changes which in turn destroy the normal functions of the living organism?' We know that a variation in temperature will not greatly affect physical changes but will profoundly affect chemical changes. A rise of $10°$ C. frequently doubles or trebles the rate of chemical change. (Hence, our home refrigerators). Let us therefore expose a living organism to radioactivity at low temperature where the chemical changes resulting will be slow and the distinction between chemical and physical change more apparent.

"Now what organism can we so cool down? Warm-blooded animals like mice have body temperatures that are cleverly thermostated. Cold-blooded animals like frogs are not thus thermostated. The temperature of frogs can be changed over a wide range without injuring them, merely by changing the temperature of the surrounding water."

Therefore, frogs were chosen for the experiment. When the frogs had been cooled to low temperatures they were exposed to intense radioactivity and were observed over long periods of time. Those frogs that were kept at low temperatures where chemical reactions are slow showed no radiation sickness. However, when they were warmed up hours and even days after their exposure to gamma rays or X-rays, sickness and damage to tissues appeared. The experiment thus showed that radiation sickness is a consequence of chemical changes which follow the primary exposure to radioactivity.

This experiment involved several aspects of the method of science. It was necessary to measure the intensity of the X-rays, and ionization meters had to be invented and developed. The per cent of the X-rays absorbed by the frogs had to be measured and calculated. It isn't accurate enough to tell how sick a frog is by looking at it and watching it hop. A technique was developed for counting the red and white blood cells, for the ratio of white to red blood cells offers a quantitative measure of radiation sickness. Not all frogs behave alike. Consequently, many frogs were used and the average blood readings determined. Probable errors were then calculated. Significantly, frogs are not mice and mice are not men. Nevertheless, their blood behavior, when exposed to radiation, is similar and it is safe to conclude that radiation sickness in men, as in frogs, involves the production of some chemical material which is detrimental to normal life processes.

* * * * * *

Various branches of science advance in various ways and not always according to the typical pattern of the scientific method. Observation, invention, intuition, hypothesis, reason, and interpretation all play important roles in research. Even chance is a factor, but it has been pointed out correctly that "chance favors the trained worker."

When a scientist embarks on a new research program, either because he is interested simply in exploring a particular field or because he hopes to find something useful, he first develops a working hypothesis and then turns to the scientific literature to see what has been done before and to discover to what extent he may build on the work of others. He usually goes through a well-indexed abstract journal. For example, <u>Chemical Abstracts</u> records researches at the rate of about a thousand a week which are summarized from all the publications of the world in the field of chemistry. If an abstract appears to be relevant, the investigator locates the original article for more details. Then he makes plans for experimental measurements and for the design and construction of apparatus he will need. Often the precision required is so great or the conditions so extreme that many months or years may be required to develop suitable equipment. Again, in some researches he can use standard apparatus from his laboratory or from a supply company. Then come long series of measurements with improving accuracy. These are followed by critical evaluation and correlation and generalization. Often the research leads to plans for practical application of the new findings.

In general there are two main types of scientific research: pure or fundamental research, and applied or programmatic research. Both are important, but applied research soon becomes ineffective unless there is a constant flow of fundamental research into our storehouse of knowledge.

Before World War II this reservoir of fundamental knowledge was filled chiefly through the published work of universities, government laboratories, and research institutions, many of them in Europe. The war greatly injured the European laboratories and turned most of our scientists to applied research. Thus, we were drawing from our capital of fundamental knowledge more rapidly than we were adding to it.

When we are in a hurry to get answers to specific questions, as in wartime, we stress applied research and are likely to throw our full resources in manpower and laboratory facilities into it. A team of scientists is assigned to tackle a given problem; the team works together under pressure for a common goal, each man ignoring the interesting sidelines that turn up. He is not free to follow up these new trails, no matter how interesting they may be. He is supposed to spend only as much time on the development of theories as is necessary for the solution of his immediate problem.

This type of applied research can be very effective and is widely used in industry. In the long run, the fundamental approach is more valuable. Even for solving specific problems it can be very effective if there is sufficient time.

The difference between the two approaches can be illustrated if we pursue a hypothetical search for a chemical that will kill a specific type of weed. The chemical must be quickly toxic to the weed, nonpoisonous to animals and to other plants, noncorrosive, cheap, and capable of quick manufacture in carload lots. If the selection must be made quickly, the staff may be turned loose to pick bottles of chemicals from the shelves to test on the weeds by "cut-and-try" or "trial and error" to find out which best meets the need for a poison. If more time is available, however, the theorists will try to explain why one type of plant is killed, why other types are unaffected, why animals are not affected when plants are. Many experiments will be carried out with other plants and other chemicals to help suggest a general theory of selective plant poisoning. From this theory, predictions of possibilities in other cases may be evolved. Now this more fundamental approach has provided all the information that would be obtained by the cut-and-try method, plus much more.

Suppose, for example, that the laboratory is called upon a second time to find a specific killer for a second type of weed. If cut-and-try was used the first time, it may be necessary to repeat the mad scramble of trying one bottle after another. However, if sufficient fundamental knowledge was acquired concerning the "why" of the behavior of both plant and poison, it may be much easier to choose another chemical to fight another weed.

Often, however, the empirical approach is necessary. Indeed, in the hands of Edison and other pioneers, it was of the utmost value. But as science advances, the fundamental attack is usually more effective.

Not only do we have different types of research, but we have different types of scientists, each contributing in his own way. In general, we have theorists and experimentalists. Some scientists are vigorous pioneers who like to explore a new field, skim the cream off of it, and move on to another field. Other scientists restrict their efforts and carry on their investigations in great detail and perfection in a limited sphere. Among the scientists we have those who can remember all the facts of previous related work. We have inventors, designers of apparatus, careful laboratory manipulators, calculators, analyzers, and co-ordinators of data, classifiers, speculators, and theorists. Then we have those who study the published works of others and write critical reviews, monographs, and books. Each of these scientists is important, and a laboratory is fortunate if it has a well-balanced team of different types of experts.

One of the hopes for the use of the scientific method is that it can be employed also to solve some of the problems that block our progress in human affairs. It would seem that human problems might be tackled with the same mental tools of many observed facts, invention, intuition, hypothesis, reason, and interpretation. Today where very extensive data are gathered, statistical and other machines help with the tabulation and correlation. Still, there are those who feel that human problems are too complex to yield to scientific study. They feel that even if they were provided with electronic calculators of tremendous size which could solve all problems presented to them, in the welter of human variables they would not know how to ask the machines the pertinent questions or to present to them the essential problems.

Of course many and various human problems have been given considerable scientific study--child behavior, national nutrition, health and disease, aspects of public education. Certainly the open mind, careful observation, imagination, and unselfish application can well be extended in further study in many social fields. Also the cautious approach, which checks conclusions by controls, is needed. The joke about the scientist who spanked only one twin and kept the other for a control illustrates the point. If any experiment is to have validity one must ask, "Where are the controls?" How do you know that your particular course of action was responsible for the observed effects? Perhaps the patient would have recovered, the political crisis have passed, without your remedy. Perhaps it was not the political party in power but a drought abroad that set your plans awry. "What are the facts?" is an essential question. Not prejudice, not political dogma, but carefully collected facts, considered by able and well-trained minds, might lift many aspects of our common affairs to a more hopeful level. As the basis of scientific advance lies in the able minds that observe and think, so the basis of social advance might well be able minds that observe and think in like fashion in the great human laboratory.

A great deal of scientific information has no practical value when first discovered. Practical applications--better foods and drugs and clothes--are made in the most unexpected and varied ways when the scientific method is put to work.

CHAPTER 6

PUTTING SCIENCE TO WORK

Farrington Daniels

To show the impact of science on our modern civilization is one of the purposes of this book. We have considered the methods of science. We shall now observe how science is put to work for the service of mankind. We shall see how advances in the laboratory are followed by engineering applications and industrial manufacturing.

Often a valuable new product comes unexpectedly as an unplanned by-product of pure research. A good example of this is hybrid corn, which is now the chief grain crop of the United States. At a time which was critical for the world's food supply, pure research in genetics resulted in a 20 per cent increase in the farmer's yield of corn.

The story goes back to 1816 in New England, when Cotton Mather observed wind pollination of corn plants. In the middle 1800's Darwin noted occasional increased vigor of the hybrid offspring over its parents. In the last quarter of the century scientists were crossing different varieties and specializing in the inbreeding of corn for generation after generation in a search for clues to the mechanism of heredity. Early in the present century, experiments were carried out on the crossing and recrossing of two purebred lines. At first the results were varied and inconclusive. It was not apparent that any practical results were near. An ear of hybrid corn would be just as likely to have extra numbers of underdeveloped kernels as larger ones. By 1918 a fair degree of stability had been achieved, but progress was slow until the 1930's.

During all this time the large expenditures of effort and money by agricultural experiment stations were justified not on the basis of practical results but on the basis of a better understanding of hybrid vigor in corn. The minds of the scientists were not closed to the practical possibilities of a sturdier, larger-eared corn for the commercial market, but they were not under instructions to try to produce such a variety. They were expected to find out what they could about the principles of inheritance in corn.

The results were a boost in annual income of 22 millions of dollars for the farmers in the state of Wisconsin alone and a potentially higher standard of living, greater purchasing power, and more food to export for a war-torn world.

The story of penicillin follows a different pattern and illustrates an accidental discovery of great importance. Alexander Fleming while making bacterial studies in England in 1929 observed that his bacteria cultures had become contaminated with mold. Now a mold growth in a bacterial culture is like a weed in a garden, but Fleming noted something peculiar about this weed and did not discard the culture. Around the mold was a clear area where the bacteria did not grow. He identified the mold as penicillin, made an extract of it and found that it contained a chemical which definitely inhibited the growth of certain bacteria.

This discovery fitted into a program designed to find a killer of bacteria which would not be injurious to man. By 1939 penicillin was being produced in small flasks at Oxford University. Then came World War II and with it the need for a millionfold expansion of production to combat pneu-

PUTTING SCIENCE TO WORK 51

monia alone. Help was sought in the United States. The problem of mass production was taken up by a Department of Agriculture laboratory in Peoria, Illinois, which found that corn-steep liquor, a by-product of starch production, favored the growth of the mold when milk sugar was added. This information was given to chemical pharmaceutical manufacturers, who then went to work on tank production of penicillin as part of the war effort. Meanwhile the Peoria laboratory sought a mold more productive than the original species and found it on cantaloupe. In a university laboratory two researchers in quest of a more productive strain altered conditions of growth and obtained No. 119, which yielded a 10-to-50 per cent increase over the original culture in Britain. These results of applied research occurred in 1944. By the end of 1948 the United States was producing over two tons per month of the dry material from which penicillin units are made.

Another story of applied research is that of dicoumarol. Cattle were dying of mysterious hemorrhages caused by eating spoiled sweet-clover hay. Through a series of patient laboratory studies under Professor Link of the University of Wisconsin it was found that the cattle sickness was caused not by bacteria but by a well-known chemical compound, dicoumarol. It was further found that the effect can be offset by administering the blood-clotting agent vitamin K. These findings led to practical uses. Dicoumarol is now an important medicine used on man to retard the clotting of blood in surgical procedures, while a related compound is finding wide use as a successful rat poison.

A further illustration of science put to work is a new process for the fixation of nitrogen. Nitrogen is one of the chief ingredients of fertilizers and explosives. There are 30,000 tons of nitrogen in the air over every acre of land, but nitrogen resists our efforts to make it combine with other chemicals so that we can make use of it. However chemical processes which will convert the free nitrogen of the air into useful compounds are known. We call these processes "fixing nitrogen." For forty years most of our fixed nitrogen has been produced in the form of ammonia by the complicated Haber process. A simpler process was started at the University of Wisconsin after years of theoretical study on the behavior of nitrogen oxides. This process has now been through engineering development, and a production plant has been built.

It was known that the nitrogen and oxygen of the air will combine chemically at very high temperatures, around 4,000° F., but that usually this chemical product breaks up again on cooling. However, if the gases could be cooled quickly enough, before there was time for this breakup to occur, the fixed nitrogen could be preserved for practical use. Dr. F. G. Cottrell suggested to a Wisconsin scientist that with pebble beds of refractory material, which are very effective in the quick transfer of heat, it should be possible to chill the gases quickly. At the same time the pebble beds would serve to preheat the air and so lead to the temperature of 4,000° F. merely by burning fuel gas in air. Moreover these same pebble beds through which the gas flowed would save fuel by holding the heat and reducing its loss from the chimney.

There were many difficulties to overcome. A suitable material to withstand these very high temperatures had to be found. Also the pebble beds became clogged with volatilized material and the economical conversion of the small amount of fixed nitrogen into useful products required much research.

Laboratory work started in 1939, the first nitrogen was fixed in 1941, and by 1944 the process was operated on a pilot-plant scale to discover weak spots and to get ready for actual production. Many industrial companies looked over the process and were impressed. Finally one company, interested in getting into the chemical production field, took the process over and after four years of research and an investment of over a million dollars solved the technical difficulties and produced continuously a ton of nitric acid per day. Then, thirteen years after the laboratory work was started, a large plant for making nitric acid was built at a cost of over two million dollars.

PUTTING SCIENCE TO WORK

This history illustrates the very large investments in time and money which lie back of modern technology's contributions to the public. Many other similar stories could be cited, and perhaps just as many ventures which failed to develop for technical or economic reasons and which resulted in loss to those who had invested money and effort. .

We are still working on many unsolved problems. Cancer and poliomyelitis are being studied intensively. We are confident of ultimate success in these fields, but we will probably have to wait until we have done a great deal more fundamental research. The chances of finding cures for these diseases increase with the amount of effort going into the researches and with the number of scientists of all types working on the problems. Success, however, is just as likely to come from some entirely new understanding gained in a laboratory of chemistry or physics or biology as from a clinical hospital.

The industries of the United States are spending a great deal of their money in applied research and increasing amounts in fundamental research in those fields that seem to promise new applications. These industrial companies find it to their advantage to support research both because of hopes for future returns and because they thus have on hand experts who can help meet emergencies. Also a few outstanding scientists help them to attract able young scientists to their laboratories and thus build up an organization which can point out new products to be made, short cuts in production, and analyses of manufacturing difficulties. A large company which does not have a research staff is likely to find itself behind, because of obsolescence and the development of newer and more successful processes. It is reported that the Du Pont company in 1942 obtained more than half its gross income from materials that in 1928 did not exist or were known only in the laboratory. The cost of research in modern industrial companies may well be charged up to the cost of operating.

A far-seeing research director seeking new things for his company to make was impressed by the published laboratory findings of a Catholic priest on the chemical reactions of acetylene. Acetylene is a gas containing carbon and hydrogen in small molecular units which tend to grow into bigger molecules--the phenomenon known as polymerization. The director hired a brilliant young chemist to extend the investigations. These researches led eventually to the production of synthetic rubber.

Again, researches on another rubber-like polymer led to the production of strings of plastics which resemble fibers. Then followed a long, intensive program of applied research which resulted in nylon, a substitute for silk. Now, after millions of dollars more of research, have come the substitutes for wool: orlon and dacron.

The large industrial companies owe a tremendous debt to science and to the universities which produce and publish scientific researches and also select and train the scientists. But science also owes much to industry for developing and making available equipment. Efficient distilling columns developed by industry in the competitive struggle to supply better gasoline are now indispensable in fundamental research on the physical and chemical properties of organic compounds. There is no end to the manufactured apparatus used--telescopes, cyclotrons, thermostats, vacuum pumps, microscopes, autoclaves, animal cages. And where would a modern laboratory be if there were a failure in the electrical supply line?

A great deal of teamwork between scientists and engineers is necessary. On the one side stand the theoretical scientists--the abstract thinkers, and on the other side, the engineers and administrators, in a certain sense the doers. Obviously both are needed. Sometimes we even need the crackpot, for every so often some "fool" blunders into a problem, doesn't know that it can't be solved, and solves it! Modern engineers trained in our universities form an invaluable bridge between fundamental research and its application. They have accomplished marvels in American industry.

The accumulation of fundamental knowledge is an expensive process. Who is going to support it? Will support take the form of taxation, gifts to universities and institutions, or of investments of private capital in old or new industries. It is interesting to note that the industrial companies themselves are realizing the debt which they owe to past fundamental research. A large company is making an annual gift of $10,000 to the departments of chemistry at several universities. The only string tied to this gift is that the money shall not be spent for research which, at the time, has any apparent commercial importance.

As we have seen from the examples given, the process of development follows a general pattern, which plainly shows how vital are the roles played by the laboratory scientists and the engineers. After a scientist or inventor has an idea which may possibly lead to a useful or economic application, a long road of further laboratory work, calculations and testing lies ahead. One writer has estimated that the laboratory phase consumes only 10 per cent of the total cost of development under present conditions. Few people realize the tremendous amount of time and investment of money necessary to convert a scientific discovery or an inventor's idea into an industrial enterprise which is of value to the public and is self-sustaining economically.

First comes a search of the scientific literature, and the chances are that the man with the idea will find that someone else has had the same idea previously. Such a finding does not necessarily deter the new enthusiast from carrying out his program. There can be many reasons why the first attempt was unsuccessful.

Next comes a detailed calculation. If it is in the field of chemistry, for example, the scientist must find out whether or not the proposed chemical reaction is theoretically possible. This he can do with the help of chemical thermodynamics, if sufficient data have been accumulated and published. If data are not available, he must make a guess and make use of empirical rules and analogies with other materials. Just because a chemical reaction is possible, however, does not mean that it will take place with practical or economic speed. The scientist must delve into the field of chemical kinetics. If the reaction seems to be too slow he must explore the possibility of using an accelerator, more commonly called a catalyst.

Then comes a preliminary cost evaluation in which one assumes the best possible conditions and attempts to estimate whether the operation can be economically successful under the most favorable circumstances. This venture, of course, involves guesses regarding market conditions, sources of materials, and similar intangible factors. If the theoretical studies and the economic studies indicate the possibility of a successful process, further exploratory research is undertaken on a somewhat larger scale and an effort is made to get quantitative data for a larger process. According to a very general rule, to which there are many exceptions, the size of the experimental plant is increased perhaps ten- or twenty-fold at a step. Since such undertakings are very expensive, one proceeds with some caution, not investing too much time, men, and money until preliminary, small-scale tests have shown the investment to be justified. When the laboratory tests have proceeded long enough, a small-scale plant is built. Such a plant is called a pilot plant.

The pilot plant is a co-operative venture involving both scientists and engineers. These larger-scale experiments may run into tens of thousands of dollars or even into millions. The pilot plant is operated for a considerable period of time. Variables are changed methodically, and yields of desired materials are recorded. Only after the pilot plant has been tested under a variety of conditions are data available for making a new evaluation of the cost of the process. If the process still looks economically feasible, other engineers are called in to make a detailed design for a full-scale production plant. Mechanical drawings are made. Every bolt and pipe, every piece of machinery, is drawn to scale. It is difficult for an outsider to conceive of the amount of detailed planning and the hundreds of pounds of blueprints which are preliminary to construction.

Even after a plant is operating, a continuing study--both technical and economic--is required. Market conditions may change, the source of raw materials may become depleted, new materials may be developed, aluminum may compete with steel, and plastics may compete with aluminum. Finally, a new chemical process is likely to be superseded by a still newer one. The industrialist must always be alert to decide when his plant becomes obsolete. Several chemical industrialists have stated that improvement in manufacturing methods is so rapid that they must allow only the briefest lifetime for the economic development of a new chemical process. Often, to offset the chances of obsolescence, the new process must show a saving or produce an income sufficient to pay off the cost of development in only a few years

The development of the idea through the pilot plant and production plant stages is much more costly than the original research. What incentive can be used to encourage the long, expensive developments which are necessary before society can reap the benefits of scientific discovery? When the government takes charge of such a development, obviously it is the tax-payers that support the project. It is proper and fitting that the federal government should support those projects which involve national defense or national health and welfare. Inasmuch as government spending is subject to public criticism and this public criticism is intimately bound up with politics, there is a tendency for the government to be conservative in developing new areas. In the development of new processes by private initiative some incentive must be found to encourage the investment of private capital--often risk capital. One important attempt to meet this need has been our patent system.

Many people have attributed a considerable measure of American industrial prosperity to our patent system. However, there are abuses, and the patent system has been under occasional criticism. It seems to me that the concept of the function of patents is not entirely clear. Patents are not needed primarily as an incentive to inventors and scientists; these men love their work and their inventive minds cannot easily be stopped. Although some merit may attach to the idea that a patent is the inventor's just reward, very frequently many different people have contributed over a long period of time to the perfection of a patentable idea. It is often difficult to assign complete originality, or full patent rights, to any one person.

Perhaps a patent system is needed primarily to encourage the investment of sufficient capital to develop scientific ideas until they make available a given product to the public. Also, in a system of private enterprise some incentive must be found to attract private capital to these venturesome projects in sufficiently large amounts. There are many failures as well as successes in new processes, and risks must be taken. If private capital is to take these risks, it has a right to expect a corresponding return. The monopoly which a patent grants for a limited period of time seems to be a practical answer. We cannot ignore the fact that present-day concern with social responsibility has caused more and more people to regard a monopoly as a public trust. Corporations which obtain monopolies are increasingly expected to discharge not only their obligations to the investors, by paying substantial dividends, but also their obligations to the public, by providing better and cheaper products.

Universities also are realizing that they have a moral and social obligation concerning the discoveries made in their laboratories. They do not usually have and probably should not have the business organization to administer and develop them. Many universities are following along the lines pioneered by the Wisconsin Alumni Research Foundation, whereby any financial gains are returned to the University for the support of further research. The Foundation, which handles patents and business arrangements, is completely divorced from the University but gives its profits to the University without strings and with no voice in the administration of the funds given.

The fruits of scientific research grow not in a vacuum but in a social world. As soon as we learned how to build the atomic bomb we had to learn how to control its use, to prevent it from destroying the very things it was created to protect. This chapter shows how the problem of controlling the bomb has raised anew the old question: Can man, having mastered nature, master himself?

CHAPTER 7

CONTROLLING THE BOMB

Farrington Daniels

The first atomic bomb was exploded on the New Mexican desert July 16, 1945. It was dreadfully powerful. Lightning-quick developments followed as the second bomb fell on Hiroshima on August 6, and the third on Nagasaki a few days later. Then came the end of the war. In June, 1946, two experimental bombs were exploded at Bikini Island in the South Pacific, where a fleet of various types of naval vessels had been assembled, some with experimental animals aboard. One bomb was exploded in the air above the ships and the other was exploded under the water. In the spring of 1951, to study the military effectiveness of still more powerful atomic bombs, two more sets of tests were conducted at Eniwetok in the South Pacific. A series of tests of weaker bombs for tactical military use was also carried out in the deserts of Nevada. Continuing tests in both areas provide important data for civilian defense and military planning. Photographs of the actual explosions at Bikini and photographs and detailed studies of the Bikini tests and the bombings of Hiroshima and Nagasaki have been released. Much more information properly remains secret.

Enough is known, however, to terrify the public. It is known that the bomb may be exploded in two general ways, in the air above the target, or under water, adjacent to the target.

The air explosion gives out extremely intense light and heat rays, gamma rays that are like X-rays, and a shock wave through the air equivalent to that produced by the explosion of more than 20,000 tons of TNT. The heat rays burn flesh and start many fires. The gamma radiation causes radiation sickness and eventual death to all animals and persons within a quarter of a mile. The shock wave causes severe to complete destruction from the target point for a radius of half a mile and causes heavy to severe damage up to a mile. The blast damage is moderate to heavy from one mile to a mile and a half, and beyond a mile and a half the damage is only slight. Within the destruction area many fires are apt to start a "fire storm" of great violence, which sweeps rapidly through the whole area. The simultaneous and instantaneous destruction of large areas of a city and the loss of fire-fighting, police, and hospital facilities and personnel causes panic and widespread destruction.

The second type of atomic explosion is the under water burst. Many experts regard this as comparatively inefficient from a military standpoint. There are no heat waves and few gamma rays from this explosion and no destructive shock waves. But highly radioactive water and mist are showered on the surrounding area, and they contain dangerous fission products. Such products from a uranium explosion emit beta and gamma rays, while unconsumed plutonium from a plutonium bomb emits alpha particles. The fission products consist of many different chemical elements with varying half lives. After one hour the radioactivity will decay to 1/160th the intensity it had at the end of a minute; after a week it will drop to 1/50,000th the intensity it had a minute after the explosion. The widespread radioactive contamination resulting from an underwater atomic explosion such as that at test "Baker" at Bikini is not too probable for most American cities. Only where a deep harbor is immediately adjacent, within a mile of a densely populated region, would the hazard be severe. On the other hand, cities near shallow lakes or rivers would not be in great danger from an underwater bomb.

Different types of radioactive hazards are produced. In the air burst, a flash of gamma rays persists for a few seconds, and then the radioactive cloud is harmlessly dispersed in the stratosphere. In the underwater burst, all the radioactive material is trapped by the water and confined to a relatively small area. In this area, however, these products can cause serious continuing damage inside the body if taken into the lungs by breathing, into the blood through cuts, or into the stomach in contaminated food.

In the early postwar years, atomic war was thought of in terms of the strategic bombing of cities and the destruction of naval vessels. Later, with the accumulation of a large stock pile of bombs the tactical use of weaker bombs against armies was considered.

The most likely method of delivery of atomic bombs is by dropping them from airplanes. They can probably be shot from large artillery pieces, from rockets, from field positions, or even from surfaced submarines. Theoretically, they could be brought into a country by truck or other standard means of transportation and exploded at a later time at will. Or they could be delivered in small pieces and assembled later. Such delivery involves a plot of a considerable number of men and is more easily noticed. Detection of a new, unexploded bomb is difficult because it will emit only alpha rays, which are easily stopped by a thin container. A bomb some months old will yield other radioactive elements of nuclear decomposition which are detectable with Geiger counters at a distance.

Authoritative writers believe these sabotage methods are less likely to accomplish widespread destruction than an aerial attack. Defense against aerial attack depends on powerful fighter planes, radar, antiaircraft guns, and guided missiles. But if a large-scale attack were launched with many bomb-carrying planes, a large fraction would probably get through to targets.

The facts of atomic warfare are ominous, but atomic warfare is perhaps no worse than biological warfare and is only worse in degree than block-busters, incendiary bombs, and chemical warfare. War itself is the real enemy. The only real defense lies in the elimination of war and the causes of war. When Bernard Baruch was asked if there was any defense against bombs, he said, "Yes, peace." The best hope now appears to lie in strengthening the United Nations.

But in the meantime, with the threat of war, there is much that we can do now in the way of civilian defense. Fear of the unknown encourages panic and makes defense difficult. Education on atomic matters can offset much of this blind fear.

The dangers of radioactivity are often exaggerated. We accept radioactivity in the form of X-rays, and there has always been weak radioactivity everywhere from cosmic rays. It is the intense radioactivity that is dangerous. When an atomic bomb is exploded in the air, the intense light and gamma radiation continue for about 10 seconds. A piece of cloth or paper will stop the heat rays and a trench or a thick wall will stop much of the gamma radiation. Every second counts in seeking quick refuge. The shock waves and the collapse of buildings follow immediately after the radiation. Reinforced concrete buildings of earthquake-proof construction will hold up quite well, but there is no reason to believe that an average American city will escape the destruction suffered by Hiroshima and Nagasaki. Underground bombproof rooms are adequate protection against all three effects: heat, gamma radiation, and shock waves. Reinforced basement shelters, with suitable exits and protection against falling debris, are next best to the underground refuges. There is no danger in an air burst from lingering radioactivity. Survivors should leave the area of destruction at once if they cannot organize to combat the fires.

In the underwater burst, the danger lies not in fire and demolishing of buildings, but in the lingering radioactivity brought in by the water. Monitoring of the radiation is necessary. Technicians with Geiger counters or other sensitive instruments must determine from time to time the areas which are safe and unsafe. People in buildings or in almost any type of shelter are protected from the first radioactivity, and as soon as the radioactivity in the streets has decayed sufficiently according to the instruments--perhaps in a few hours--the people should leave their shelters and get out of the area to a safe distance as rapidly as possible.

The only permanent civilian defense against atomic bombs lies in the decentralization of cities and industries. Fortunately there are already efforts in this direction. High city taxes, automobiles, busses and good roads, attractive suburban developments and urban parking problems have all contributed to a spreading out of the population from American cities. Taxes, labor conditions and improved truck transportation, too, are causing industries to locate many new factories or branch factories on the edge of cities or in smaller towns. More and more, the assembly lines are collecting their special parts from smaller factories spread through many cities and towns.

These trends are desirable for many reasons and particularly from the standpoint of defense against aerial bombing. Yet decentralization is so unpopular, particularly with urban property owners, that accelerated decentralization by government edict is unlikely. Even in Washington, which is a particularly vulnerable target, and where one has a right to look for leadership in these matters, the well-laid plans for moving some of the government offices to near-by

Maryland and Virginia have had to be postponed. Certainly, though, the government should use every power in its possession to prevent further congestion of people and manufacturing facilities. For example, financial loans for construction and the award of contracts for new defense plants should be denied in those cases that would make civilian defense still more difficult.

On the whole, the progress made in civilian defense is pitifully small. In spite of favorable trends which could have been strengthened, our target areas in industry are becoming more vulnerable every year. The situation is serious. The fact that much of Germany survived two years of severe bombing is not entirely relevant, for in atomic warfare two years of bomb damage could be inflicted in one night and dispersal made impossible. The situation calls for an aroused public opinion and courageous government leadership. Are we responding?

* * * * *

The military effectiveness of atomic warfare, the vulnerability of the United States and the moral problems involved in the use of atomic power were the objects of vigorous discussions and serious conferences among the atomic scientists for months before the bomb over Hiroshima presented these questions to the general public. The scientists held conferences with a panel of a few national leaders called by Secretary of War Stimson to advise the President regarding the use of the atomic bomb in Japan. After the war, when legislation for the ownership and control of atomic energy was being debated in Congress, atomic scientists went to Washington, took an active part in an education program there, and urged upon Congress the control of atomic energy by a civilian commission rather than by the military branch of the government. The founding of the Bulletin of the Atomic Scientists, which gives thoughtful consideration to every aspect of atomic power, was one of their early activities.

Atomic energy is a power that must be controlled nationally for the safety of the country and internationally for the survival of the world. The Atomic Energy Act of 1946 is one of the most drastic and revolutionary laws ever passed by the Congress of the United States. It was necessary to meet drastic new conditions. All uranium and other fissionable materials belong to the United States government. Private laboratories and manufacturers can have more than 10 pounds of uranium in their possession only with special permission. A special five-man commission, appointed by the President, was set up as the United States Atomic Energy Commission and was given complete responsibility and authority for formulating policies and carrying them out. A large administrative staff is now functioning smoothly, and the budget amounts to over a billion dollars a year for construction, engineering, and research. There are many checks and balances, and close liaison is maintained with the military heads and with Congress.

The Atomic Energy Commission has much to do. It is fully aware of its heavy responsibilities and realizes that it has a monopoly on atomic energy and that part of its program is not subject to public criticism because of secrecy. The progress of the atomic energy program is told clearly in the series of semi-annual reports made to Congress and available to the general public at a nominal price.

As a general rule, the Commission works through private contractors, such as the Carbon and Carbide Company, which runs the diffusion plant and the laboratories at Oak Ridge, or the University of Chicago, which operates the Argonne National Laboratory near Chicago, to name only two of several hundred contractors. These contractors are skilled in the technical work which they are hired to do, and they are experienced in the administration of large groups of men.

The Commission is responsible for developing practical devices and weapons of war and for getting an adequate supply of uranium and other raw materials. It encourages peaceful uses of isotopes and industrial power. It seeks to insure fundamental research in the whole field of atomic energy. It encourages the growth and dissemination of knowledge of atomic energy while at the same time keeping highly secret certain items of military and strategic importance.

The problem of secrecy is a difficult one. Security is much more important than secrecy. Uninformed people have clung to a dangerous and false belief that we would have been safe if the United States could only have kept "the secret" of the atomic bomb. But no one can hide a law of nature as if it were a magic formula or a legal paper. Other nations were bound to find the laboratory facts and thus become able to build bombs. The original hope was that if we kept back the information and the technical know-how, other nations would be slowed in their production of bombs and there would be a breathing spell in which the nations of the world would get together and arrange for their mutual benefit a system of control.

The Atomic Energy Commission has adopted a wise policy and declassified--that is, removed from the class of secret--much harmless scientific material which may be of use to American industrial development and of interest to those scientists who are not working under secrecy restrictions.

A great many of the facts of atomic warfare have now been officially released. In a democracy where the people make the decisions, the people should know the facts. When they don't know the facts they are apt to imagine affairs to be worse than they really are. Fear often paralyzes good judgement, and when people are frightened they may do foolish things. They may look for spies among innocent, loyal friends, and they may even listen to those who try to make political capital out of dramatic but irresponsible public accusations against public servants.

It is readily realized that an international armament race with atomic bombs is the greatest of tragedies--yet this came to pass. What possible ways out are there? If neither party in a cold war trusts the other and if agreements cannot be made, the building up of a stockpile of atomic bombs becomes accepted as a tragic but necessary measure. Retaliation and the fear of retaliation, however, are precarious deterrents. And to have a large excess of bombs over those of an enemy is not of much importance if both have enough to destroy the major opposing targets, and with them much of the urban life and productive capacity of both countries.

The most satisfactory solution seems to be international control of atomic energy, trying always and in every way to work out friendly relations with other powers. An eventual solution is to build an effective world governmental organization.

International control has worked in other fields, in maritime regulation, in public health measures, and in narcotic control. Chemical gas warfare was outlawed and the agreement was honored during World War II. International control of atomic energy by the United Nations, with inspection and punishment, seemed to offer the best hope of agreement, but Russia has found this inacceptable.

Possibilities of such control were first explored in preliminary thinking by the atomic scientists before Hiroshima. Then came the brilliant and far-reaching Acheson-Lilienthal report of the State Department in June, 1946. It was incorporated into the expanded Baruch plan, which was next proposed by the United States to the United Nations. According to this plan, the United States would relinquish all its bombs to an international agency of the United Nations and give all its know-how. The United Nations would own and control all the uranium and thorium of the world and any other fissionable material which might be made into bombs. The United Nations would use this fissionable material to operate atomic power piles in strategic places around the world for the generation of useful electricity. Inspection by United Nations experts would have to be free and easy at any time or place in any country. Fissionable material could not be allowed to accumulate in a given country except with the permission of the United Nations Atomic Authority. Otherwise, in a matter of weeks technically skilled violators could take out the atomic fuel from a furnace that is generating electricity and convert that fuel into bombs. Infraction of the United Nations Rules would call for immediate and severe punishment. While inspection for illicit manufacture of bombs would be extremely difficult technically, it was thought to be possible since small manufacturing units for fissionable material are impractical, and the diffusion process of uranium 235 calls for such a huge consumption of electric power that it would be noticeable. Large nuclear reactors for plutonium can be detected by their radioactivity.

This proposal for effective international control of atomic energy was drastic. It called in reality for world government in a limited area, and, as will be shown in a later chapter, such an achievement is exceedingly difficult. Nevertheless, so great was the threat of atomic warfare that most of the nations of the world struggled long and earnestly to try to bring about this great step toward peace After 240 meetings of the Atomic Energy Committee of the United Nations, however, further attempts were abandoned because unanimity could not be obtained. An alternative proposal by Russia was carefully considered and rejected. Instead, 45 of 50 nations agreed to try a somewhat modified plan retaining most of the features of the United States proposal. Throughout, Russia and its group insisted on the veto power when considering punishing an aggressor. The United States replied that the power of veto by any nation would wreck the security which the whole plan strove to achieve. Russia also objected to the right of UN inspectors and police to travel at will in a sovereign country to ascertain the status and amounts of fissionable material. Perhaps the most serious disagreement of all was over timing. The United States said in effect, "Set up a really effective organization to prevent atomic warfare, and we will progressively give up our bombs," while Russia said, "Throw your bombs away first and then we will work out an agreement for international control."

On September 23, 1949, President Truman announced that Russia had effected a nuclear explosion. Shortly afterward, the General Assembly of the UN ordered the Atomic Energy Committee to try again to reach agreement, but agreement still seemed to be impossible. All this time, other nations continued to develop their own techniques and acquire a supply of atomic bombs. Our know-how and our proposals were becoming less valuable as a bargaining tool.

It is important to know that uranium 235 and plutonium now being accumulated for bombs can eventually be used for generating electric power. Every pound is equivalent to a train load of coal for manufacturing and industry that will raise standards of living around the world--just as soon as effective peace can be established.

It was the dream of the atomic scientists that the impelling need for control would lead to international agreements, that these agreements would become stronger in time and lead to further agreements for the control and outlaw of other weapons of war. This hope is dim indeed for the immediate present, but it still exists.

It may well be true, as Churchill and other experts have so often claimed, that the stockpile of atomic bombs in the United States has been the chief deterrent to military conquest of Europe by Russia. Through this threat of a superior atomic arsenal that offsets the superiority of men and military might we have been able to have years of time in which to urge peaceful settlement of differences between the East and the West and to rearm against armed aggression.

But we must not put our reliance on atomic bombs; they may well turn out to be a Maginot Line, and they can certainly be a boomerang. If we place too much confidence in the efficiency of atomic warfare, we may fail to try our utmost for peaceful solutions. We may also be tempted to neglect other important means of military security. Our cities and factories are much more vulnerable to attack than are those of nations like Russia. Moreover, our numerical superiority in atomic bombs can be greatly decreased in the years ahead. Let those who cry loudly for the quick use of atomic bombs be the first to disperse our cities and decentralize our manufacturing!

> *In seeking to master his destiny, man has taken up a problem less dramatic than controlling the bomb but possibly more important: controlling science itself, to best serve mankind. In the United States we have taken one approach to this problem.*

CHAPTER 8

CONTROLLING SCIENCE IN THE UNITED STATES

William B. Sarles
Department of Bacteriology

Our Federal Government conducts research in its own laboratories, finances research in university and private laboratories, and controls the research work of many scientists. Although these activities are related, they are not as centrally directed and related as they may become in the future.

Before considering the control of research, it may be well to ask why science has become so important to our government.

In 1950, Mr. Kimball, the Undersecretary of the Navy, and Mr. Dean, the Chairman of the Atomic Energy Commission, issued the following statement:

> One very essential condition for maintaining our national strength, whether for peace or for war, is that the research in the sciences which is basic to all technological progress be kept at a high level. Such research is now in progress in many universities, private research estab-

lishments, and other laboratories throughout the nation. By this research we add to our store of scientific knowledge and increase the number of highly trained persons available to the nation in time of need. The scientist in his laboratory and the research professor with graduate students are performing a service which may make a critical difference to our country in the difficult years ahead....

This same attitude toward research in the sciences is contained in George Washington's first inaugural address, in which he said: "The arts and sciences are essential to the prosperity of the state and to the ornament and happiness of human life. Every lover of his country and of mankind should be encouraged to support the advances of science."

It is not possible in the space of a few pages to describe how the present 41 bureaus or agencies representing 18 different departments of the federal government became engaged in scientific research. Neither is it possible to give the history of the current practice of providing federal grants to support both basic and applied research in universities, private research institutions and industries. But some idea of the federal government's stake in research can be gained from the fact that in 1950, $1,323,752,311 of federal funds were spent on research projects and contracts. It might even be pointed out that this represents support of science on a scale that would have amazed George Washington.

The taxpayer may well want to know if these expenditures are necessary. At the same time, scientists, who are also taxpayers, are concerned over control by the federal government of their work and their liberties. This concern of scientists is not selfish. It is based upon the realization that excessive or improperly employed government controls may harm the scientific work of the nation. Therefore, the citizen needs to share this concern.

* * * * *

Control of scientific research by means of financial support provided by the federal government is as old as the history of such aids. This form of control has been accepted by scientists without question until the years during and following World War II. It has now become apparent that strong federal support of applied science and development work, with relatively little support for basic, fundamental research, may produce serious imbalance.

It is believed that the need for balance between basic and applied research is even greater than that required between defense and nondefense scientific activities. Definition of what constitutes defense research as contrasted with nondefense work is not easy to accomplish. In addition, projects which start out to be defense work may prove to be of great nonmilitary significance, and of course the reverse may also be true. But in any scientific work there is a difference between the search for new knowledge, and investigations that are made to use known facts in the development of a better process or a better product. Applied research and technology are dependent upon facts which are supplied mainly by basic, fundamental work.

The need for greater federal support of basic research was recognized in the second session of the 81st Congress, which passed Public Law 507, The National Science Foundation Act of 1950. This is an "Act to promote the progress of science; to advance the national health, prosperity and welfare; to secure the national defense; and for other purposes." These described objectives are broad, and at present the National Science Foundation is starting a program which includes support of basic scientific research, provision of fellowships to graduate students in natural sciences, and completion and bringing up-to-date of a roster of the nation's scientific manpower. It is hoped that Congress will support the National Science Foundation degree that will provide adequate, needed aid to fundamental science; it has not done so during the first two years.

What are the possibilities of control through financial support? It was pointed out that federal aids might have a decisive influence upon the subject matter of research; that scientists might work on problems for which federal financial support could be obtained and neglect those for which needed funds could not be secured.

Would it also involve the training of graduate students in sciences? If the subject matter of the research carried on by principal investigators who are faculty members of colleges and universities is defined by federal support, then the only research open to graduate students who are employed as research assistants on such projects turns out to be some part of the main, federally financed program. Therefore, the control exerted through financial support may involve the highly important graduate training program of a university. It may lead to overemphasis upon supported projects and neglect of those which cannot be used for training purposes because of lack of funds. It is even possible that graduate students who are not sincerely interested in scientific research may be induced to get into such work because it offers financial security. Such educational errors would be harmful to the students and would yield inferior results.

There is great need for research workers to consider with care the full significance of federal support of their work. Their freedom of choice of subject matter, the flexibility of their investigations, and the educational aspects of their research activities may be involved.

Administrators of colleges, universities and research institutions would do well to accept Dr. Vannevar Bush's advice. In his "Report of the President of the Carnegie Institution of Washington for the year ending June 30, 1951, Dr. Bush said:

> Many universities are carrying the bulk of their research, and the salaries of their graduate faculties, on government funds. Numerous government agencies, quite independently, are furnishing the lifeblood of our advanced univeristy work in science and technology by grants and contracts. There is the definite

pitfall of greed, and scientific eloquence is sometimes preferred over scientific merit.

Government control, thus far, has not been very onerous. But centralized federal control of research has inherent potentialities that are very dangerous, and bureaucratic control could in time become onerous indeed. Dependence on variable and uncertain yearly government appropriations increases the dangers of control, tends to emphasize the ephemeral, could blight the whole growth, and could put our universities into very serious financial and organizational difficulties.

In the great laboratories created for military purposes we see the most direct methods of governmental control of scientific work and of scientists by security regulations, secrecy restrictions, and loyalty checks. Such controls have as their objective the protection of national security through prevention of transmission of information of potential military value to an actual or possible enemy of the United States. These controls may be established in one or more of four main ways:

(1) Restriction of research classed by the government as secret to government installations which are protected by civilian or military armed guards.

(2) Compartmentalization of research to such an extent that only a few key individuals understand the objectives and progress of the entire program. Workers in any one department are not informed of the results obtained by others engaged in closely related activities.

(3) Classification of the results of research and committing these results to security control that permits them to be seen only by "authorized" persons. Such results cannot be disclosed to "unauthorized" individuals who are not "cleared" for acceptance of the information. Obviously, classified results cannot be published.

(4) Loyalty checks to determine that scientists and other workers engaged in government-supported research are trustworthy and that they will not transmit classified information to real or potential enemies or to fellow citizens who are not authorized to receive such information. Loyalty checks represent the best efforts of a research agency to make sure that an individual will transmit information of importance to the security of the nation only to those entitled to use it in the national interest.

It is these four direct controls of scientific work and of scientific workers that are most troublesome and dangerous, and yet most important. They are troublesome and dangerous because they affect the freedom of inquiry and of publication, because they may stifle rather than stimulate advances in science, and because they impinge upon the freedoms that we are trying so diligently to protect.

Maintenance of secrecy by putting research and development establishments and even production facilities in guarded government reservations is an almost absolute method of control. It can never provide total secrecy, however, because the guards are human beings and hence may err. Also, the scientists or other workers who leave the reservation for any reason may prove to be irresponsible, careless, or even dishonest and thereby disseminate accidentally or purposely the information they have promised to keep secret.

Compartmentalization of research and division of work among many groups or numerous individuals is an effective means for maintenance of secrecy. But it is a costly, frequently inefficient operation because teamwork may be needed to get some jobs done, and compartmentalization is incompatible with co-operative effort. Compartmentalization also requires agreement to keep results secret, because it would not be too difficult for a curious and intelligent enemy agent to piece together odd bits of information and to fit them into a revealing pattern. Here again the integrity, loyalty, and dependability of the individual scientist or administrator become the key to success of the effort to maintain security control.

Classification of the results of research as "top secret," "secret," "confidential," or "restricted" involves security control in descending order of magnitude and difficulty. Such classification implies that someone, or some group of persons responsible to government authority, must determine the qualitative and quantitative aspects of secrecy required. Furthermore, it is necessary for someone or some group continually to review security classifications and to decide when classified information may be designated as "less secret," and finally as free, unclassified knowledge which may be published.

These are difficult tasks to perform, and as the quantity of classified information grows, the complexity of the classification and declassification procedures becomes greater. Those who have been or are now engaged in classification or declassification of information subject to security control will recognize this description of the problem as a gross understatement. It is a monumental labor for even a specialist to differentiate between those results which must be kept secret in the interest of national security and those which should be released because they are of value to the health or welfare of everyone.

This is an activity in which calculated risks must be taken to prevent deposition in a sort of "deep freeze" of all new scientific knowledge. At the same time, it is an activity which must be performed with skill and efficiency to maintain national security in an age when results of at least some scientific research may disturb the delicate balance of military power.

The security classification of some kinds of scientific work and of the results which it yields involves an additional danger. It is entirely possible for poor, inefficient, inaccurate, or even dishonest work to go on under the protective cloak of secrecy. Such work may use up large sums of money and keep needed manpower tied to jobs that yield nothing of value. Under ordinary peacetime circumstances, a scientist, if he is honest and sincere in his work, hastens to report his results at meetings or to publish papers which tell why and how he investigated a problem and what he discovered. If his work is poorly done, if his results are inaccurate, or if the conclusions he draws from the results secured are wrong, he is soon corrected by someone who is able by experimentation to prove his fallibility. But secrecy may protect mediocre or poor work, and if it is used for such a purpose it is bad.

The final method of direct control, the use of loyalty checks to determine who can engage in work of immediate or potential security value, is the most difficult and dangerous of all. Furthermore, it is a necessary procedure because the honesty, integrity, loyalty and responsibility of the individual provide the foundation for the success of any method of direct control.

In present practice, the agency which is responsible for the work to be done requests the Federal Bureau of Investigation, and possibly additional investigative branches of the federal government, to get all of the information available on those qualities of a person's character, behavior and background that will reveal whether or not he is eligible for a position of trust. The individual must be completely honest in reporting upon his own background and experience. The investigators must be thorough, accurate, and objective in their work. Finally, the loyalty board of the agency concerned must study with care and with fairness the information provided by the individual and by the investigators. The final conclusion of such a study must be either that the individual can be trusted or that he is a poor risk and should not be "cleared" for work in which information which may affect the security of the nation is involved.

Unfortunately, loyalty checks are to some extent based upon evidence or reports that may be difficult to prove. Consequently, dishonest, disloyal, or inefficient workers occasionally are entrusted with key jobs. It is also possible for capable, honest, sincere scientists to be kept from positions of trust or to be removed from important jobs because they are judged as poor security risks. When this occurs, the government loses a valuable worker, and the individual suffers severely from the effects of his disqualification. Consideration of the possibilities for error in personnel security investigations and evaluations leads one to confess pleasure and pride that so many are found to be worthy of positions of trust. However, the mistakes which have been made force one to the conclusion that investigation and evaluation of a citizen's loyalty are tasks that need continual study and improvement.

Control of the individual scientist may not end with clearance on loyalty grounds. After he is employed, he may find that his freedom to criticize policies, programs, projects, experimental work or conclusions drawn from such work is restricted. For the intensely individualistic, original, inventive scientist such restrictions may prove to be so damaging that his value to the government is impaired. This does not imply that all good scientists are sensitive prima donnas who cannot stand criticism or control. However, it must be kept in mind that many scientists are restless, dissatisfied persons who believe that almost anything can be improved; furthermore, they are impatient to get at the job of improvement. When such a person is told that he cannot question or criticize, his mildest reaction is one of incredulity, Reference to some scientists as geniuses or as near geniuses may be overdone, but the fact remains that many of the best workers--those who have original ideas--are high-strung, sensitive persons. It is not possible to control and to regiment scientific workers without encountering the danger of losing the new ideas which they might provide if they were given freedom to question and to criticize.

During the past hundred years, when American science made its phenomenal growth, the scientists breathed a free air. They increased in numbers until the members of one scientific society alone numbered sixty-nine thousand. They have multiplied journals in every field. They have met frequently and in large numbers to give and discuss papers in every specialty and branch of science. Most of their scientific laboratories have been freely open to interested visitors. There has been freedom of inquiry and co-operation to a marked degree.

Perhaps the first limitation of publication came in the large industrial laboratories where some of the findings were held as trade secrets.

The greatest limitation came with World War II and the building of immense installations with military significance, where secrecy was required.

It is not the aim of this chapter to give the impression that science in general in the United States is at present subject to government controls which are onerous and destructive of scientific progress. The main purpose in pointing out the kinds and amounts of governmental control of science and of scientists is to aid in the eternal vigilance that is required to preserve our freedom of thought and of inquiry. For freedom to investigate, to report or publish, to work co-operatively, and to criticize the research of others are freedoms which must be guarded zealously. Of course, scientists, like all citizens in a democracy, must carry on their work under the common controls which may be called freedom under the law.

The future of government support of science in the United States is great and challenging. As Pasteur once said: "It is characteristic of science and progress that they continually open new fields to our vision." To develop these new fields and to continue the progress of science, which is so necessary to our national health, welfare and security, demands unremitting effort of all concerned. Keeping science and scientific workers free from controls that may inhibit or prevent progress is everyone's responsibility.

The scientist in Russia appears to be a public servant, bound by totalitarian obedience to intellectual control. Yet we'd be foolish to forget that, year by year, scientists are adding to Communism's strength.

CHAPTER 9

CONTROLLING SCIENCE IN RUSSIA

C. Leonard Huskins
Department of Botany

The issue before us today is really the issue of coercion versus freedom of thought, of authoritarian thought control versus the right of man to seek and to find facts and to follow wheresoever they may lead. It is an issue wider than science as ordinarily conceived and certainly wider than the one science, genetics, that was recently subjected to direct Politburo control in the Soviet Union. Yet much understanding of the barrier between East and West can be reached through analysis of the official destruction of genetics in Russia.

The foundation of Western science is, as we have seen in earlier chapters, its "method of verified hypothesis." This has both negative and positive aspects. On the negative side, it rejects authority as a criterion for the establishment of truth. This does not mean that authorities are scorned or neglected, but that in any issue wherein authority is questioned it is the evidence, not the opinions of the authorities, that decides the issues. On the positive side, the formulation of hypotheses is encouraged but these must be verified by observation, and preferably by experimental confirmation, before they can attain scientific standing.

Data obtained by observation and experiment must be tested statistically for significance and then connected in a rigidly logical framework.

Thus are our "truths" obtained. Scientific "laws" (or "generalizations" as they might better be called) do not imply finality but are subject to continuous revision as new data are obtained or new ideas linking diverse existing data are tested.

By contrast, in the U.S.S.R. today authority plays a very important part in scientific interpretation, and data frequently have to be fitted into political frameworks if their discoverer is to avoid condemnation. The "confession" in the Academy of Sciences of one of the geneticists dismissed because he practiced and taught Mendelian principles in plant breeding reads in part: "I admit that I held an incorrect ideological position ... The speech of Vasilenko showed me how important it is at this time to uphold the authority of President Lysenko." The authority of Stalin was recognized in matters of music, history, art and various sciences. Authority, as in any dictatorship, is not merely moral; neglect of or deviation from it usually involves penalties. The concept basic to the Soviet political ideology is applied to science. Of that, Lenin wrote: "The scientific concept of dictatorship means neither more nor less than unrestricted power, absolutely unimpeded by laws or regulations and resting directly on force." In Russia today an authoritative statement by the Presidium can arbitrarily become "truth" and thereafter be regarded as a reality.

The attack on genetics and its destruction has significance for all of science and for all that pattern of thought which we call Western. It has been accompanied by attacks on theoretical atomic physics, on all schools of psychology and physiology which the Presidium does not approve, on unorthodox writers, artists, and musicians.

Of course, the two initial attacks were on all forms of religion (except Leader-worship) and on the Western democratic tradition which, in theory at least, puts the individual above the state in according him certain fundamental or "inalienable" rights which the state cannot abrogate except in moments when its own existence is in extreme danger.

The basis of the ideological issues dividing us from Soviet Russia is a clear-cut difference in the roles as--signed to authority and the degree of liberty allowed to individuals to question authority and to seek and to record the truth as they see it. That today some of the loudest-mouthed American opponents of Communism have views and use tactics that are as anti ethical as is Russia's Communism itself to the scientific attitude and to the American ideal should not be a surprise--the Devil is said to quote Scripture.

Walter Lippmann states the thesis well:

> This is the creative principle of freedom of speech, not that it is a system for the tolerating of error, but that it is a system for finding the truth. It may not produce the truth, or the whole truth all the time, or often, or in some cases ever. But if the truth can be found, there is no other system which will normally and habitually find so much truth. Until we have thoroughly understood this principle, we shall not know why we must value our liberty, or how we can protect and develop it. . . . If we are to preserve democracy we must understand its principles. And the principle which distinguishes it from all other forms of government is that in a democracy the opposition not only is tolerated as constitutional but must be maintained because it is in fact indispensable . . . . A good statesman, like any sensible human being, always learns more from his opponents than from his fervent supporters. For his supporters will push him to disaster unless his opponents show him where the dangers are. So if he is wise he will often pray to be delivered from his friends, because they will ruin him. But though it hurts, he ought also to pray never to be left without opponents; for they keep him on the path of reason and good sense.

An essential implication is, of course, that both science and Western democracy are ever-changing, dynamic systems. All authoritarianism, on the other hand, carries an implication of finality.

* * * * *

Any discussion of either ideological or political or even scientific differences between East and West is made very difficult by different meanings given to words. The "Peoples Democracies" behind the Iron Curtain are far from democratic in our sense of the word--and it was our word before it was theirs. Even "Communism" itself seemed to have different meanings in Stalin's Russia from what it had in Lenin's day or in the Communist Manifesto of 1848. Between all of these, there is, however, much less difference than between any of them and the meaning of the word communism to the early Christians or later utopian movements.

So it is in science and philosophy. For instance, heredity for us is the process or processes by which the hereditary materials are transmitted to and cause their effects on successive generations. To Lysenko, who is the dominant opponent of genetics in Russia today, it is all materials of which an organism is composed and which it uses in reproduction, which is called "the heredity." This is almost as bad for obscuring thought as if one were to refer to all the materials that went into construction and operation of a hydroelectric plant as the "electricity."

Similarly, genetics is obviously a materialistic science in the sense that its laws of hereditary transmission are based on the transmission of chromosomes and genes in the reproductive cells, and on the union of the two parental contributions in the process of fertilization. Yet Lysenko calls it "idealistic"--apparently only for the reason that this is a term of abuse or of ridicule in the U.S.S.R.

Whether or not genetics is called materialistic or idealistic makes no difference, of course, to its progress as a science.

In the West we manage to keep a fairly clear separation between a man's scientific work and his philosophy, which we consider a personal matter. We therefore demand that his scientific work meet the standard tests of demonstrability, reproduceability by others and logical consistency. Of his philosophy we demand at most consistency and usually care not a jot about even that, provided his work meets the tests.

In the U.S.S.R., however, all activities must fulfill the philosophical tenets of dialectical materialism. We therefore had (before he was "reconstructed") the spectacle of Zhebrak, a university teacher of dialectical materialism who was also a geneticist, arguing that genetics is in full consonance with dialectical materialism and that the teachings of Lysenko are grievously not. Prezent, who is Lysenko's philosophic mentor, argued that genetics is antidialectical.

Confusion is compounded when the ideas of a very few eugenists who sought to apply genetics to human population in Hitler's Germany are seized upon and imputed to geneticists in general. Though in a free society no one person or group can speak for all its members, a statement which was drawn up at the 1939 International Genetics Congress in Edinburgh and signed by a group of us from various Western nations (including H. J. Muller, the Nobel-Prize-winning American geneticist who drafted much of it) is at least not unrepresentative. It reads in part:

> There can be no valid basis for estimating and comparing the intrinsic worth of different individuals, without economic and social conditions which provide approximately equal opportunities for all members of society instead of stratifying them from birth into classes with widely different privileges. The second major hindrance to genetic improvement lies in the economic and political conditions which foster antagonism between different peoples, nations and races. The removal of race prejudices and of the unscientific doctrine that good or bad genes are the monopoly of particular peoples or of persons

with features of a given kind will not be possible, however, before the conditions which make for war and economic exploitation have been eliminated. . . . Before people in general, or the State which is supposed to represent them, can be relied upon to adopt rational (eugenic) policies, we shall also have to have a far wider understanding of biological principles and a recognition of the truth that both heredity and environment constitute dominating and inescapable complementary factors in human wellbeing.

Yet in 1949 an official Russian publication said:

American racism basing itself on Mendelian genetics is entering into open warfare with the slogan of democracy. It is currently poisoning the mind of the American petty bourgeois, engendering in him a bestial chauvinism, racial intolerance, and contempt for the culture of other peoples. Having covered themselves with infamy in the eyes of all progressive mankind, it is impossible for the American Mendelists to conceal their bloody relationship with the Hitler scholar-beasts. Mendelian genetics, eugenics, racism and the propaganda of imperialism are at the present time inseparable. That is why the destruction of Mendelian-Morganism at the August session of the All-Union Academy of Agricultural Sciences of V. I. Lenin aroused such hatred in all the reactionaries in politics and science throughout the entire world.

Almost all of Lysenko's attacks on genetics are couched in terms of denunciation or are nonspecific charges or generalities that are hard to pin down, especially since he is not consistent. They have not been neglected, however. Th. Dobzhansky and C. Zirkle in the United States and Julian Huxley and Hudson and Richens in England have published translations and analyses of Lysenko's works and met his arguments. Many of his experiments have also been repeated but without success.

It appears that most of Lysenko's objections to genetics are due to his very limited understanding of it and of mathematical probability. He also seems to have no understanding of the standards of evidence acceptable in a science.

Following Michurin, a successful plant breeder who was the Russian counterpart of Luther Burbank, Lysenko claims that he has been able to improve the hereditary make-up of many plants by improving the conditions under which they are grown and to "educate" plants to grow under new conditions.

Many similar claims were made in the West up until about thirty years ago. By that time carefully controlled experiments and advancing knowledge of the mechanism of heredity had shown that the causes of the changes which occur in some cases are quite different from those which were first assumed. For instance, the environment naturally affects the development of a plant or animal, and natural selection acting on a mixed population comprising many different genetic types can, of course, pick out for survival those that are best suited to the environment in which they have developed. Thus there appears to be inheritance of characteristics acquired by a plant in the course of its own development. That this is not the true explanation is shown by the simple experiment of growing a really purebred or "homozygous" stock of plants under similar conditions; it is then found that, apart from fortuitous changes, successive generations have the same genetic constitution.

Many efforts are being made by Western biologists, and especially by geneticists, to produce directed changes in the germ plasm of plants and animals. Changes can readily be made by radiations and by some chemicals, but changes directly adapted to the environment have never yet been obtained in any ordinary plants or animals.

The theory that evolution depends upon characteristics <u>acquired</u> by an organism during the course of its development being passed on to its descendants was first clearly enunciated by the great French biologist J. B. Lamarck half a century before we had any knowledge of the mechanisms of heredity.

With the development of genetics it has become clear: (a) that there is almost no possibility that the inheritance of acquired characteristics can occur in ordinary multicellular plants and animals and (b) that apparent cases of such inheritance can satisfactorily be explained by well-known processes of fortuitous changes in the germ plasm which is being acted upon by natural or artificial selection.

There is abundant positive evidence against the inheritance of acquired characteristics and also negative evidence against it, in that it has been shown to be an unsatisfactory interpretation for results that superficially may appear to support it. To cite only one problem which has been attacked in both ways: William Macdougall, a psychologist, conducted experiments with rats learning to escape from a simple maze. He thought that the learning was biologically transmitted to the offspring, but detailed analysis of his results showed that this interpretation was not necessarily the only one, nor was it the most probable. Further, two independent groups of workers used similar methods, except that they started with pure-bred rats. They failed to obtain similar results, though they tried for many years. On the other hand, a selection experiment conducted by Tryon in California has shown very clearly that there exist genetic differences between ordinary laboratory rats in their capacity to learn to escape from a maze. Selection and interbreeding of the most rapid learners leads to the production of still more rapid learners within a very few generations. Selection and breeding for slowness of learning likewise leads to greater slowness.

Actually, the official adoption of the theory of the inheritance of acquired characteristics is an example of what Churchill calls the "riddle wrapped up in an enigma" that is Soviet Russia of today. If this theory were true, it would follow (a) that the Russian proletariat, having been illiterate, oppressed, and culturally backward from time immemorial, would be of lower intelligence than the people of the more advanced Western European countries, who have long had more widespread literacy and culture; and (b) that the "intelligentsia" and nobility that the Communists "liquidated" were superior in some sort of hereditary, inborn intelligence, and culture to the proletariat and peasantry. Of course, no geneticist would believe either of these things and the Presidium would be the first to deny them. If there is any rational answer to the riddle, it must be that they really believe their people are inferior, but dare not admit it, and that they expect rapid educational and cultural advances to produce equally rapid advances in inborn, hereditary intelligence. But this is absurd.

Lysenko, like Michurin, also claims to have made new hybrid forms by grafting together very diverse species of plants. Fairly diverse varieties of plants can be grafted on one another and the grafting of high quality but perhaps delicate buds or shoots (scions) of apples, oranges, plums, and peaches on hardy but otherwise low-quality stocks has, of course, long been standard horticultural practice. There are, however, no established cases of true hybrids arising in this way.

It is clear from the Proceedings of the Soviet Academy of Science meeting of August, 1948, when genetics got its final coup de grace, that the issues are not scientific but ideological, "philosophical," and above all political.

Following a statement of his views by Lysenko, 58 speakers glorified him and the principles of dialectical materialism, condemned all foreign biology and particularly anyone who had ever disagreed with Lysenko. Three of them to some extent straddled the fence and three were fairly outspoken against Lysenko's theories, though all of them gave him considerable credit. When they finished, Lysenko summed up:

> Inheritance is determined by a specific kind of metabolism. Inheritance changes with changed metabolism. It has been proved that all living cells and all portions of the organism, not only the chromosomes, have an effect upon heredity. Even the sap exchanged between stock and scion in a graft hybrid possesses hereditary properties. According to Mendelism mutations are regarded as accidental and fertilization is not a matter of choice, but is due to the chance meet-

ing of sexual cells which leads to a chance segregation of characters in the hybrid offspring. By purging Soviet science of Mendelism the element of chance is being purged from biology.

He then announced that his initial statement had received the prior approval of the Politburo. In other words, his opponents had been trapped into expressing opposition not only to himself but to the government and to Stalin.

Pravda immediately came out with a terrific denunciation of his opponents. The recantations that followed have a horribly familiar ring to those who remember the "confessions" of Radek and the Old Bolsheviks in Stalin's political purge or the later "confessions" of recalcitrant churchmen in Hungary and Bulgaria. One example will suffice: remember that this statement is made to scientists at an Academy meeting by a scientist accustomed to speaking in terms of evidence for or against the views which he holds and note that there is not a word about scientific proof or disproof of the scientific problems at issue:

> I want to make it clear that this statement is not influenced by the statement in Pravda today. Day before yesterday I spoke out against Michurin; it was also my last speech with an incorrect biological and ideological position (applause). My article 'Darwinism' was written in a dialectical manner, to which our president answered. This took me from the region of the ideological battle into the region of personal offense.
>
> ...my speech was not worthy of a member of the Communist Party, and a Soviet scientist. I admit that I was taking an incorrect position. Yesterday's wonderful speech by Lovanov was addressed directly to me, "we are not on the same road as you are,"--and I consider Lobanov a great government man. These words upset me very much. His speech threw me into confusion, and a sleepless night helped me to think over my actions. The speech of Vasilenko also had a similar effect on me because he showed me how Michurinism is tied up with the people, and how important it is at

this time, to uphold the authority of the president Lysenko. So convinced of the rightness of the session and its demonstration of strength, and of its relation with the people, and of the demonstration of weakness of the opponents, it is for me obvious that I will fight--sometimes I am capable of fighting--for Michurin's teachings. I am working for the committee for Stalin prizes, in the Council of Ministers, and therefore I think that I have a great moral duty--that is, to be an honest Michurinist, to be an honest Soviet biologist. If I say that I am going over into the ranks of Michurinists, and that I will defend them, I do this honestly. I declare that I will honestly perform what I declare today. Those who know me know that I do not do this out of cowardice. An important facet of my character was always a great sensitiveness. Everybody knows that my nerves are impressed by everything. Therefore you will believe me that this session really had an enormous effect on me.

It was then announced that all of the opponents of Lysenko were to be relieved of their positions (the recantations did not help them) and that several of the biological institutions were to be abolished. A letter was sent to Stalin praising him for his interest and his guidance of biological research, and special point was made that Michurin biology was to be furthered and the unpatriotic genetics ideology to be rooted out. "Opposition between the two ideas has taken the form of an ideological class struggle between socialism and capitalism on an international scale and between the majority of the Soviet scientists and the few remaining Russian scientists who have retained traces of bourgeois ideology on a smaller scale. There is no place for compromise."

Lenin laid down the concept of dictatorship resting directly on unrestricted power, as quoted earlier, and we know Lord Acton's famous dictum, "All power corrupts, absolute power corrupts absolutely." For a politician to want to get rid of his opponents is nothing new. But why purge a science? Soviet Communism has always glorified science, has stressed that its own advance must depend upon industrialization, which in turn depends directly upon the advances of science. Why then should a science be destroyed and the fundamental attitudes and methods that have made modern science so successful be abrogated and ridiculed?

To get any understanding at all of this riddle we must examine further what we mean by the word "science." It happens that in Russia the word, as in the original Greek, means all knowledge. The Politburo obviously was not attacking that. Far too many people believe science means only the applications of science: gadgets and chemical products, cures for human diseases and ills, the production of new and better varieties of crops, and so on. It is not this type of science, either, that the Politburo was attacking.

I turn to that astute observer of the American scene of the early nineteenth century, Alexis de Toqueville, for a wider view. In his "Democracy in America" he writes:

> The mind may divide science into three parts. The first comprises the most theoretical principles, and those more abstract notions whose application is either unknown or very remote. The second is composed of those general truths which still belong to pure theory, but lead nevertheless by a straight and short road to practical results. Methods of application and means of execution make up the third. Each of these different portions of science may be separately cultivated, although reason and experience show that none of them can prosper long, if it be absolutely cut off from the other two.

He went on to say that for the then foreseeable future Americans would surely develop the second and third of these because they had the practical job of building a New World, and they could draw on the Old World for their theoretical principles.

In the latter part of the nineteenth and early part of the twentieth century when the original Soviet Communist ideology was being formulated and when literacy was being extended to the masses in Europe and America as it is in Russia today, the overwhelming success of the applied sciences was obvious everywhere. It is these that are most important in Russia today--in all spheres except atomic physics, of which more later.

Until very recently there has been available such a store of fundamental, theoretical, and as yet unapplied data that it was easy to forget the necessity for maintaining that store. The necessity was not widely realized in this country until near the end of World War II. The 1945 Report to the President by Vannevar Bush, entitled, "Science, the Endless Frontier," marks the turning point in American public thinking away from that reported and predicted by de Toqueville. We haven't yet proceeded very far from it in some fields! It is evident from the propaganda literature of the U.S.S.R. that Russian thinking on science is in a phase very like that of nearly all Americans in the earlier part of this century. Stories of the development of new varieties of wheat, of citrus fruits that will grow in the Arctic, of new and better subways, canals, power dams, and all sorts of machines fill their press.

The Russians do not, however, ignore pure science. But just as the Nazis claimed to have a distinct "Nordic science," so the Russians claim to have a dialectical-materialist science that is independent of Western democratic, or international, science. There is one difference from the Nazi situation: "German physics" was expounded in the Nazi press, but German professors in general had enough influence to prevent its being foisted on university students; their science remained international. Lysenko's genetics is, however, being foisted not only on Russians, but on all the satellite nations, and they have been "purged" of international genetics.

Much internal and external propaganda on the superiority of "Soviet science" over "bourgeois science" was made in association with the report some years ago of the discovery of new fundamental nuclear particles, "varitrons," having masses 100 to 25,000 times that of an electron. For this the 200,000-ruble Stalin Prize was awarded to Professors Alikhanyan and Alikhanov. Western physicists were very dubious about varitrons, and last year the Russians announced that their supposed discovery rested on erroneous interpretations of experimental data. As the New York Times says: "Experimental data may play second fiddle to ideology in genetics, but in nuclear physics--the foundation of atomic bomb production--the Kremlin is willing to face reality and to follow canons of scientific logic accepted in all lands." The significance of this for us is not the error but its official acknowledgement.

A translation in Nature, (pp. 92-94, Jan. 19, 1952) of a resolution adopted on June 12, 1951 by a conference of the Chemical Science Section of the Academy of Sciences of the U.S.S.R. reads in part:

> The chemists, and also physicists, of our country have not given sufficient attention to the struggle for the establishment of the dialectical-materialism world-view in chemical science and allied branches of physics, in theoretical chemistry and, in particular, in organic chemistry, and, as a result, some Soviet chemists have been ensnared by the unsound, idealistic 'theory' of resonance.... In recent years there has been a spread in organic chemistry of a concept developed by Anglo-American scientists. This has done harm to Soviet chemistry. It has diverted the efforts of chemists into useless, pseudoscientific directions and created a harmful illusion of explaining many facts and laws, which are in reality not explained at all. The Conference considers it necessary to point out also a number of serious defects in the report of the Committee. Thus, it is not shown in the report that the ideological perversions in matters of chemical theory are closely related to the hostile theories in biology and physiology, and that, taken together, these present a united front in the fight of reactionary bourgeois ideology against materialism.... The development of theoretical organic chemistry, and above all, of chemical structural theory must proceed in a state of positive struggle against idealistic and mechanistic theories in chemistry on the basis

of the world-view of dialectical materialism....
Under the guidance of the party of Lenin and Stalin,
Soviet chemists will honorably carry out the directions of the great leader of the workers, the scientific genius, Joseph Vissarionovich Stalin.

* * * * * *

In dealing with the Communists we are dealing with a highly intelligent group of men quite unlike the cunning but relatively unintelligent fanatics who surrounded Hitler. Probably the chief limitation of the Kremlin and, almost paradoxically, the chief source of its danger to us is its acceptance and authoritarian enforcement of an outmoded nineteenth century ideology.

Marx took from Darwin mainly the ideas which the development of modern genetics has modified or outmoded. Many economists think he did the same in their field. Certainly the development of trade unions and of social security in America has changed the Marxian picture of an oppressed proletariat that would inevitably arise to overthrow capitalism in bloody revolution. Certainly also, the U.S.S.R. is getting farther away from the classless society which Marx foresaw after the proletarian revolution. Is it not possible that the "men in the Kremlin" are intelligent enough to change their ideology in one fundamental respect in which it is actually more ancient Russian than Marxian. Could the discovery of errors in "Soviet Science,"--the inevitable discredit which must fall on Lysenkoism as its absurdities are revealed and as Western genetics progresses to more successful application such as hybrid corn--lead to a deeper consideration of the handicap which authoritarianism places on the authorities who impose it? If so, could this lead to a realization that in a dynamic world no one system of anything can for long have a monopoly of the truth, in science, political theory, or economics? Could they realize that if adaptive change is the basic law for survival, of individuals or societies, as they themselves state in theory, then the existence of variation must be of value in itself? Could they realize that different political and economic systems flourish under different conditions of time and place because best adapted thereto? Could they admit that the Marxian dogma of the inevitable collapse of capitalism in the West is as outmoded as the dogma of the withering away of the State has so far proved to be in Russia? Could they see that Michurinism and "dialectic materialism" are limited and outmoded scientifically and philosophically?

The Russians have at times stated that Soviet Communism and the modern modified and ever-changing capitalistic economics can co-exist. Could they come to believe this to the point of being prepared to act on it? Certainly in the atomic age the alternative to co-existence is not suppression of the one by the other, but elimination of both. Maybe multiplication of atom bombs by both will enforce peace by reason of fear. But fear has rarely been an effective source of reasonable conduct in the past. Are there any possible bases for hope? I think there are some.

In pre-revolutionary Russia, many great advances were made in pure or theoretical sciences, and the ever-doubting, freely challenging spirit of science was widely accepted. The leaders of the 1917 revolution were brought up on and subscribed to that tradition. With the triumph of Stalin there came a change. Nationalism developed. With the rapid spread of literacy and the enormous expansion of Russian science and technology, official appreciation has come to focus on the immediate utility of science. It is true that lip service is paid, as in the Revolution in Chemistry, to theory and fundamental research, but the practical and immediate outcome of theories and their ideological soundness are the only tests applied. It is obvious that if non-Russian data and theories are so generally ridiculed or ignored, the Soviet theories are not being tested, as with us, by the widest possible range of data.

This nationalistic trend of science in Russia is a relatively new thing and is not a necessary concomitant of Communism. On the contrary, one of the first acts of Lenin after the Revolution was to send N. I. Vavilov (later liquidated) to America and all parts of the world to collect information and species and varieties of plants and then to set up in Russia one of the finest systems of botanical research institutes that has ever existed anywhere. In the 1930's foreign geneticists went to Russia and found amazingly fine facilities. Outstanding genetic researches were published up until the outbreak of the war in 1941, though the opposition to genetics had been gathering strength since about 1936. .

* * * * *

As recently as 1944, Ashby in his Scientist in Russia could report that "international" theoretical or fundamental botany was flourishing despite the war. In 1945 there was a great international conference in Moscow at which the outstanding Russian physicist, Kapitsa, said:

> What will the consequences of this Conference be? The U.S.S.R. appreciates the achievements of British science. Our achievements are not so great because we are younger. But there is really no such thing as Soviet science, or British science: there is only one science, devoted to the betterment of human welfare. Science must, therefore, be international. The U.S.S.R. has been the first to recognize this, by calling together scientists from all over the world immediately the war ended. The Soviet appreciation of international science is well illustrated by these celebrations. Foreign delegates have been brought here from their own countries by Soviet planes, housed, fed, and transported by the Soviet Government. What other country is able to do this for international science? This is proof that the U.S.S.R. intends to take a leading part in international science.

Earlier a leading Communist wrote something that if fully recognized and acted on in Russia today would certainly prevent attempts to control or direct science by authority and that might give East and West a philosophical and ideological basis for co-existence: "Truth is a process. From the subjective idea man attains objective truth by way of practice and technique. Understanding is the continuous approach of thought towards the object." The writer of that was Vladimir Lenin!

Engels and Marx at various times expressed a similar philosophy. Said Marx: "One no longer permits oneself to be imposed upon by the antitheses, insuperable for the still common old metaphysics, between true and false, good and bad, identical and different, necessary and accidental. One knows that these antitheses have only a relative validity; that that which is recognized now as true has also its latent false side which will later manifest itself, just as that which is now regarded as false has also its true side by virtue of which it could previously have been regarded as true." Engels declares, "With each epoch-making discovery in the department of natural science materialism has been obliged to change its form."

Herbert J. Muller in his Science and Criticism said that while the system of Marx, like a good scientific hypothesis, provided in its premises for future development, revision through self-criticism, and adaptation to inevitable change, Marx ended, like Martin Luther, in an absolutism as despotic as that he had set out to demolish. "And if Marx accordingly needs to be rescued from his own excesses, he needs still more to be rescued from Marxists. Instead of subjecting his program to the constant criticism that dialectical materialism itself calls for, his followers have made it still more like a religion and less like a science, and chiefly wrangled over the proper interpretation of the holy text. He rationalized a myth; they mythologized his rationalization." Lenin likewise at different times expressed both a liberal philosophy and an illiberal, unscientific, tyrannical attitude.

It is clear, though the trend seems now all one way, that there are ways wide open for ideological reversals within the system itself. The atomic age seems to demand one. If by the fiascos in Russian science that will surely result if present trends continue, a successor of Stalin should ever be jolted to a sufficient realization of where authoritarianism leads, he might go back to early Marx and those parts of Engel's and Lenin's philosophies that are in substantial accord with modern Western scientific points of view. The transference of lessons from science to politics would be very difficult but not impossible.

The ideology of modern Western science is, as I have hoped to show, very similar to that of the American Ideal. Some aspects of modern scientific philosophy were expounded by earlier Marxians. We and the Russians might yet find in them common ground for a co-existence in which our differences would provide the experiments that are necessary to determine the best adaptive changes to suit a changing world. Incidentally, the hope of any good scientist is not to become an authority but to initiate developments that others can carry on from the point where he leaves off. I think that is also the aim of really great statesmen! Is Stalin's successor intelligent enough to see that in the long run authoritarianism defeats the authorities that practice it, whereas the evidence from 400 years of science is that the free interplay of ideas, the adoption of what we call the scientific attitude, seems capable of leading to almost unlimited advance in human welfare and understanding. It may seem a slim hope but I see none better for the long term.

PART TWO

Nations in Turmoil

> *Modern technology is a result of putting science to work. In a hundred years it has created or crippled nations by opening up continents with the railroad and shifting men's attention from food to mineral resources. We have only just begun to mold the world.*

CHAPTER 10

MAN MOLDS THE WORLD

Abbott Payson Usher
Departments of Economics and History

The changes in systems of production that have resulted from the development of technology can be described in two general categories.

The earliest forms of economic organization centered around the production of food, with the use of animate sources of power supplemented incidentally by the use of wind and of minor sources of water power. Recent forms of production are based upon an intensive use of minerals and of mechanical forms of energy derived from mineral fuels, such as coal and oil, or from major water powers. We may characterize these systems of production respectively as a food economy and a mineral economy.

The _food economy_ emerges before the dawn of history in the nomadic cultures based on livestock and in the sedentary cultures based on the cereals. What were their sources of energy and power?

Systematic use of animal power began at least as early as the beginning of the Christian Era, both in the Mediterranean World and in Asia, although it came into use perhaps earlier in China than in the West. Water power was used in the West at about the same time, though neither animal nor water power came into general use until much later. Metals were used, but their use was restricted, and per-capita consumption was small.

For many centuries the social structure was dominated by agriculture, but it is an error to describe the food economy as self-sufficient. Characteristically, population was limited by the food supplies available locally, though there were supplementary imports of foods in some regions served by deep-water transportation.

Even at the beginning of the eighteenth century, woolen workers consumed a greater weight of material in food and domestic fuel than the combined weights of all the materials entering into their woolen products. Trade was restricted largely to industrial raw materials and to finished products. Movements of cereals and edible fats and oils were limited.

Industry in the food economy was closely associated with agriculture. Where food was abundant, specialized industrial workers consumed the stocks that were in excess of the needs of the agricultural workers. If the productivity of agriculture was low, the workers were obliged to engage in supplementary industrial pursuits to provide an adequate income. Arable agriculture in temperate climates rarely provides more than 200 days' field work per year, so that about one third of the possible working time was available for supplementary employment. Even in Asia, in areas of rice culture in India, China and Japan, the close association of industry and agriculture emerged. Different soils and climates can support different numbers of people, but the general features of the food economy remain. These characteristic features persisted down to the nineteenth century, even in the West, and much later on the other continents.

MAN MOLDS THE WORLD

Until recently, there has been a tendency to generalize carelessly about the use of power. Thus the use of animal power was given little attention, and the importance of water and wind as sources of power was underestimated. The production and use of energy in the United States in 1850 illustrates conditions in a country which had not passed beyond the food economy in its original form. The relative importance of animate and mineral sources of energy at this date is shown on the accompanying graph, along with the vastly changed picture of energy sources in the fully developed mineral economy of 1944.

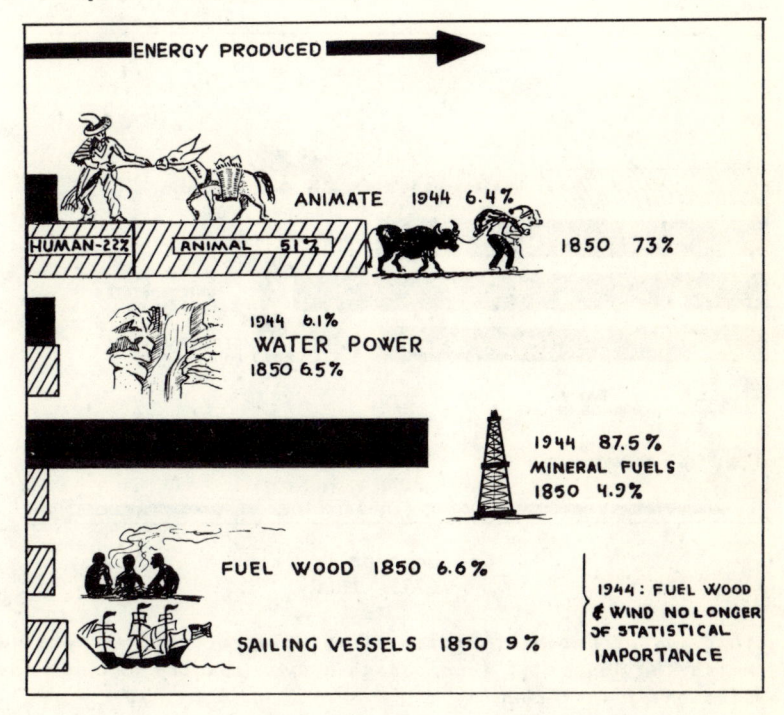

```
ENERGY PRODUCED →

HUMAN--22%  ANIMAL 51%   ANIMATE 1944 6.4%
                                  1850 73%

              1944 6.1%
WATER POWER
              1850 6.5%

                         1944 87.5%
                         MINERAL FUELS
                         1850 4.9%

FUEL WOOD 1850 6.6%      1944: FUEL WOOD
                         & WIND NO LONGER
SAILING VESSELS 1850 9%  OF STATISTICAL
                         IMPORTANCE
```

Sources of Energy in the United States
1850 -- 1944

While the proportions altered radically among the sources of energy between 1850 and 1944, the total amount of energy produced jumped enormously. This is one way of describing the transition from a food economy to a fuel economy.

Another indication of the difference between the food economy and the fuel economy lies in the per-capita consumption of iron. In 1735, before the Newcomen steam engine was in general use and before any large development of coke in the smelting of iron, the consumption of iron in Great Britain is estimated at 15 pounds per capita. In England, in 1864, the per-capita consumption of iron was 169.4 pounds. In 1900, the per-capita consumption of iron iron in Great Britain amounted to 292.0 pounds; in Germany, to 289.7 pounds; in the United States, to 351.3 pounds.

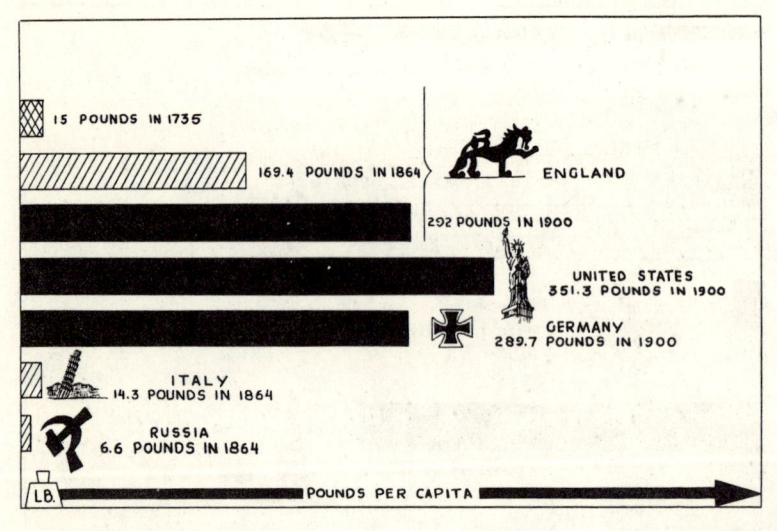

Consumption of Iron
1735--1900

Another way of noting the rise of the mineral fuel economy is to match the amount of iron consumed by a country against the population of that country.

The above graph shows the tremendous rise in the use of iron by some nations during the nineteenth century.

In the world as a whole, inanimate sources of energy are now the primary factor in the production of power: Asia, excluding the U.S.S.R., derived 50.5 per cent of its power from inanimate sources. Africa produced 60.9 per cent mechanically, and South America secured 62.3 per cent. But despite the extensive diffusion of techniques of engineering and important movements of mineral fuel, the differences in the productive power of the regions of the world have increased rather than decreased.

We have no means of estimating the effective output of energy under the food economy. Areas of great agricultural fertility undoubtedly achieved relatively high rates of productivity <u>per acre</u>, but broad regional comparisons should give consideration to the rates of productivity <u>per capita</u>. Actually, the differences in these figures would be moderate, because the poorer districts engage in stock raising, which yields high rates of return for the relatively small numbers of men employed. Productivity per acre is more significant as an index of the general level of economic activity, while product per person is a better index of the effective opportunity for the individual.

In 1937, careful estimates of energy used for productive purposes gave a world average of 1,250 kilowatt-hours of energy per person. The highest figure for any large area was 6,996 kilowatt-hours used in the United States. China, excluding Manchuria and Jehol, used 164 kilowatt-hours of electricity per person, or its equivalent. Some small areas consumed even less energy. The range from low to high levels of use must be much greater than differences that existed under the food economy, which was essentially dependent upon organic products and organic energy.

These changes in the general conditions of productive activity are not the only kinds of technical changes to be considered. The application of power to transportation has been of utmost importance. It has provided massive, heavy-duty transport at speeds and costs never before available. It has enabled man to create a comprehensive transport network capable of serving entire continents. Before the development of the railroad, heavy-duty transport was confined to the oceans and the inland waterways.

The resistances that once prevailed to movement of heavy goods were only in part a matter of cost. The accompanying graph shows how animal power was not capable of handling large tonnages. While certain natural waterways could do better--as much as nearly four million tons of freight per route-mile per year in a few cases--waterways do not run anywhere and everywhere. The railroad, using mineral fuel, changed the picture. It became a close competitor of water transport almost from the beginning. As early as 1834, the heavy freight locomotive in the United States was capable of moving 3,280,000 tons per route-mile per year on a single track with grades not exceeding 0.2 per cent. The Baldwin freight locomotive of 1845 was capable of moving nearly 9,000,000 tons of freight per route-mile per year on a single track. Yet these potentialities were not realized in practice, because the demand for service was not great enough to require full utilization of capacity.

Furthermore, passenger service was an important feature of railway operations, and the demand for speed leads to a sacrifice of potential tonnage movement. No single figure can be given for the traffic capacity of a railroad operating both passenger and freight services. Capacity to move freight is the best means of comparison and analysis. Precise comparisons of railroads with waterways are complicated by dates when important technical changes in the service occurred.

Water transport greatly benefited, of course, from the application of steam power. Major improvements were made in the regulation of the great natural waterways: The Ohio-Mississippi system, the Seine, the Rhine, and the Danube. Speed of movement greatly increased, as did the size of the units. We must remember that when it is possible to move large numbers of barges in single units, the physical capacity of the best rivers is clearly greater than the capacity of a four-track railroad. But such conditions

MAN MOLDS THE WORLD 109

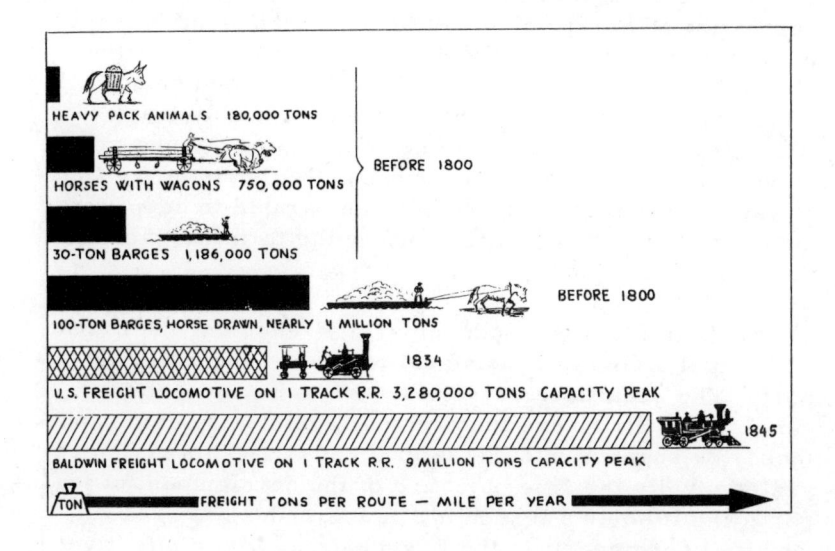

```
HEAVY PACK ANIMALS   180,000 TONS
HORSES WITH WAGONS   750,000 TONS        } BEFORE 1800
30-TON BARGES   1,186,000 TONS
100-TON BARGES, HORSE DRAWN, NEARLY 4 MILLION TONS    BEFORE 1800
U.S. FREIGHT LOCOMOTIVE ON 1 TRACK R.R. 3,280,000 TONS CAPACITY PEAK   1834
BALDWIN FREIGHT LOCOMOTIVE ON 1 TRACK R.R. 9 MILLION TONS CAPACITY PEAK   1845
         FREIGHT TONS PER ROUTE — MILE PER YEAR
```

Movements of Heavy Freight

Freight was hauled in increasingly massive quantities during the 19th century--another indication of the rise of a mineral fuel economy.

Note that animal power is insignificant alongside coal and oil in land transport.

Railroads possess this advantage over waterways as heavy haulers: they can form a network over the land, while waterways cannot. This transport network opened up the continental masses to industry, agriculture and commerce on a scale unprecedented in history.

of river service are rare. Few waterways are capable of supporting a larger volume of service than could be supplied by a railroad. Through most of its active life the Erie Canal moved more freight than a railroad on a single track, but less than could be moved on a double track. When fully regulated, the Rhine, Seine, and Danube might move more freight than the Erie Canal. Parts of the Ohio-Mississippi System were nearly comparable to deep-water navigation, which is limited only by the terminal facilities that can be provided.

Early in the eighteenth century, French engineers had a vision of a comprehensive network of inland water transport. The great river systems were to be connected by canals, and the rivers themselves regulated by dams and locks, or supplemented by lateral canals. This vision revealed vividly the true objective of the development of transport, and it holds a lesson for us. For despite great ingenuity in engineering, the French dream of an effective interconnected system of water transport was never realized. It was possible to make connections, but the flow of traffic was impeded by locks and by the lack of uniformity in the dimensions of the barges. Only the smallest barges could move freely over the whole system, and the small units were not economical.

In the development of a comprehensive transport network, the railroads succeeded where the canals failed. Their capacities to provide heavy-duty service were adequate to the needs of any economy in which the demand for transport exceeded certain critical amounts. The problems created by topographic resistances were less serious than in the case of canals.

It was originally presumed that grade reduction must be carried to very low percentages. George Stephenson early in the nineteenth century set the grade limit on the Liverpool and Manchester Railway at 20 feet per mile, or 0.38 per cent. The French in 1835 similarly set a limit of 0.3 per cent. In practice, some concessions were made, but restrictive limits were not substantially relaxed until

American experience had demonstrated the possibility of using much steeper grades. As early as 1853, railroads had occupied the primary passes of the northern Appalachians, and in the late sixties the Rockies and Cascade mountains had been crossed.

It is now recognized that grades are not a serious operating problem even up to 0.8 per cent, and operable lines can be constructed up to 3.0 per cent. A definite loss of capacity and an increase in costs of operation occur beyond 1.5 per cent. Some mountain barriers still constitute a serious obstacle to the movement of primary heavy traffic, but the surveys of the American engineers established a technique that opened to heavy-duty transport all the great continental areas of the world.

The effect of these developments in transportation upon the world economy were first clearly shown by the great agricultural depression of the late nineteenth century. New railroad connections made it possible for wheat and corn from north central United States to enter British and European markets in a large way. The serious crop failures in Great Britain in 1878 made heavy imports essential. Though subsequent years were not so bad, harvests fell below older standards for a considerable period, both in Great Britain and in Europe. The resulting volume of imports from the United States and southern Russia was so great that prices fell to new lows. The disaster was widespread. Heavy losses were incurred, and much arable acreage was abandoned in England. There were severe strains from low prices both in northern Europe and in the United States.

This episode marks both phases in the transformation of the world economy. First, limitation of major commodity movements to the maritime fringe of the continents had come to an end. Henceforth, the deep interiors of the continents were definitely in the world market for all classes of commodities. Secondly, specialization in economic activity was carried to new lengths. The great interior grasslands were opened up to specialized production of the small grains. The areas of possible wheat culture were so enormous that since 1870 there has been scarcely a decade in which the area of wheat culture was not expanding more rapidly than the demand for wheat. The farmers of Great Britain and Europe were faced with the necessity of a complete reorganization of their systems of cropping. The farmers of the United States were tantalized by visions of prosperity that were never quite realized.

The true meaning of this episode was not perceived by the diplomats and political essayists of Europe. The issues of power politics as conceived in the decade preceding the first World War continued to be couched in terms of a maritime world that had really passed away. It was presumed that the primary political problem lay in the division of the tropics among the European powers and in the creation of a number of imperial systems that would be maintained primarily by sea power.

Despite projects for an expanding sphere of influence overland through the Balkans to Turkey, even Germany took the position that her future was on the water. None of the diplomats seemed to realize that the position of Europe in the world was really the paramount issue. They did not see that the European economy could achieve prosperity only by presenting a united front to the continental economies that were emerging in North America and in Asia. It is a lack of vision that has persisted into the middle of the twentieth century.

Very likely no person in responsible position could have detached himself sufficiently from contemporary attitudes to see in stark reality the implications of the primary economic changes that were inexorably taking place. But there were men in Germany, France, and England who put forward moderate policies looking toward adjustment of differences rather than toward conflict. Even without full insight into the future, they might have possibly chosen measures leading to harmony. These would have given time and opportunity for further development towards co-ordination and ultimate unity.

The wars have sharply revealed all the political consequences of the transformation of the world economy, but the record of aggressive diplomacy does not give us satisfactory clues to the causes of this transformation. We can best see the basic economic and social causes of the change if we glance at the differences between present energy production and probable energy resources still unused over the world. This will give us a rough yardstick by which we can measure the present position and the future potentialities of the various continents.

Trustworthy figures for energy production are available only for 1935 and 1937, the last years when truly world-wide information was available. The accompanying graph matches distribution of primary energy sources against their use. While the values given are not up-to-the-minute, habits of energy consumption have not yet changed so radically as to alter the basic proportions presented. Now, as then, these figures demonstrate the instability of the present world economy and underline the political tensions that are a consequence of economic change.

Careful analysis can free us from the dangerous idea that the economic and political relationships of the late nineteenth century were sufficiently stable to endure. If we are to deal effectively with the problems of the present world economy, we must understand its primary characteristics and accept these new stage settings for our economic and political activities. It is not enough to try to apply obsolete ideals inherited from the nineteenth century. Those who think in terms of Victorian liberalism and those who think in terms of Marxian socialism are alike victimized by the errors and illusions of a period that is past. Despite great achievements in philosophy and science, only the greatest intellects were ready to recognize that the achievements of the nineteenth century marked new beginnings and not the final formulation of truth. For general popular thought, the new outlooks have hardened rapidly into dogmas that have been the more dangerous because they purport to be the findings of pure reason and not a mandate of authority.

114   THE CHALLENGE OF OUR TIMES

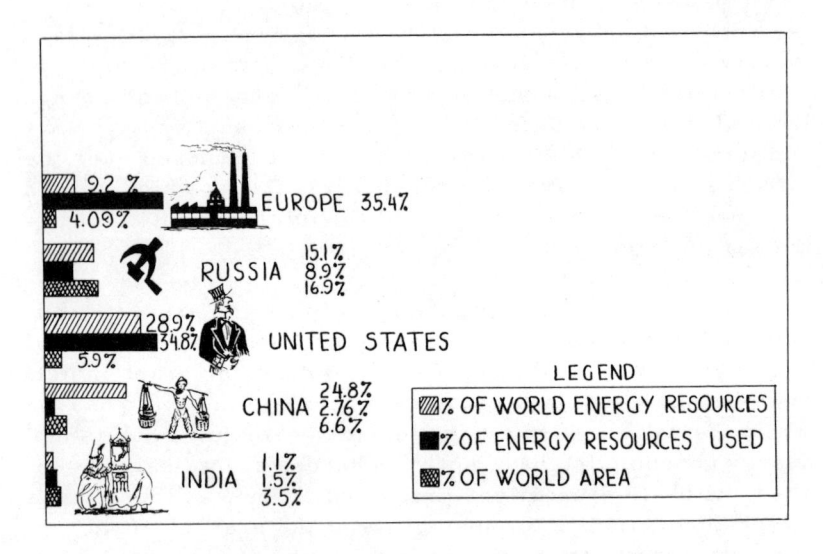

```
            9.2 %
         4.09%
                          EUROPE  35.4%
                          15.1%
                  RUSSIA  8.9%
                          16.9%
            28.9%
            34.8%         UNITED STATES
         5.9%
                                        LEGEND
                          24.8%    ▨ % OF WORLD ENERGY RESOURCES
                  CHINA   2.76%    ■ % OF ENERGY RESOURCES USED
                          6.6%     ▦ % OF WORLD AREA
                          1.1%
                  INDIA   1.5%
                          3.5%
```

Instability of Present World Economy

The present international balance of industrial power is not permanent. China, for example, possesses vastly greater energy resources than Europe, but has scarcely begun to tap them. The United States is in a strong position today because of the enormous energy resources it not only possesses but uses. Yet domestic demand continues to rise, impelling industries to import increasing amounts of goods and energy materials.

Because of the uneven distribution of world energy resources and the time it takes to develop them, the world is most productive when it is a freely trading, peaceful economic unit.

We cannot infer the immediate military potential of the Soviet Union directly from its economic position. Nor can we estimate the immediate appeal of Soviet ideology. Its underlying concepts are certainly vulnerable to serious critical examination, and its authority is limited in effect by external conditions even though its executive officers have no clearly defined responsibilities to other branches of their government. Obscure as the future may be, it is difficult to imagine a world economy in which Europe and North America will not be major centers of economic and political activity.

In the present world of continents, Europe occupies a position very different from that held by her in the maritime world of two centuries ago. But it is still an important position. While the Soviet Union will clearly possess great importance in the world economy, much of her unused potentiality must be devoted to home use if her standards of consumption are to be built up to levels comparable with the standards of Europe and the United States.

The limits of the world economy have been greatly enlarged as a result of man's use of mineral fuels in industry and transportation. But economic problems are still concerned with the wise administration of scarce resources, and power politics--even when most cynical--must be directed towards the intelligent use of limited resources.

> *In 1798 Malthus raised an issue still unsettled: must hunger and famine alone limit the size of human population? Since then, as this chapter shows, the issue has become more complicated. The world population has continued to swell while scientific agriculture produces more food, modern medicine cuts back death rates, and scientific technology raises living standards. The challenge, however, remains as simple as the title of this chapter.*

CHAPTER 11
MOUTHS TO FEED

Noble Clark
Associate Director, Agricultural Experiment Station
and
James F. Crow
Department of Genetics

Two thirds of the people in the world are undernourished. Some of these have sufficient food to prevent actual hunger, but their food does not contain the proteins, minerals, vitamins, and other factors essential for health and comfort. And for almost half of mankind--a billion people--actual hunger is a reality. Food, or the lack of it, is the basic problem of most of the world's people. To add to the difficulty, the world population is increasing at such a rate that there are about 75,000 more births than deaths every day.

Hunger is nothing new in the world. Probably mankind has been putting up with it one way or another since the first human being evolved. But one thing is new: that is the widespread and growing belief that something can and should be done about it. The historian, Arnold Toynbee, has predicted that this century will be remembered particularly as the first time in which people "dared to believe it practicable to make the benefits of civilization available for the whole human race."

The Communists have seized on this world-wide craving for the benefits of science and technology. They try to tell the hungry and the underprivileged peoples everywhere that these benefits will come only if the present governments are overthrown in a communist revolution. There is probably no other factor in the world today which is so powerful an aid to Communism.

It was a century and a half ago that a British clergyman, Thomas Robert Malthus, published an essay which has since been the subject of great controversy. Assembling what facts he could find on the rates of population growth in various countries, he concluded that human beings increase faster than their means of subsistence. He believed that humans were little different from lower animals in their urge to procreate, and that only the inherent checks of inadequate food supplies, disease, and wars prevented populations from increasing indefinitely. But inherent in these checks is the bitter fact that they are expressed in high death rates, in low levels of living, and in widespread misery for the great masses of the people.

Malthus could see no real solution to the problems involved except in measures to reduce the birth rate, primarily by postponement of marriage until women were near the end of the child-bearing age. He called this "moral restraint."

It is not strange that most people greeted the thesis of Malthus with little enthusiasm. He did not recommend a happy procedure and he was widely regarded as a great pessimist or gloomy philosopher. But it was difficult to refute his logic.

However, human experience during the next century and a half in Europe (the area he discussed chiefly in his essay) did not bear out his dire predictions. Population numbers more than doubled. The level of living of nearly all Europeans was raised, and for many, raised greatly. It appeared as if Malthus was wrong. But was he?

Three developments had major influence in enabling Europe to increase its population and at the same time raise the standard of living of its people. The opening up of the new agricultural lands of the United States, Canada, Australia, New Zealand, and South America enormously increased the world's food supplies. The development of railroads and other transportation facilities enabled Europe to supplement its own production with food from all over the globe.

The second new factor in the food situation was the bringing of science to the farms of Europe and other advanced nations of the world. Commercial fertilizers, improved strains of crops and livestock, and the control of pests and diseases resulted in greatly increased yields from the areas already in production.

The third major development, perhaps most important, was the coming of the industrial revolution, which provided profitable nonagricultural employment and gave millions of urban workers the income with which to purchase food.

Malthus could not have anticipated these developments. They were new elements in the picture. But are these developments of such a nature that they can result in the indefinite postponement of the time when populations will press on the food supply? Or was Malthus correct, after all, and should we expect hunger and famine to become the limiting factors in population increase now that most of the more productive lands of the world have been put under the plow? This is a hotly debated question. It is worthy of the attention of scientists, economists, public officials, and all of us, wherever we live.

First of all it must be realized that most of the populations in the world can be classified into two contrasting types. The first includes those with a high birth rate and a high death rate--populations such as are exemplified by China and India. The second group comprises those areas in which the birth and death rates are both relatively low, such as the United States and Western Europe. There are also intermediate populations that have reduced their death rate but still have high birth rates. These are the transition areas, such as Puerto Rico.

With industrialization and scientific advance there has been in country after country a trend from high-birth-high-death rates, through high-birth-low-death, to a low-birth-low-death status. Why have birth rates fallen? Because the level of living was raised and the people had the opportunity to choose between having more children or having fewer children better provided for and more of the comforts, conveniences, travel, education, and other benefits of industrial society.

Actually, death rates have fallen much sooner than birth rates, giving rise to a two-or three-fold actual increase of population. There is thus a serious question as to whether the production of the necessities of life can keep pace with the increase in population.

The issue, then, is this: On the one hand it is argued that as soon as the world's standards of living are increased the birth rates will automatically decline and the population eventually become stable. On the other hand, it is maintained that in many parts of the world the major hindrance to economic development is the overpopulation itself, which prevents the raising of living standards.

These arguments agree in the assumption that birth rates cannot be permitted to stay high forever. Both arguments depend on an eventual decline. The difference lies in whether the primary attack should be on the economic problems, with the assumption of a fall in birth rates as living standards become higher, or whether the attack should be directly on the birth rates themselves. It is our conviction that both approaches must be tried, simultaneously and with vigor.

Can the world's food supply be increased sufficiently while populations accomplish these desirable transitions which will reduce human misery? Food production in the world has increased markedly in the last few decades. However, the greatest advance has been in those areas in which production was already high. If all the food-producing lands in the world could be made as productive as the farms in such nations as the United States, Holland, and Denmark, the world could go a long way toward solving its immediate food problem.

Improved varieties and methods of farming in agriculturally efficient countries have led to substantial increases in the yield of almost all important crop plants. One of the largest advances has been in corn production in the United States, where there has been a per-acre yield increase of some 30 per cent in the last two decades. Some of the increase was undoubtedly due to improved cultural practices, such as the use of more and better fertilizers, but the sudden rise in production when hybrid corn became popular indicates that genetic improvement was the major cause. As a result, about 500 million additional bushels of corn are raised yearly in the United States on 15 million fewer acres than twenty years ago.

Similar improvement has been made in wheat and other grains, due to high-yielding varieties and to better methods of fertilization and cultivation. A spectacular increase in productivity has occurred in the potato because agricultural experiment stations and growers have improved the methods of controlling diseases and insects.

It must be remembered that the energy content of food is not all that is important. People need carbohydrates, fats, high-quality proteins, vitamins, and certain minerals. At present, animal products--meat, milk and eggs--are the best sources of many of these necessary elements. Unfortunately, animal products are in much shorter supply than is food in general. Furthermore, it takes several pounds of plant material to produce a single pound of meat, milk, or eggs. Feeding the world a well-balanced diet will necessitate greatly increased supplies of those products which are more expensive to produce, both in terms of acreage and labor involved.

Scientific advances in greater use of the sea and inland water resources may be expected, particularly more efficient production of fish, which may supply some much-needed proteins to supplement cereal diets in various parts of the world. There are also possibilities in expanding tropical and subarctic agriculture. Finally there may be ways of using forest products and water plants such as algae as direct or indirect sources of food. All in all, it is likely that science and technology can find ways of materially increasing the food supply of the world.

All this means that research in ways of improving crop yields and increasing the efficiency of livestock production must be expanded. New sources of food that yield more energy and essential nutrients are needed, and many can surely be found. But research costs money, and the public must be prepared to increase its support of research if these goals are to be reached.

Likewise necessary is a world-wide soil-conservation program. We need to conserve the topsoil on which plant and animal life depend. Farmers in all parts of the world need to be educated to those practices which maintain the soil at high productivity. Each generation has an obligation not to impair the agricultural base on which future generations are directly dependent.

The first and most important requisite for increased world food production is the provision of basic education for those who operate the farms. An efficient agriculture requires that farmers have at least the rudiments of an education. They must be able to read and understand the instructions which the manufacturer sends out with his farm machine or his insecticide as well as use the bulletins from agricultural research institutions. Unfortunately, most of the world's farmers are still illiterate.

Assuming that scientific methods for improving food yields exist and that still more are being discovered, the problem is not automatically solved. The knowledge must be put into practice. Even if enough food is raised, freedom from hunger is not assured. For hundreds of millions the serious question remains whether they have the money with which to buy food or the productive capacity to enable them to provide goods in exchange.

A particular problem for a region like Western Europe, which must import much of its food, has been the recent tendency for agricultural nations to develop their own industrial enterprises. It is reasonable for these nations to want to avoid selling cheap raw materials in exchange for needed manufactured goods. Australia, for example, has decided to import from Great Britain the machinery with which Australians can make their own woolen cloth and blankets rather than to continue to send their wool to Britain for processing. More and more nations plan to develop industries at home and thus give their own citizens the higher incomes which are provided by skilled industrial occupations.

Even if all these difficulties could be solved, the problem would still remain as to how the immensely complicated economic and political arrangements could be worked out so that the food would move freely from surplus areas to those places where it is needed. It is likely to be even harder to overcome the social, political, and economic obstacles than to find ways of raising more food, difficult as that is.

We conclude that substantial increases in food supply are possible. But the practical problems of production and distribution are tremendous. There is serious reason to wonder if sufficient food can be produced and distributed to keep up with the demand of an already hungry and rapidly increasing world population. We cannot evade the sobering fact that agricultural recovery since World War II has not been enough to bring per-capita food supplies to the prewar levels. Total production is greater today than ever before, but world population numbers are increasing even faster than gains in food production.

The implications of the preceding section are obvious. Any increase in the world's food supplies will be of no advantage in terms of human health and well-being unless population numbers can be kept from increasing just as fast as the food supply grows.

The major problem concerns the future of areas with high birth and death rates. What happens when the death rate falls but the birth rate stays about the same? This is the usual result of an improved economic situation: death rates are much more responsive than birth rates. We have such an example in Puerto Rico, where the birth rate is among the world's highest though the death rate has fallen almost as low as in the United States. The rate of population increase in 1951 was in the vicinity of three per cent per year. If this same change occurred in all the high-birth-rate areas, the world population would increase tremendously. If the rate were to continue for 500 years the world would be packed with people. There would be literally standing room only--about a person per square yard.

A geometric increase in population cannot exist for long. The present rate of growth of the world's population is about one per cent each year. This doesn't sound particularly large, but it is an accelerating growth. Even this rate could not possibly have existed more than a few hundred years in the past, and it cannot continue long in the future without disastrous consequences.

The difficulty is to get from a high-birth-high-death status to one with low-birth-low-death rates--and to do it quickly. It took Europe over a century to make the transition. But if the rest of the world takes this long there is no foreseeable way of feeding the additional billions of people born during that period. The world should not, and we believe will not, tolerate the high death rates now prevalent in many of the most populous lands. Thus any hope that hunger is to be reduced is dependent on whether these overcrowded areas can find ways of promptly reducing their birth rates.

Many persons do not realize the staggering waste of material resources and human effort which occur in a society with high birth and high death rates. There is little that a child can contribute in the way of work before he is twelve years of age. Before that his consumption is almost completely at the expense of those older than himself who are producers. In India, where the life expectancy is less than 30 years, in contrast with the United States and Britain, where it is nearly 70 years, it is apparent that individuals in the productive years of their lives must create goods and services for a much larger number of dependent persons than we do in this country. Remember, too, the very high infant death rates in India and the number of children who are sick and dying. Add to this the fact that most Indians are so inadequately nourished that while they may get enough to live on, they do not get enough to enable them to do hard work. Beyond all of these material factors there is the human suffering and sorrow inevitably associated with widespread sickness and death.

It is much easier to point out that world birth rates are too high than it is to suggest specific procedures for lowering them. What are the factors that cause variation in family size from one population to another? What is it about industrialization and urban society that leads to lower birth rates? Can the factors be found, and if found can they be applied in densely populated, agrarian countries? Are the causes of high birth rates economic, cultural, social, or religious, and to what extent are they capable of modification without disrupting the society? Are high birth rates due to the lack of desire for a limited family or to the lack of means? To what extent is the high birth rate due to the absence of a cheap, harmless, simple, and effective way of limiting family size? Is it possible to influence birth rates without infringing on important individual liberties?

We don't have the answers to these questions. A great many people from a great many countries will need to devote time and thought to this problem before we can expect anything like a solution. This requires much basic research. Even with greatly increased knowledge the application is almost certain to be difficult, but it would be worse than foolish to follow a do-nothing policy and hope that some miracle will save humanity from the inevitable results of man's unwillingness to face the problems caused by his own actions.

The answer to the question, "Can the world feed its people?" must be accompanied by provisos. We can answer "yes," provided science and technology are used throughout the food-producing areas of the world--and provided man can control his numbers so that the increases brought about in food supply will be more rapid than the increases in human population. We must answer "no," if most of the world's agriculture remains as unscientific and as inefficient as at present, and if population numbers continue to increase at the current rates.

To alleviate the world's food shortages there are many things that the United States is doing and many more that it can do. We can continue to ship our agricultural surpluses to other areas. But even our own population is growing, and we may not always have surpluses. At any rate, we cannot hope to make up for the food shortage of the whole world. We can encourage international trade so that there may be more free movement of food supplies from regions of plenty to regions of want. We can take all possible steps to conserve our own topsoil and mineral resources and encourage other countries to do the same. Finally, and perhaps most important, we can provide American technical advice to other peoples--the idea embodied in the well-known and widely-discussed Point Four Program.

In his 1949 inaugural address, President Truman said:

> Fourth, we must embark on a bold new program for making the benefit of our scientific advances and industrial progress available for the improvement and growth of under-developed areas.... Our aim should be to help the free peoples of the world, through their own efforts, to produce more food, more clothing, more materials for housing, and more technical power to lighten their burdens. We invite other countries to pool their technological resources in this undertaking. Their contributions will be warmly welcomed. This should be a co-operative enterprise in which all nations work together through the United Nations and its specialized agencies wherever practicable. It must be a world-wide effort for the achievement of peace, plenty, and freedom.

There are those who say a Point Four Program, unless population increases can be checked, would only increase the problem by lowering the death rate and consequently increasing the number of mouths to feed. They would say that it is useless (or even criminally irresponsible) to try to improve living conditions in high-birth-rate areas. However, most people would not consider this an argument against Point Four Programs but rather an indication that finding means of increasing food supplies is not the only problem.

What the United States can do to put a check on the high birth rate in much of the world is not nearly so clear as what it can do to improve the means of subsistence. Family size is intimately tied in with the customs, beliefs, religion, and personal habits of people, things not easily influenced by outsiders. Suggestions from the United States are not likely to be taken too kindly or seriously by the rest of the world, particularly when they concern something as personal as family size. Most of the initiative in a country will have to come from local leaders who have the confidence of the people.

The United States can and should insist that the subject of population control be discussed in the United Nations and elsewhere and should encourage the world-wide education on which this as well as other aspects of progress depend. Also it can encourage greater research into the causes and control of variation in family size, for the answers can come only as a result of painstaking scientific study.

The solemn fact is that population pressures are responsible for a very large portion of the world's present human misery. We cannot have a healthy and peaceful world until mankind gets into better balance with the available food supply. Recognizing the fact that the food supply is not likely to keep pace with the present increase in numbers, it would seem only reasonable that we in the United States, together with those nations which will co-operate with us, should no longer allow our reluctance to discuss these highly personal matters to stand in the way. Mankind has too much at stake, for the welfare of future generations is in large part dependent on what we are able to accomplish.

It would be tragic indeed if man were able to use science to control the world in his interest, yet could not find a way to control himself. The twin problems of increasing the world's food supply and preventing a runaway increase in the population <u>must</u> be considered together.

Why is our world a world of nations in turmoil? It is partly because populations, food, mineral resources, and industrial technology are not evenly spread over the world. Unevenly spread, they form significant patterns that project into the future.

CHAPTER 12

WORLD PATTERNS IN POLITICS AND GEOGRAPHY

Richard Hartshorne
Department of Geography

In the centuries since the great explorers encompassed the world, it has been increasingly One World. Yet it is still true that remote distances and broad oceans tend to separate countries and lessen the importance of their relations to each other. In even greater degree large land areas of sparse population or poor transportation tend to prevent contact between the contries they separate. Generally speaking, areas close to each other have common interests--economic, political, and strategic.

It is pertinent therefore to examine the geographic pattern of the world, to recognize its major divisions and within each of these to analyze its pattern of independent states and dependent countries and to note its problem areas.

The accompanying map shows four major and four minor realms, based on community of interest.

It may be appropriate to start with our own. This includes all of North America (including Central America) and the West Indies, together with the Caribbean countries of South America; for the islands and shores of that sea

POLITICS AND GEOGRAPHY 129

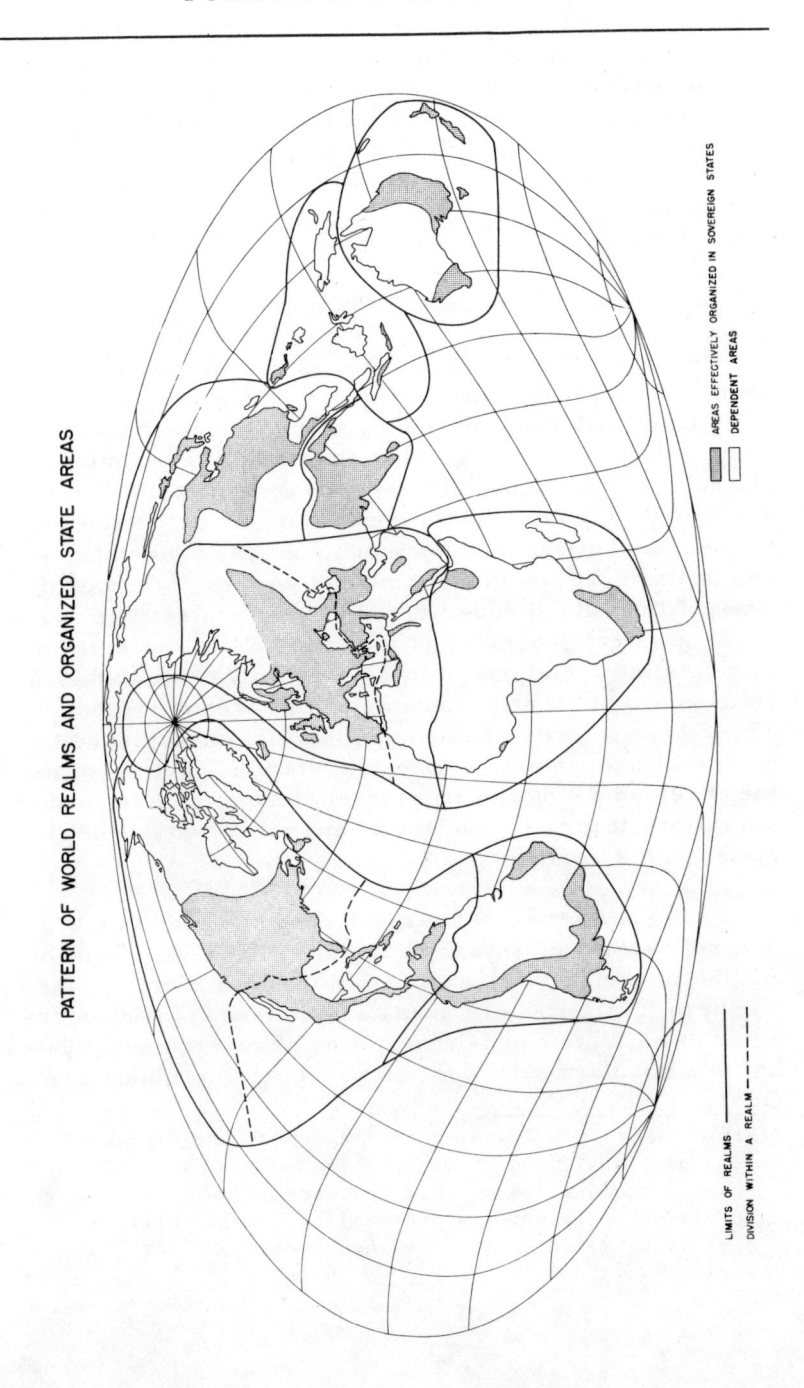

PATTERN OF WORLD REALMS AND ORGANIZED STATE AREAS

AREAS EFFECTIVELY ORGANIZED IN SOVEREIGN STATES
DEPENDENT AREAS

LIMITS OF REALMS ―――
DIVISION WITHIN A REALM ―――

are in close economic relation to the United States and belong inseparably to the strategic area of North America. Possessing a total population of more than two hundred million, this is the fourth of the major world realms in terms of mere numbers. But in terms of total production and hence of material power it is easily the second most important.

By far the greater part of the productive power of this realm is found in its northern portion, the United States and Canada, where the population is predominantly European in racial origin and even more predominantly English in culture, and where technological development and machine production are highest in the world. The United States is of course one of the very large states of the world whether measured in area, population, or production.* Canada has but one tenth as much population but rates as one of the most significant "minor" powers of the world. The political division between these two states runs counter to the physical geography of the area so that there are many intricate interrelations in local proximity of settlements, transport routes, and economic and strategic interests. These have forced--and common political background together with a century of peaceful relations have permitted-- the development of closer interrelations of policies and operations than has been true of any other two independent states in the world.

Each state possesses large dependent areas in the sparsely populated subarctic regions. If the territory of Alaska is obviously separate from the United States, the northern territories of Canada are no less colonial in character of population and organization of government. Throughout this northern part of the first realm no problem areas exist.

---

* *Four "very large" states in the world have a population of 150 million or more. Eight "large" states have 40 to 80 million. Sixteen are "minor": 12 to 28 million. Twenty-two are small: 4 to 11 million. Some twenty-five, with less than 4 million, are "very small."*

In the southern, Middle American, portion of the realm the situation is in many respects opposite. The population is predominantly either Indian or Negro, in the different parts, and while generally Spanish in culture--other than in the small British or French possessions--has also large ingredients of native Indian culture. Levels of production and standards of living are very low and most settled areas are overpopulated.

Politically the area contains twelve independent states, none of which is large. Mexico, with a somewhat greater population than Canada, has far less production. All the others are small, most of them very small. In addition are numerous small dependencies of the United States, Great Britain, France, and the Netherlands. Whether all of the independent states are in fact "going concerns" may be questioned, but their small size and their small productive power prevent any resultant problems from being of much concern beyond the United States.

Throughout the entire North American realm the supremacy of the economic, political, and military might of the United States is so obvious as to be universally recognized. This is a unique situation, a situation that can easily give Americans a false sense of security. Further, if we add to this realm, as we do commonly in our thinking, the apparently adjacent realm formed by the rest of South America and map the two as the Western Hemisphere, we appear to have a half of the world in which we are entirely secure if not the potential master.

It is however an error (though a natural one and very common in American thought) to consider the South American realm as our next neighbor. On the maps we commonly look at, it appears nearest. For decades we have heard of the increasing trade with South America. We like to think of those states politically associated with us as republics. And ever since the promulgation of the Monroe Doctrine we have tended to think of this realm as most important in our strategic defense.

In reality, the well-populated portions of South America are farther from the United States than are the countries of Europe. Our trade with that realm has always been much smaller than that with Europe. Although the Latin American states have imitated us in drawing up republican constitutions, the great differences in cultural origin and population characteristics have actually resulted in forms of government that are very different from ours and that have little influence on our political thinking. In contrast, the government of many European states, whether called republics or monarchies, have paralleled our own political development, and currents of political thought in Europe and North America have had pronounced influence on each other. Finally, the concern of the United States for the independence and strategic security of South American states has from the beginning been caused by our dominant concern for security from European powers.

The European states, therefore, must be considered as our nearest and dearest neighbors--whether dearest friends or dearest enemies. The countries of Europe are those with whom North American countries have the closest relations, relations that are the most valuable economically, politically most influential, and strategically most dangerous relations.

The fact that this realm as marked on the map corresponds roughly with the conventional area of Europe is not without significance. For Europe is the single one of the conventional continents that owes its name not to the map of land and sea masses but to the facts of human geography. In the western portion of the Eurasian land mass there is unbroken continuity of human settlement. Farms and cities are interconnected by roads and railroads, interrupted only by narrow seas, and all are similar in agricultural and urban economies and technology. This area extends from the Atlantic eastward beyond the conventional border of the Urals into Western Siberia.

Inhabited by more than 500 million people, this realm has nearly three times the population of the North American realm. It is second in population only to the East Asian realm. It includes the greatest area of agricultural land and has by far the greatest total capacity of mineral and industrial production of any world realm. It is also the largest area of the world effectively organized into states that function as going concerns. If it were organized into a single power unit or block, it would constitute by far the greatest power in the present world.

Europe, however, has never been organized politically as a unit. In 1938, the area and people of Europe (Europe in the conventional sense) were divided among 28 independent states, and the number today is only slightly less. Politically speaking, Europe is a collective word to describe a group of states located close to each other. But in most other aspects of human geography, Europe is a unit region. In this contrast lies the core of its problems.

Because of great variations in the size of its countries, the pattern of division is extremely complex. The eastern third forms the major portion of one very large state, the Soviet Union, which extends great distances beyong the European realm into Central and East Asia. In western Europe, before the Second World War, there were four large states, one of minor size, and ten small or very small states which were fairly well scattered through that portion of the continent. But between western Europe and the Soviet Union, from Finland on the north to Greece on the south, was a zone of 13 states, none of which were large, most of them quite small.

The weakness of this so-called Shatter Zone presented the opportunity for expansion to an aggressive Germany, then the strongest state in Europe and in the critical central location. Because Hitler could not admit the failure of this venture until Germany itself had been brought to ruins over his head, no power remained to check the expansion of Russian control throughout the greater part of this belt. The Soviet Union absorbed the three very small Baltic states and established puppet Communist governments in most of the others, as well as in the eastern zone of Germany.

The major powers of Europe today are therefore found at opposite ends of the realm, with a large and productive area between them that is not independently organized. This power vacuum of central Europe is by all odds the problem area of most critical importance in the world today. No other area offers such possibilities of great increase in strength to whatever power secures its support or control. And nowhere else are great powers, on both sides, so close to the contested area.

This explains why we adhere to past convention in considering Russia as part of Europe. Whatever means may prove effective in preventing further expansion of Soviet power in the rest of Europe, that can not be accomplished by the verbal device of redefining the word "Europe" to exclude Russia, or--with even less logic--to exclude whatever areas happen to be under Soviet control. There is no escaping the essential unity of the total European area. To be sure, there is at present a sharp political cleavage between western Europe and the Communist lands behind the Iron Curtain. It is also true that throughout European history there has been a marked difference in cultural history in the western and eastern portions of the continent. But we are not here concerned with such cultural differences, all too readily exaggerated by those who forget that Communism as a doctrine was a product of western, not eastern, European thought.

The basic facts are the continuity of rural and urban settlement throughout, together with the interconnection of transport routes and the common use of the same tools of agriculture, industry, and transport. These result in a trade situation in which eastern Europe is interconnected with central Europe(except for the Iron Curtain), and central Europe is very closely interconnected with western, Atlantic Europe. These facts have produced a unity of strategic geography; all of Europe forms a single theater of war. In every major war in Europe since the middle of the eighteenth century, nearly every power in Europe was involved, from Britain on the west to Russia and Turkey on the east.

In this strategic sense and to a large degree also in the economic sense, the European theater extends into North Africa and the Near East. The sea routes of the Mediterranean are among the more important trade routes between different European countries. They also lead to the narrow fringe of populated areas that lie along the southern and eastern shores of the Mediterranean, backed by the desert. These routes are of paramount importance in the naval strategy of European war and as routes of transport for land forces. In consequence, this belt of countries, with a population of over 100 million, is here added to the European realm, in spite of the great difference in culture, religion, economy, and political development.

The western portion of this Mohammedan belt has long been a dependent area under control of European states, primarily France. Incipient nationalist movements among the native population suggest that this may constitute a problem area in the near future.

The eastern portion of this belt, once included in the Turkish Empire, extends from Egypt to Turkey, through the states of the Levant coast. With these we may include the similarly semi-arid and Mohammedan countries that extend through Arabia and Iran to the gates of India.

Since the collapse of the Turkish empire in the first World War, some eight countries have emerged as independent states, together with Iran and Afghanistan. In comparison with the great neighbor on the north, the Soviet Union, or with the external sea powers, all these states are small, most of them very small. Particularly critical is the smallest of all, the new Jewish state of Israeli in the midst of larger Arab neighbors.

Small bits of this area, notably in Arabia, remain directly or indirectly under British control. In addition Britain has retained some degree of control in one or more of the independent states, notably at the Suez Canal. On the northeast, Czarist Russia had penetrated far from its European base into the outer margins of this belt both in the area south of the Caucasus and in the belt of oases south of the Caspian-Aral deserts. These non-Russian territories are now firmly included in the Soviet Union.

The new independent states of the area are constantly disturbed by conflicts among themselves or by internal unrest. Hence the region as a whole represents a problem area of major importance, caught between the pressure of the great land power of eastern Europe on the north and the seapowers of western Europe on the south. Actually this belt represents an extension of the Shatter Zone of east central Europe eastward through Turkey to the gates of India.

In terms of population and productive capacity the area is not important. But its great petroleum resources are vital to western Europe. Its location is strategically of great importance since it lies athwart the routes from western Europe to India and the far East, and also the routes to or from the Soviet Union, whether via the seaway through the Straits and the Black Sea, via land routes through Turkey or Iran, or from air bases within the Middle East. As long, therefore, as the Soviet Union appears to be a threat to central and western Europe, the Middle East remains a problem area of major concern.

Two of the minor world realms are located one on each side of the South Atlantic. These are: most of South America, with a population of little less than 100 million, and Negro Africa--the main bulk of that continent south of the empty Sahara--with some 150 million people. Both areas include large regions that are very primitive, sparsely populated, and of little significance at present in world affairs. But both include areas of surplus production of foods and raw materials critical for western Europe. In their vast areas of undeveloped lands they offer perhaps the most promising opportunities for future support of the industrial countries of the North Atlantic.

In political organization the two realms are in sharp contrast. Africa is predominantly an area of dependent territories ruled by outside European powers. South America is theoretically organized into some eight independent states. In reality each of these eight governments represents only the realtively small portion of its territory that is effectively settled by sedentary population although it controls as colonial territories the larger portions that are sparsely populated by primitive peoples. Although one of these states, Brazil, covers vast territory, and counts a population of nearly fifty million, neither it nor any of the others can rank, in terms of productive capacity, as more than a minor state power. Neither could any possible combination among them amount to more than a minor total power.

In each of these two realms, relations among the countries within the realm are far less important than relations with outside areas. These relations are predominantly with western Europe in both cases, but also with the United States in the case of South America. Increased industrial development in Argentina and Brazil may tend somewhat to offset this situation, but lack of fuel and the extraordinary obstacles to land transport within South America (in contrast to the ease of sea transport) may cause this situation to continue.

There are in both realms possibilities for considerable difficulties, both present and future. In southern South America, an aggressive power in Argentina might operate as a local "great power," dominating landlocked Paraguay and threatening the other smaller neighbors, Uruguay and Chile, possibly even Brazil. Such efforts could hope for success only if the great powers of the North Atlantic were tied down by greater dangers nearer home.

In parts of Negro tropical Africa, the very successes of the colonial administration have inevitably led to the development of native nationalism. Here one must anticipate the appearance of genuine problem areas unless effective transition is skillfully handled. The most insoluble problem, apparently, is that presented by the Union of South Africa, where a minority group of European origin operates an independent state in which those of native race and culture are excluded from economic advancement or political influence.

These four realms, two major and two minor--North America, Europe, Africa, South America--may all be included in a single hemisphere drawn with its center in the Atlantic Ocean (somewhat north of the equator). This is the hemisphere of most concern to Americans. With the important exception of Australia and New Zealand, this "Atlantic Hemisphere" includes practically all of the lands of the world of Western civilization. In total, it comprises approximately three fourths of the land areas of the world (excluding ice-covered Antarctica), about one half of the world's population, and nearly 90 per cent of the world's manufacturing industries.

The opposite half of the world consists largely of the waters of the Pacific and Indian Oceans, and ice-covered Antarctica. In the lesser area of land included within it, however, live one half of the people of the world. These are found in two major realms on the continent of Asia, in the minor realm of the islands southeast of Asia, and in the apparently misplaced, but very minor, realm of Western culture in Australia and New Zealand.

In southern and eastern Asia are two of the four world regions of very large populations. In no other realms are there such large and dense populations dependent primarily on agriculture and possessing little industrial or military power. Nevertheless, because of sheer numbers of people and because of future potentialities for development, each must be considered a major realm.

The East Asian realm--extending from Japan and Manchuria south to Indo-China and Siam--is the larger of the two. Its population of nearly 600 million is almost as great as that of the entire European realm, including its trans-Mediterranean and Near East extension. In total production of all kinds of materials it is far inferior to either of the North Atlantic realms. In basic resources--

coal, iron ore, petroleum, and water power--it also appears less well endowed but may well prove to be third among the world's great regions. Only in Japan and Manchuria, as a result of Japanese control, have major steps been made toward industrial development based on these resources.

In political organization, all parts of this realm are at the moment problem areas, though for different reasons. Japan, prior to the destruction which it brought upon itself by attempting to bring all the other areas under its control, was the single and striking exception. It was an effectively organized sovereign state and the only one in that half of the world commanding major power. Its advances in modern technology and industry, as well as its long experience in effective political organization, may enable it to assume again its former position of superior power. But if the signing of the peace treaty with the United States reestablished the Japanese state, the independence of that state was markedly curtailed. So long as the Soviet Union refuses to recognize the situation, so long as it maintains its objection to the use of Japan as an American military base, and so long as the economy of Japan depends on American subsidies, we must continue to consider that country in some degree a problem area.

China, the largest state in the world from point of view of population and also one of the oldest, has been an enigma on the world political map for more than forty years. Though its status as an independent state has never officially been disputed, other than by Japan, since the First World War, the inability of its government to establish effective control over its territory and people have made it continuously a problem area of major scope. If the Communist regime which now controls the greater part of its mainland area fully establishes itself, will China become at last an organized independent state? Or will it be simply an organized dependency of an outside state, directed from Moscow through the intermediary of Chinese Communist officials? Or again, is it to become a field of international conflict? Upon the answers to such questions depends the future power pattern of the entire East Asian realm.

Lesser problem areas are Korea and French Indo-China, where solutions have been sought by the clash of arms. Korea, only lately a dependency of Japan, found itself the first battleground of outside opposition to the expansion of Communism. In Indo-China, peoples formerly under effective colonial control of France are engaged in a struggle for independence, a struggle confused by conflicts among local ethnic groups and by the issue of Communism.

On the northern margin of this realm, a narrow belt of recently settled land along the Trans-Siberian railroad represents a landward extension of European Russia into this otherwise Oriental realm. The population, east of Lake Baikal, is less than six million, or less than three per cent of the total of the Soviet Union. This constitutes a very small, but strategically significant, element in the East Asian realm.

In south Asia, the great subcontinent of India plus Burma and Ceylon comprises a major realm, whose dense population is strikingly cut off from the rest of the continent by the surrounding mountain areas. Most notable are the unbroken lofty ranges of the Himalayas, the high semi-arid plateaus of Tibet, and the rugged mountain ranges that lie between Burma and China. While this area may appear close to China, it faces the Indian Ocean exclusively. It remains today--as throughout history--largely isolated by land from most of the rest of Asia.

In population it is the third major realm of the earth, possessing nearly 450 million people. Thanks to the long period of British control, the area has developed considerably in modern technology, notably in its railroad system and more recently in industry. In these respects it is far more developed than China, though less than Japan. But its industries total hardly more than those of Belgium.

This realm has seen the greatest change in political pattern in the years following the war. It now consists of four independent states: United India, Pakistan, Ceylon, and

Burma. While the first three remain voluntarily in association with Britain in the Commonwealth, Burma refused and operates entirely independently.

The separation of Burma and Ceylon presents no major problems, but the division of the main Indian area on religious grounds into United India and Pakistan creates serious disruption of previously close economic bonds. The split of Moslem Pakistan into two parts widely separated by a main portion of United India is unique on the political map of the world. This situation is sufficient to make this a problem area of first rank--even if the two countries can arrive at final agreement on the disputed region of Kashmir.

United India, with nearly 350 million people, constitutes three fourths of the total South Asian realm, and population-wise is the largest political unit of effective organization in the world. This alone gives it great psychological influence and prestige as a leader throughout all the non-European world, even though its productive capacity for economic and military power is still small.

South and east of the Indo-Chinese peninsula is the island realm of the Philippines, the East Indies, and the Malay peninsula, which is attached to the continent only by a narrow neck of land. With a population of about one hundred million, this realm is comparable in numbers to Negro Africa or South America. Like each of them it includes large areas of extremely primitive development and sparse population. But the island of Java and some of the Philippines show an intensity of agricultural development, and consequently extremely dense populations, comparable to conditions in South and East Asia. In others the most successful plantation areas of the world have been developed. It is not surprising that its total economic importance to the outside world, measured by export of surplus products, has been greater than of any other part of this half of the world, exclusive of Japan.

This island region is in a state of radical transition in nearly all its parts. Up to the second World War the entire realm consisted of dependent areas under control of west European powers or the United States. Further, this control appeared to be strongly established. No major native opposition existed. The economic and technical development under outside control had resulted in great increase in production and population as well as economic benefits to the outside world.

Since World War II, however, almost the entire area has been reconstituted as independent states--either on the basis of mutual consent, as in the Philippines, or as a result of armed revolt following the withdrawal of the Japanese, as in the Indonesian Republic. In the most important area remaining under colonial rule, the Malay peninsula, armed revolt continues to present a major problem.

Recent developments in the two new independent states of the Philippines and Indonesia indicate continuing problems there. The island of Java, thronging with nearly fifty million people who share a common economic structure, can perhaps be effectively organized together with the smaller population of Sumatra into an indigenous state. But the remaining islands of Indonesia differ entirely in race, culture, and stage of economic development. In their present primitive development, they must of necessity be organized from the outside. A major problem in the negotiations with the Netherlands has been whether such outside control shall come from Java, the Netherlands, or some kind of combination.

The last realm to be considered is a geographic paradox. The realm of Australia and New Zealand, though closest to Indonesia and Southern and Eastern Asia, and farther from Europe than any other realm, is more completely European in race, culture, and character of development than any other realm outside of Europe itself. Its economic connections are overwhelmingly with Europe and its political association in the world-wide Commonwealth is primarily significant in maintaining a strategic tie with Great Britain.

The small desert-divided continent and the pair of distant islands each organized as a single independent state, have together barely ten million people, the size of a small European state. The high productivity per capita, however, together with the concentration on production for export makes this realm proportionately much more important to the economy of the outside world. There are no problem areas at present, but Australians fear a future danger in the vacuum of the unpopulated tropical northern part of their territory, so close to the over-populated lands farther north.

Unlike all the other oceans of the world, the western Pacific contains a vast number of very small islands. These lie for the most part in the tropical waters east of the Malay Archipelago and Australia and reaching as far as Hawaii. Their combined area is less than that of Cuba and their population is only one million, of whom nearly half are in the Hawaiian Islands. Except for the latter group none of the islands has more than very slight economic importance. Many of them, however, have long been recognized as strategically important for possible naval operations in the Pacific and, as was repeatedly demonstrated in the last war, almost any of them may have such importance for air transport and warfare.

All the inhabited islands, and in recent years many tiny islands that had not been inhabited, have been brought under the control of one or another of the major naval powers. Today almost all the islands north of the equator are under American control, as possessions or as trusteeships. Most of those south of the equator are under British control, as possessions of the United Kingdom or trusteeships of Australia or New Zealand. A much smaller number of the southern islands are possessions of France or of the United States.

The discussion of the eight realms has made clear that however important may be the relations among the countries in each realm, the relations between them and those in other realms may be equally important.

This is true of the relations between European and North American realms. The United States has more trade with Europe than with the remainder of North America, and far more than with any other realm. In economic, political or military matters it is impossible for major developments or cataclysms in either to take place without profound effects upon the other. They face each other from their most productive portions, across the relatively narrow North Atlantic Ocean. Over its swells passes all but a minor part of the overseas trade of both realms. The security of these routes of shipment is of vital importance to the countries of western Europe and to every one of the North American states.

The same waters have been available since Columbus to armed forces intending to invade across the dividing but not separating ocean. They were so used by European forces during the earlier periods of our history and were likewise used by millions of American forces during each of the two World Wars. That the route has been used in our time only eastward is due not to any superior power of North America over Europe, since exactly the reverse is the case, but rather to the fact that European powers were in conflict with each other and the United States was allied with the strongest naval power in Europe. As long as the states of western Europe together are weaker on the land than any one state seeking control of all Europe, the security of both western Europe and North America depends on the combined forces of both, united across the North Atlantic.

Until recent years all the connections between the two realms were by sea across the North Atlantic. These provide still the important peace time connections, but two additional routes have become significant. One is the circular route via the northeastern coast of South America, the 1,600 miles across the narrows of the Atlantic to the coast of West Africa and thence either to Europe or to the Middle East. The use of this route for air passage during the last war extended that portion of South America which is of strategic concern to the United States to at least the bulge of Brazil and--for the first time--to the Atlantic coast of Africa.

The other route lies across the Arctic Ocean. Here, where the two realms approach each other most closely, Arctic ice and barren lands once formed an impenetrable barrier. Now they provide possible routes for land-based air attacks.

The development of air transport and air reconnaissance over the North Atlantic has caused small and even tiny islands to become critically important. These include the very small independent state of Iceland, the Portuguese Azores, and the single little British island of Ascension, just south of the narrows.

In contrast to the close interrelationships of the European and North American realms is the lack of relationship between the South Asian and East Asian realms. From our distance, the peoples and civilizations of southern and eastern Asia may appear much alike, but in reality the differences between them are far greater than those between the two North Atlantic realms. Likewise, their trade relations are far fewer. In spite of increasing trade with Japan, southern Asia still has its most important trade relations with Europe, as does eastern Asia with North America. The extraordinarily strong strategic separation of the two realms is illustrated by the desperate efforts during the war to establish a trickle of support from Burma and India to China, over the Burma road or over the Hump.

All the minor world realms, regardless of location, have their most important connections with either Europe or North America, or with both. Economically this is bound to be true as long as the only areas of great surplus industrial production (and hence of great markets for food and raw materials) are in western Europe and eastern North America.

The interrealm connections are by sea. This is true even where such land connections as the Isthmus of Panama exist. Air transport can carry but small amounts of freight over long distances. Air-bombardment at long range, however important a threat against aggression, is not believed capable of forcing final military decisions. We must therefore recognize the continuing vital importance of sea routes in the present economic and strategic geography of the world.

Minor exceptions are two land routes that lead from Europe to India, but neither of these has a through rail connection. The route leading through the Middle East, across the highlands of Turkey and Iran, parallels the sea route and is not likely to be important save for air transport. The other leads from the major populated area of the Soviet Union across the desert east of the Caspian to isolated irrigation districts on the Soviet frontier. From there it is but a short but very difficult route across Afghanistan to Pakistan and India.

Far more important are the Russian land routes across Siberia to China and the Pacific. Whether by the main line of the Transsiberian Railroad to and around Manchuria, or by branches that reach at several points to the borders of Sinkiang or Mongolia, these routes must cross vast and nearly empty and barren areas. They have very limited capacity and the latter route has no rail connections on the Chinese side. But they are effective in supplying the needs for limited war and in spreading political ideas through innumerable points of contact along the longest land frontier in the world.

Russia's early expansion along these routes made it a European power with colonial dependencies in the heart of Asia and on its north Pacific coast. Increasing development under the Soviet regime has gone far to integrate these remote possessions into the national unit. If the vast area of China is now to be joined to Moscow, we have a political realm of two major cores in separate geographic realms, separated by the vast expanse of nearly empty land in Central Asia. What does this portend?

In the distant future, eastern Asia--and south Asia and the island realm as well--may attain a much higher degree of industrialization and political organization. In time these areas may become major power factors in world affairs. Thus the greatest issue of the next half century may prove to be the contest between the Soviet power block and its opponents to win these future powers to one side or the other.

But in that contest for the minds and hearts of men, the issue will not be decided by military force. Rather, the outcome will hinge on the power of genuine ideological, economic, and political support. Whether we can offer such support depends on the outcome of the current struggle for independence and security in the Atlantic hemisphere. For the immediate future, the areas of the Asiatic half of the world are important in the world power pattern to the degree that they provide aid to one side or the other in that vital struggle in the Atlantic. Always we return to the key question of the Atlantic struggle since World War II: Will the western half of Europe be brought under the same domination as Eastern Europe or will its power, combined with that of North America, and supplemented by South America and Africa, be sufficient to keep western Europe free and North America secure?

> *If the only forces at work among men were the scientific, technological, and economic ones described in the preceding chapters, the picture would be complex enough. However, there are other forces, namely, ideological differences.*

CHAPTER 13

RUSSIA AND THE COMMUNIST WAY OF LIFE

Michael B. Petrovich
Department of History

It has become commonplace to observe that we live in a time of crisis. Prophets of doom have cried ominous warnings foretelling the decline and fall of Western civilization. They confront us either with a deluge of "neo-barbarians" from "the East" or else with the atomic obliteration of the whole human race.

It is hard, in the face of such dire prophecies, for us to remember that ours are not the only times that have tried men's souls. How often in the past have men cried peace when there was no peace? We only know with painful certainty that we live in unsettled times, and that we understand all too imperfectly the perilous forces which prey on our security. We are the mightiest power in the world-- a nation which seemingly but yesterday emerged victorious and relatively intact from the most devastating war in history. Yet we are sinking into uneasiness, suspicion, fear, and even panic. How came this to be so?

For many the answer is all too simple! Russia. We are somewhat like that well-heeled suburban couple in the New Yorker cartoon who are sunning themselves in uneasy comfort on their back lawn and wearily wishing that Russia did not exist so that they might peacefully enjoy what they have. Evidently our experience with Nazi Germany failed to teach us that Hitler was not so much a cause as a symptom of evil. Had we learned that lesson, many of us would not now indulge in the primitive delusion that Russia is the root of this world's troubles. It is true that the present dictatorship in the Soviet Union has not brought its promise of bliss but rather a grinding misery to much of the world's population. Yet totalitarian ideologies such as Communism do not cause the hunger, want, disease, social inequalities, lack of opportunity, racial and religious prejudice, economic and political servitude, and frustrated national ambitions upon which they feed. All these are ills which atom bombs cannot cure. We must be careful of those among us who would train our eyes solely on the Communist menace while the very evils which have given rise to it go unattended.

On the other hand, we cannot ignore the fact that the Soviet Union and the Communist ideology do indeed confront the democratic world with a perilous challenge. Common sense requires of us a thorough awareness and understanding of that challenge. Who does not realize that today peace depends largely on the relations between these two world powers--the United States of America and the Union of Soviet Socialist Republics? Let us, then, examine some of the bases of that relationship in an effort to discover what may lie ahead.

The present tension makes it difficult for us to recognize certain similarities and to realize that the history of the relationship between America and Russia offers some cheery episodes. Looking back over the panorama of two centuries, we find that whenever these two countries took notice of one another, the dominant theme was more often one of friendship than discord.

How many Americans know that not only France but

Catherine's Russia came to the aid of the Thirteen Colonies during the American Revolution? It must be admitted that neither of our allies acted so benevolently out of love for our revolution but rather out of hostility to England. But international relations have been, after all, basically a matter of self-interest.

It is good to think of a time when Benjamin Franklin was a corresponding member of the Russian Academy of Sciences, when Jefferson and Czar Alexander I wrote each other admiring letters, when Russia sympathized with us in our war with Britain in 1812, and when we in turn sympathized with Russia in the Crimean War in 1854. It is good to remember that Russia publicly mourned Lincoln's assassination and that our emissaries to the Russian capital were the favorites of St. Petersburg society. And when Russia was beaten by Japan at the beginning of the century it was at Portsmouth, New Hampshire, that Theodore Roosevelt helped ease the bitterness of the Russian defeat.

It is incredible how many Americans do not know that our country greeted the Russian Revolution of March, 1917, with enthusiasm. What could be more natural than for our own revolutionary republic to approve the downfall of an oppressive monarchy?

It was the October Revolution, the Bolshevik revolt against a middle-of-the-road government, that we so strenuously opposed. Despite our opposition, the American Relief Administration during the devastating famine of 1921-1922 saved literally millions of Russian lives.

The Bolshevik regime admired certain aspects of American life as much as it detested our economic and political system. There was nothing the Soviet Union could not accomplish, Stalin once declared, if Russians would only learn to combine their socialism with American efficiency.

Russians were genuinely pleased when, at the beginning of Franklin D. Roosevelt's presidency, this country at last decided to recognize the Soviet Union. A low point in our

THE COMMUNIST WAY OF LIFE

relations was reached when the Soviet Union attacked Finland and signed a pact with Nazi Germany in 1939. Yet the fortunes of war brought us together in a strange alliance which gave many Americans reason to hope that we would yet be friends with the Soviet Union.

It was especially during this honeymoon that we became conscious of our similarities. When G.I. Joe and Ivan Ivanovich met on the Elbe River in 1945 they might have recognized a certain kinship which went beyond their comradeship in arms.

Both the United States and the Soviet Union are huge continental powers whose influence must in the very nature of things transcend their borders. Both think in superlatives. Both talk incessantly about the biggest, the best, the fastest, the strongest, the tallest--much to the annoyance of a sophisticated Europe, which regards both Russians and Americans as noisy adolescents. Many observers have been struck by a certain similarity between the broad Russian nature and the expansiveness of the American character. Both countries include peoples of many different races, ethnic stocks, and cultures, and both proudly offer their unions as examples to a divided planet. Both the United States and the Soviet Union are young, growing countries with whom progress is a sacred word. And by this word both of us more often than not mean material progress.

Despite these similarities, the differences which separate us are far more basic and serious. Our American political heritage is founded on the sacredness of the individual, the inviolable rights of minorities, the freedom to differ, to criticize, and to participate in government.

In Russia the autocracy of Byzantine Caesars, Tartar khans and divine right monarchs has made it all the easier for the Communist Party to impose on a basically democratic Russian people a completely totalitarian state. Russia has long been a land in which the individual has counted for little, in which minorities were regarded as pernicious, and in which a privileged state bureaucracy lorded it over the population. It is difficult to see eye to eye with a country whose political concepts so conflict with our own.

In economic structure, too, the Soviet Union and the United States differ markedly. The basic economy which has developed our resources, commerce, and industry has become a modified capitalism. The story of capitalism has often been far from a pretty one. Yet it must surely be recognized that much of our strength and greatness rests on a numerous and inclusive middle class which emerged as the result of private enterprise.

Russia never knew a middle class like ours until late in its history, and then that class hardly had a chance to survive in the face of a traditional authoritarianism. The Soviet government's monopoly on trade is nothing new in Russian history. Ivan the Terrible instructed his ambassador to England, Nepeya, four centuries ago, "Tell my sister Elizabeth that I am the only merchant in Russia." What private enterprise there was under the czars certainly disappeared under the commissars. It is difficult to do business with someone who does not share with us a single notion as to how business ought to be done.

We and the Russians have always been literally worlds apart in civilization. We are the beneficiaries of Western Christendom, Scholasticism, the Renaissance, the Reformation, the Counter-Reformation, Rationalism, Humanism, Free Trade, and parliamentary government. Russia is the heir of Byzantine autocracy, Greek Christianity, the Tartar invasion, a would-be enlightened despotism, serfdom, agrarian collectivism, and absolute state control. It was almost a century before the Bolshevik Revolution that a famous Russian thinker, Chaadaiev, wrote: "We have never walked hand in hand with other nations. We do not belong to any of the great families of mankind, either to the West or to the East. We do not have the tradition of either. We exist as if beyond the limits of time and as if we were never touched by the universal education of humanity."

The Russians have copied and continue to copy foreign

techniques. They have been far less successful in adopting the Western way of life. Indeed, Russia's best minds have consciously rejected the West in the past. Communism is only the latest in a long line of barriers which have separated our worlds from one another. Even when we understand each other's language, we fail utterly to understand one another's meanings. There is no translator at the United Nations so skillful that he can make the word "democracy" mean the same thing for the American and the Soviet delegations. He would have to change a thousand years of history to do that!

Despite these basic differences in our political, economic, and cultural heritage, our chances of living in peace with Russia would be immeasurably heightened were it not for Communism. It is truly ironic that Russia received the Communist ideology from the West. When the founders of that ideology, Karl Marx and Friedrich Engels, issued the Communist Manifesto in 1848, they hardly dreamed that peasant Russia would one day claim to be the incarnation of their creed. When Karl Marx helped found the First International in 1864 in St. Martin's Hall in London, he and his comrades could never have guessed that Moscow would one day be the headquarters of world Communism.

What are the basic tenets of this ideology? Very briefly, Communism sees all of man's past as the history of class struggle. Capitalism is denounced as the final stage of man's exploitation by man. The workers of the world are urged to unite against their capitalist governments, to nationalize the means of production, and to establish a state based on the dictatorship of the proletariat. We would think it a damaging charge indeed to accuse a country of being a dictatorship. The constitution of the U.S.S.R. proudly proclaims that the Soviet state is a dictatorship!

It is no secret that Communists the world over believe in the violent overthrow of all non-Communist governments, including our own. "In order to overthrow the international bourgeoisie and to create an international Soviet Republic as a transition stage to the complete abolition of the state," say the statutes of the Third International, which was founded in Moscow in 1919, "the Communist International will use all means at its disposal including force of arms." The Communists may work openly or subversively, they may press forward or beat temporary retreats, but they will never do anything without keeping in mind the ultimate advancement of their goal. The Communists are certainly not the first to have subscribed to the proposition that the end justifies the means. However, none before them has ever proclaimed and published it with such an unconcealed contempt for ethics.

This circumstance makes it particularly difficult for our nation to deal with the Soviet Union. If American relations with the U.S.S.R. were just a matter of adjusting international differences, our ability to arrive at some agreement might be much greater. The chariot of Soviet foreign policy is pulled not by one horse but by two. There is not only the white horse of historic national ambitions but the red horse of world revolution. Russia has been interested for centuries in warm-water ports, free passage through the Dardanelles, a system of buffer states on its western border, a sphere of influence in Iran, and many other such ambitions. The whole question has been considerably complicated by the fact that Moscow has become the headquarters for world revolution. At times the white horse pulls faster; at times the red horse is given free rein.

* * * * *

In the past three and a half decades the Soviet Union has exhibited extraordinary contrasts in its foreign policy. We can speak of at least seven distinct policies. From 1917 to 1921 the Russian Communists, who were waging a revolution and a civil war at home, openly called upon the whole world to revolt. The results were disappointing. Outside Russia there were a few abortive revolutions--the Bela Kun government in Hungary, the Spartacus Putsch in Berlin, and the complete fiascos of Bavaria and Slovakia. In Russia itself a war-exhausted country needed a respite, and Lenin called a retreat both abroad and at home during the so-called New

Economic Policy 1921-1927. Soon after Stalin came to power in 1923 the new leader declared the doctrine of "Socialism in One Country" forced by what he termed the temporary stabilization of world capitalism. In other words, in a time of Western strength and their own weakness, the Soviet Leaders discovered that the peaceful coexistence of Communism and Capitalism was possible, at least for a time.

With the inauguration of the Five Year Plan in 1928, however, Stalin reversed himself and adopted once again a more aggressive and militant policy of fomenting world revolution. The Third Communist International was turned completely into the instrument of Soviet foreign policy. The banner of world revolution was unfurled once again.

It was not long before the Soviet leaders had occasion to change their minds--and for two reasons: the failure to arouse workers in other countries to destroy their own governments, and the growing threat of Fascist Italy, Germany, and Spain. So a fourth policy was born. In 1935 the Seventh Congress of the Communist International or Comintern proclaimed the policy of the Popular Front. Communists everywhere were instructed to make friends, if they could, with the non-Communist Left and to form an anti-Fascist alliance. Fearful for her own safety, the Soviet Union joined the League of Nations in this period.

In 1939, as Hitler was ready to launch his military might against Poland, France, and England, Stalin abruptly and dramatically shifted to an agreement with Hitler. In late August of that year Fascist Germany and Communist Russia signed a so-called nonaggression pact which contained then secret clauses in which the two partners divided the loot of eastern Europe.

The world was amazed at the bizarre sight of the leader of world Communism joining hands with the leader of the world's anti-Comintern forces. Also amazed were many Communists and fellow travelers in our country who had joined the good fight against Fascism in the previous Popular Front period. Thousands of them took this opportunity to break with the Communist Party. But the loss was not too great. The Communist Party does not count its strength in numbers and votes anyway. Most of those who stayed on in the party even after the Russo-German pact could be counted on to stomach anything, to explain away everything, and to obey orders without question.

During this fifth period of Soviet foreign policy, all the invectives that Communists had once hurled against Hitler and Mussolini were now cast against the West. In our own country Communists and the most conservative isolationists found themselves repeating the same line--that the United States had no business coming to the aid of Hitler's victims.

All of that suddenly changed, however, when on June 21, 1941, the German Wehrmacht attacked the Soviet Union. After all, Hitler was also a disciple of the creed that the end justifies the means. Overnight the imperialist war of decadent capitalism became a war to save democracy. The Popular Front policy was dusted off wherever necessary and Communists the world over either joined or organized a common action against Germany and Italy. This was, for example, the origin of such guerrilla movements in embattled Europe as Tito's Partisans in Yugoslavia. To allay natural Western suspicions, the Comintern was officially abolished in May, 1943, though it became evident later than the organization had never really ceased to function.

This was the period of the strange alliance between capitalist, democratic America and communist, totalitarian Russia during which well-meaning Americans sincerely felt that to understand Soviet Russia one had to admire it. Few Americans realized at the time that we and our Communist allies were really fighting two different wars, even though we were fighting at the same time and against the same enemy. We thought that all of us were engaged in something we called, for the want of a better name, the second World War. Meanwhile the Soviet Union, which was caught up in a nationalist fervor of its own, was waging what it called the Great Fatherland War.

It became obvious as soon as Germany was beaten in May, 1945, that our alliance had had only a single real basis, the fight against a common enemy. This marked the inauguration of the Soviet Union's seventh and present policy--the extension and consolidation of its own sphere of influence, the encouragement of revolts in Asia and elsewhere, obstruction in the United Nations, and the weakening of the non-Communist world wherever and however possible. As far as the Soviet Union itself is concerned, one may well characterize its present policy by a phrase out of its history in 1917--"no war, no peace."

There is a simple lesson to be learned from this review. The Soviet Union has been most aggressive when the non-Communist world has been weakest, and it has been most co-operative when the non-Communist world was strong and determined.

* * * * *

Today there are many sources of friction between the Communist and non-Communist world. In the Far East and Middle East a long smouldering nationalism is now aflame. The Soviet Union is naturally eager to encourage this unrest and to exploit it. In Korea, Malaya, and French Indo-China, Western forces are being kept on call while the Russians need not expend a single man. India and Pakistan, Iran and the Arab states are all raw and sensitive areas. In Europe our troops and those of our allies stand face to face with the Red Army along a most unnatural boundary. A precarious balance of power has thus far survived incident after incident. How much more strain this balance can stand only the future will tell.

In the United Nations the Soviet Union and its satellites have created an obstructive bloc which has made use of the veto power wherever oratory has failed to persuade. This has been frequently. A particular source of friction between America and Russia has been the question of atomic control. We have put forward the Baruch Plan, which calls for the international supervision of atomic production. Despite the fact that the Soviet leaders fear our superiority in atomic weapons, they could not afford to risk international inspection behind the Iron Curtain. The result is an armaments race the like of which the world has never seen. It is little wonder, then, that so many inhabitants of this great globe feel as though they were on the threshold of catastrophe. Two opposite poles of the planet are gathering their forces and stand poised to destroy one another. What are the choices that stand before us?

A few voices have been raised in favor of a "preventive" war against the Communist bloc. To these advocates an immediate showdown appears preferable to the present tension in which the other side appears to be growing in strength. Even if this school could prove that its calculations were absolutely correct, it is extremely doubtful that Americans are morally capable of such a deliberate action. Even more pertinent is the consideration that our own aggression could hardly win us the support of a world that is crying for peace.

At the other extreme are those small numbers who advise peace at any cost. This course depends on the supposition that we are dealing with a force that can be appeased. If this were a matter of satisfying the traditional ambitions of a nationalist Russia, appeasement might be possible. Surely our experience with Hitler must have taught us the futility of so shameful a policy. It is the appetite of the red horse that cannot be satisfied. World Communism has but one goal--the world.

What, then, is the alternative? If we must avoid war and yet cannot expect peace with the Soviet Union, what is there left? Precisely what we have--no war, no peace. Before lies a prospect which nervous Americans will find a dismal one--the stabilization of bad relations by parrying thrusts wherever they may appear. We must prepare for a series of Koreas in which we have little choice but to build up as much strength, both material and moral, as we can muster. If war with the Soviet Union itself must come, the choice must be theirs and not ours. Judging by past Soviet policy, if we are strong and determined enough, the Russians will not choose to fight.

What is it that the Soviet leaders are after in their relations with us? They wish to harness us into a position of weakness while they grow in strength. This is all the more reason why during this impasse between democracy and dictatorship, we must evaluate our weakness and strength as well as theirs. It is disturbing that we have shown so little faith in ourselves and such unreasoning fear of our opponents. We have actually frightened ourselves into believing that the Kremlin is inhabited by an infallible master-mind whose limitless authority commands millions of obedient slaves. On the other hand, our own newspapers loudly cry out our apparent disunity, disagreement in high and low places, and errors in our policy.

One depressing result of this has been that those very Americans who have preached the defense of our democracy the loudest have shown so little faith in that very democracy that they would curtail it. The American citizen must resist attempts to impose on our own people and even on our allies an orthodoxy of opinion, any deviation from which is regarded as treason.

We must resolutely reject the doctrine of fighting fire with fire if that means becoming more and more like the Soviet Union. It is our democracy--our two-party system, our respect for the rights of minorities, our willingness to permit unpopular as well as popular opinions to circulate freely in the market of ideas, our belief in the sacredness of the individual--that makes us stronger than any dictatorship. It is conceivable that Communist Russia may in some future time be as industrially productive as America. It is impossible, however, for dictatorial Russia ever to know the strength that democratic America has gained through its respect for life, liberty, and the pursuit of happiness. To relinquish this source of power in the mistaken belief that we will thereby become stronger is to contradict our whole history.

We must make an appraisal of Soviet strength. It is

erroneous to credit the Kremlin with either infallibility or unlimited power. The Soviet Politburo was guilty of a succession of bad guesses and mistakes. Consider the Russian failure in the first Iranian crisis, the Berlin blockade, the Cominform's expulsion of Tito, our resistance in the Korean War, and a whole series of setbacks in the United Nations, of which the Japanese peace treaty is but an example. Each time their error consisted of underestimating the strength of their opponents.

To the outsider the Soviet Union must appear a completely unified monolithic machine capable of deadly efficiency. More astute observers see the Soviet Union as beset by serious problems which rarely find their way into our press. The Soviet press itself reveals many sources of dissatisfaction inside the U.S.S.R.--a low standard of living which Soviet leaders cannot much longer attribute to the last war, increased pressure on the collective farms, and growing social inequalities that come with the fostering of a privileged bureaucracy. Even more obvious is the dissatisfaction which is rampant in the satellite countries. Millions of Poles, Czechs, Slovaks, Hungarians, Bulgars, and other East Europeans are bitterly opposed to their own Communist leaders. Judging by Tito's break, the rulers themselves have ample reason to be dissatisfied with the treatment they are getting from Moscow.

Undoubtedly one great source of Communist strength has been the ideology of Communism itself. The fanatical allegiance which Marxism-Leninism has been able to command in the past did create a resolute group of revolutionaries who were capable of the highest ideals and most desperate sacrifices. Only three and a half decades have produced a radical change. Reality has forced such tortuous reinterpretations of Marxism that much of the theory has become a liability. The Soviet Union today is managed by a generation of Malenkov's and Gromykos. There are no more bitter opponents of the U.S.S.R. today than a wide variety of Marxian socialists who have come to feel the present Soviet regime is a betrayal of their faith. Tito is but one Communist rebel who has accused Stalin's followers of being not "scientific" Marxists but power-hungry opportunists. The sectarian struggles which rend world Communism today must be a source of grave concern to Moscow.

Even more serious is the fact that Communism has turned into a rigid hierarchy which in Eastern Europe, at least, no longer attracts the idealist but the opportunist, the bureaucrat, the climber, the yes-man. Not even in the most trusted ranks of the Communist Party is disagreement nearly as possible as it once was. The result is that the Communists have hamstrung themselves by their own lack of freedom. They have been shackled by their own chains. Both their necessity to believe in what is not so and to pretend belief in what they know is not so places the Communists in a false position which can lead to defeat.

That is why the free countries of the world enjoy a distinct advantage in their freedom to discuss and to act without being bound by fear.

* * * * *

Two tasks stand before us: to contain the physical expansion of the Communist world and to supplant Communism as an ideology everywhere. The first task calls for the extension of our military preparedness. Experience shows that strength alone can force the Soviet Union to compromise. Why any but the most innocent optimists should expect any other basis in our relations is inconceivable.

Yet while negative measures may stop the Soviet Union, they cannot stop Communism. Only by helping the world rid itself of hunger, disease, ignorance, poverty, social inequality, racial prejudice, and political oppression can we make it impossible for Communism to exert any appeal. To do this the United States must continue its economic assistance to less fortunate allies--out of self-interest if not humanitarianism. Above all, we must help the free world to help itself. Far more important than our money is our positive moral leadership. The United States must not become identified solely with negative measures.

Our country was born in revolution no less than the Soviet Union. The American has become known the world over as a fighter against political tyranny, as a rebel against domestic restrictions on his dignity and freedom of action, and as a trail-blazer pushing out against both physical and intellectual frontiers. There are millions of people in the world who wish to throw off the same fetters that once bound us. What appeal can our country make to these millions? Certainly none as a defender of old regimes, reactionary parties, tottering imperial schemes, and an outmoded colonial system.

We are mistaken if we think that Communism is the cause of unrest all over the world. Historic changes are in the air. If our democracy allows Communism to pose as the defender of change while we become identified with ancient evils, then we will not only lose, we will deserve to lose. It is our task to convince the world by positive action that it is _we_ who stand for political, economic, and social progress while the Soviet Union stands for a way of life as old as the caveman: brute force. The garbage heap of history is piled high with nations that have lost faith in their own dynamic principles. As long as we are faithful to an ever-living democratic heritage, we have little to fear from Communism.

Unlike science, politics does not permit the citizen to remain an impartial observer. Recognizing this, the democracies urge the citizen to participate in an ingenious government in which the majority rules but guarantees the right of a responsible minority to be heard and to become the majority if its views win acceptance at the polls. Why does this system work so successfully and inspire such loyalty?

CHAPTER 14

THE WAY WE THINK IN THE DEMOCRATIC WEST

Llewellyn Pfankuchen
Department of Political Science

The Western peoples have been so distracted by the expansion of the Soviet Union, and so disturbed by its ideologies, that sometimes they do not seem to state their own case effectively. This is strange, because during the nineteenth and twentieth centuries the peoples of the United States and western Europe enjoyed a better standard of living, more opportunity for the individual, and a more varied freedom of spirit than did peoples at any time or place in previous human experience.

Is it possible that the development of the West happened without system, organization, or ideas? Or does the West have a structure, system, and doctrine capable of a statement that can claim men's attention and allegiance? The question is important. No framework of human effort and institutions can long endure if the people who live and work with it feel that they do not understand and accept it; if they cannot explain or defend their communities and give reasons for the faith that is in them. This chapter is a modest inquiry, therefore, into the structure and validity of Western institutions and the Western way of life.

The world before 1914 consisted of some fifty odd independent political communities. Each of these had its own set of social, economic, and political institutions, developed out of its own history and experience. Each prized highly-- probably too highly--its freedom of action towards its neighbors. Yet most of them were bound to near and distant neighbors by trade arising from a mutual and expanding division of labor. They were bound also by the conceptions of a rudimentary international law.

This period has since become regarded as a sort of golden age. Standards of living had been steadily rising. Though barriers existed to trade, new goods and services were appearing in most quarters of the earth. Surplus capital from wealthy countries, though accompanied with some abuses, flowed into underdeveloped areas. The international gold standard provided a stable world monetary system. Men and ideas moved rather freely from one part of the world to another. Social and economic life seemed well on its way to be internationalized in practice. Most important, the situation seemed to most people to be stable, secure, and permanent.

This great achievement came about as the result of the growth of industry, capital, and domestic and international investment and trade that occurred in the security of the century following 1815. During that time there were only local wars. The system began to break up, however, as the result of the failure of the balance of power to keep peace in 1914. It was accompanied by a breakup of trade and the growth of economic and political nationalism.

The sense of well-being revived briefly until about 1929

and then began to decay again in the presence of the world depression. World War II and its aftermath of rivalry so shattered the atmosphere of normal peace and trade, that governments and peoples now struggle with the greatest difficulty to restore it. Yet the ultimate restoration of this system or its equivalent is much of the essential meaning of UNRRA, the British Loan, aid to Greece and Turkey, the International Bank, the International Monetary Fund, and the European Recovery Plan.

What are the ideas, the doctrines, the structures that give meaning to this effort? Let us begin with our ideas about capitalism.

Capitalism, as a system of organizing the production, distribution, and exchange of goods, superseded older systems of government control with the advent of the Industrial Revolution in the eighteenth century. Its great theoretical statement is in Adam Smith's <u>Wealth of Nations</u>, published in 1776.

Smith held that there exists in nature a harmony of economic laws which operate to achieve the welfare of all when each individual strives for personal gain. Individuals should be permitted by the community to engage freely in the search for profit under competitive conditions. Competition between producers will secure a constantly increasing quantity and quality of goods at lower prices, prices being fixed at a natural level by the higgling of the market between buyers and sellers of goods and services. Internationally, there should be free trade.

The role of government under the theory was limited. Internally, government was only to maintain order, maintain the property rights necessary to the operation of the system, and prevent invasion. It was not to restrict trade. Internationally, governments were to impose no limitations on the free import or the free export of goods, by tariffs, subsidies, or other methods, except possibly those necessary to the military security of the state.

This theory of the economy was the one on which most governments purported to act during the nineteenth and early twentieth centuries, although there were many exceptions. Particularly on the international side, many countries enacted tariff laws and restrictions on international trade which contradicted the theory. As the nineteenth century wore on, many criticisms of the theory were heard.

The most sweeping criticism came in a frontal attack by Karl Marx on the whole laissez-faire doctrine of Adam Smith. In essence it claimed that the evils of capitalism were incurable by the system itself, either in their national or international aspects. It declared that a violent assumption of social and political control by the workers was necessary and inevitable in order to bring about higher standards of living and freedom from wage slavery, both in the metropolitan countries and in their underdeveloped dependencies.

A second and less drastic criticism of practical capitalism was developed in the twentieth century by the late John Maynard Keynes. Lord Keynes believed that the recurring booms and depressions of capitalist society were due to an inherent instability in the system which uncontrolled private enterprise could not remedy. Two tendencies produce this result, he said. One is the tendency for investment in capital goods (factories, plants, machinery) to be subject to wide fluctuations, because the demand for these is not continuously self-renewing as is the demand for consumers' goods like food or clothing. The other is the tendency of established industry to become increasingly rigid and stagnant, "enterprise" taking the form of protecting existing markets and building up monopolies rather than of experimenting in new demand and building up new capital.

These results occur: there is a permanent instability in the important capital investment in heavy industry and a slowing down of its pace until there is almost none of the new capital development necessary to keep the economy in movement and alive. But without a high and stable level of investment in heavy industry, and in capital goods as opposed to consumption goods, industrial society is unable to avoid recurring crises of unemployment. These crises begin in the laying off of men in the capital goods industries. Through the resulting falling off of demand, they spread to the industries producing consumers' goods, and presently the whole economy is involved in a downward spiral of unemployment and declining demand. And since unregulated capitalist society produces no automatic corrective to these two tendencies, it must inevitably fall into recurring crises of depression and mass unemployment. *

Many facts in the twentieth century economic scene tended to support this conception. The theory differs from Marxism in that it traces depressions to definite and identifiable causes with which governments, acting for peoples, can effectively deal. If private investment in heavy industry lags, the government, using funds raised by taxation, can invest in heavy industry as a justified expenditure of public funds to keep the economy going in the interest of the general welfare. Or if the case is very bad, the government can even take over heavy industry. If monopolistic tendencies stifle new capital development, the government may offset this by investing tax funds in industries that seem promising from the point of view of either becoming self-sustaining or contributing to the public welfare. To this extent, government planning supplements private planning under laissez-faire capitalism. Whether such development becomes socialism depends upon its extent. It need never become communism as long as it is controlled by the majority of the people as determined in honest regular elections and under conditions which permit discussion and the possibility of the minority's becoming a majority.

Keynes' doctrine, too, has international applications. If capital investment lags in one country for any reason,

---

* *This summary leans heavily on B. Ward, "Europe Debates Nationalization," Foreign Affairs, Oct., 1946, pp. 47-8.*

whether depression or the destruction of war, it may become desirable for a more prosperous country to make government investments in the form of loans to the country in need. Such loans may be made directly by governments, or they may be made by private lenders with government guarantee. They may be a form of international planning.

They are made on the theory that low standards of living and unemployment in one country promote low standards of living and unemployment in other countries, while rising standards of living and employment in one country tend to spread to others. In the long run this will be possible only if the borrowing state is permitted to repay the loan. If tariffs prohibit the repayment of the loan in goods or services, it becomes impossible for the borrowing country to enrich the standard of living of the lender. At this point <u>laissez-faire</u> and Keynesian economics become one: both support the idea that a most important contribution of the United States to a stable economic Western order will be its continued support of measures increasing world trade. In practice, particularly after World War I, many governments acted according to these doctrines in their internal policy. Such phenomena as the Dawes and Young Plans, Lend-Lease, and the Marshall Plan illustrate the philosophy of Keynes.

* * * * *

While the Western world was laboring to establish an adequate concept of its economy, it was also establishing a well-developed theory of national and international political life, although practice sometimes fell short of the theory.

In the first place, the West accepted the self-determined and sovereign national state as the standard and normal unit of organized society. Such states seemed to furnish the most satisfactory environment yet achieved for human endeavor, and the establishment of such states became the general aspiration of those peoples which did not already have them.

In the second place, the principle that a people should

choose the form of government under which they would live had led to the increasing acceptance of constitutional democracy.

In the third place, it was widely believed that the international action necessary to keep the world a going concern could be achieved through the voluntary co-operation of the sovereign states, through such instruments as international law and treaties, the League of Nations, and the United Nations.

The great ideological conflict of our time rages mainly around the second of these principles: whether within the national state, constitutional democracy is to be preferred to communist organization. Politically the peoples of the United States and western Europe share a common faith in democratic constitutionalism. This creed may be summarily stated as follows:

> First, the majority of a people--as this majority is determined in honest and regularly held elections--is entitled to wield political authority in the nation. The existence of regular elections, the freedom of these elections from force and fraud and arbitrary disfranchisement, and confidence in the honesty of the count are indispensable to the determination of who is to govern.
>
> Secondly, once the majority is ascertained, minorities concede the right of this majority to rule. Minorities are not entitled to resist the policies, laws, and administration of the majority by force, but are bound to obey these policies and laws and their administration.
>
> Thirdly, on the other hand, minorities must be free to discuss and criticize the policies, laws, and administration of the majority, by speech, press, radio, and other means of communication. They must be free to hold meetings and to form party organizations. In short, the minority must

have the right to become the majority, if it can do so by <u>persuasive</u> means, in another honest election. This principle is as much a life principle of democracy as is the principle of majority rule. For it makes it possible, if one government becomes unsatisfactory, for this government to be replaced peacefully in an election by a more satisfactory government. The vitality of a democratic community lies largely in the fact that there is always an alternative government available to replace an unsatisfactory one, if a minority group can succeed in becoming a majority in an election. In a totalitarian government the only way of making a change is by violence or revolution.

Fourthly, the majority in power must respect and even protect those rights of the minority that enable the minority to become the majority, and that guarantee freedom of speech, press, assembly, and party organization. <u>This is the price the majority pays for the peaceful acceptance by the minority of the majority's right to rule.</u> The minority obeys the majority, but only because the minority has the protected right and opportunity of itself becoming the majority. This is the basic bargain and social compact in democratic communities.

Fifthly, the system is workable only if majorities and minorities both observe these rules. This is what makes democratic systems the most difficult of all to operate. They require understanding and self-restraint on the part of practically the whole people. This system requires the greatest self-control on the part of the majority to protect those rights of the minority that may result in supplanting that majority. The greatest self-control is required for a minority, impatient for power and perhaps in control of important sectors of a community's public and private services, to keep from using its strategic position to take over the government by force without waiting for a ballot. The need for self-control is so great that democratic communities are justified in protecting minority rights by special institutions, such as the judiciary, that are not immediately susceptible to majority pressure. But if minorities are entitled to such protection, it is at least arguable that the right of the majority to rule should also be protected. If certain minorities have proved that they will not observe the rules, majorities may be expected to argue that the only remedy is to deprive them of participation in the ballot until they prove that they will observe them. The argument will be used that the principle of majority rule is too important to be sacrificed to those whose real intention is to destroy the essential nature of the system.

This ideology of democratic constitutionalism is already shared by the United States, the British countries, France, the Scandinavian countries, the Low Countries, Italy, and Austria. In some countries of eastern Europe it has been displaced only by force. Given a chance, it might appeal to Germany. In form it is accepted in Latin America. It has been received at least as an aspiration in Asia and in depressed communities throughout the world. At present it is a beleaguered ideology that has lost ground even since the conclusion of World War II. Yet it is far from being a dead doctrine, and it can claim to provide the peoples of the world with greater rewards than any alternative being offered.

The best proof of this is that a country operating under democratic constitutionalism has a wide variety of choices as to the form of economic organization it will adopt. The only forms which are really excluded are the two totalitarianisms of fascism and communism. And they are excluded not so much because of their economic organization as because a one-party state, with its elimination of opposition, denies the life-giving possibility of peaceful alternations in the conduct of government and policy. But aside from fascism or communism, the majority of voters in a democratic society may adopt one of several types of economic organization. They may proceed as rapidly or as slowly as they desire in adapting to any of the forms and may shift from one form to another.

A democratic majority may adopt <u>laissez-faire</u> capitalism. In many underdeveloped countries this is still the basic system. Among leading countries it is still strongest in the United States. But everywhere majorities in democratic communities have been modifying this system in the last hundred years.

A democratic majority may also make a series of decisions leading to what is normally called "modified capitalism," a "mixed economy," or "creeping socialism." Such decisions have sprung from feelings that <u>laissez-faire</u> capitalism led to evils requiring the intervention of the state. These evils include principally depressions, with consequent unemployment and suffering, and monopoly, with consequent high prices and a tendency to maldistribute income and lower the standard of living.

Under a mixed economy most industry may be carried on by private enterprise, but the state may interfere to cushion the effect of depression and monopoly and to regulate wage and price levels and labor relations generally. The state may engage in some enterprises or services considered unsuitable for private enterprise, such as regional power development and conservation of natural resources. Frequently the state owns and operates banking and credit agencies, transport and communications facilities, and other public utilities. Often the state subsidizes private business for desirable public purposes, such as the maintenance of a merchant marine, or it socializes losses in important fields, or utilizes its taxing power to influence the organization of production.

No modern industrial nation has escaped this trend, especially since the first world war. Since the depression in 1929 the private character of business in the United States and many other countries has been definitely modified in this direction. The characteristic method is change brought about by currently dominant majorities, not on the basis of adoption of any complete new social doctrine, but rather on more or less pragmatic analyses of particular problems.

As another possibility, a democratic majority may adopt socialism as its goal in a single outright decision, which is then implemented in practice by a series of separate and subordinate decisions over a period of time. For want of a better name this may be called evolutionary socialism. Political parties supporting this view ordinarily accept the Marxian postulate that capitalism must collapse of its own evils. But they insist that the necessary changes be by regular democratic majorities produced at honest elections, after full discussion by a free opposition. They bitterly oppose the communist conception of the seizure of power by a small disciplined organization claiming to represent the proletariat, which then abolishes all opposition and establishes socialism through a dictatorship ruling society, economy, and government. Thus Great Britain, ruled from 1945 to 1951 by a Labour government with a socialist program, had not a single Communist in the House of Commons, the last two having been defeated in the election of 1945.

The center of this socialist doctrine is the requirement that the ownership and control of the primary means of production, distribution, and exchange should be vested in the people and operated by representative agencies of government. This public ownership and control is to be acquired in successive stages in which the principal resources and industries of the nation will be purchased--not confiscated-- by the nation.

First on the list of acquisitions would be public utilities such as light and power, munitions industries, and the banking system. Then would come natural-resource industries such as mining, lumbering, petroleum. Then would come capital goods industries like steel, and all industries in which monopolies had been established. Small-scale distribution, handicraft, and agriculture would not necessarily be taken over. Private ownership of personal property, homesteads, and family farms would not be affected. Planning agencies would administer the system, estimating the nature and volume of needed production, allocating machinery, materials, and technical advice, and co-ordinating the needs of consumers with the need for expanding the means of production.

As one looks at the unfolding picture of political and social changes in western Europe since the war, one is struck by the extent to which these countries have, by the action of freely voting majorities, adopted solutions farther along the road of socialism than those adopted in the United States. But these acts are in the same direction taken by the United States since 1933. Thus we followed Britain in the adoption of a broad social security program, but Britain is following us in the extension of broad educational opportunities to its people. Britain has nationalized the Bank of England, coal and steel, transport, cable and radio communication. France has nationalized railways, parts of munitions and aviation, certain coal mines, the Bank of France, gas and electricity production, and some of the insurance companies. Italy, through an Industrial Reconstruction Institute, controls large sectors of the steel industry, telephones, and banking. Nationalization programs of an extensive character exist in Austria and did exist in Czechoslovakia before the Communist coup d'etat. On the other hand, there is little tendency in this direction in Belgium, the Netherlands, or Greece.

On this side of the water Canada, which engaged in many kinds of government industry during the war, has not since nationalized a single industry, although there was real sentiment favoring the nationalization of coal. In the United States the tendency since the war has been to relax most controls. Although there is some interest in extending social security and health programs, no industry has been nationalized except atomic energy. Nationalization of important industries is not likely, though rearmament has brought a revival of controls.

In sum, the general picture of the economically organized Western societies is one of variety. Independent peoples analyze their own needs and make their own decisions as to the kind of economy they will have. We must understand how important the right to make such decisions is to these peoples and how much this may mean in enlisting their co-operation in rebuilding their societies, as opposed to solutions imposed by force or brought from the outside. Much of our wealth, strength, and courage lies in the variety we have of regional and local cultures, governments, and powers of decision. The question may well be raised whether the very variety of the national societies, working together for common ends, may not be the greatest source of ultimate strength and understanding in the Western community.

The international organization of the national states for necessary co-operative activity likewise depends on the consent of each sovereign state. This is the traditional principle of treaty international law. It is the principle likewise recognized in the Covenant of the League of Nations, in the Charter of the United Nations, and in such regional defense arrangements under the United Nations' Charter as the North Atlantic Pact. These are based not only on the consent of the states to the original treaty provisions, but also upon the individual judgment of each of them in particular situations in actual operation.

In only one field--the international control of atomic energy--has a limited type of world government been responsibly proposed by a majority of the United Nations. But this proposal foundered on the rock of Russian sovereignty. It seems unlikely for many years to come that national states will concede any substantial portion of their sovereignty to international institutions, or that they will willingly be bound to anything to which they have not consented.

The state of international organization thus portrayed may seem to many a prophecy of doom. Yet this is not necessarily the case. It may mean only the extension to the international organization of the principle of consent which we hold within the sovereign state.

It is true that there are important differences. Yet the sovereign states have given their consent to a large number of international procedures for co-operation in the international organizations related to the United Nations. They have consented to burdensome sanctions in Korea. In the United States consent has been given to enormous economic and military burdens in the general interest as well as our own. And in western Europe the peoples have accepted freely the merging of many previously inviolable interests in a common cause.

The process is slow and faltering, and the outcome cannot be foretold. But to say that in our present world a state cannot be bound without its consent, is not at all the same thing as to say that sovereign peoples, with all their variety of life and thought, will not respond to generous, enlightened, and responsible leadership.

In a world where there has been so much destruction, dislocation, and despair, and where the possible imminence of an atomic war sobers the minds of all those who think about the future, it is easy for men and women to forget the value of what they have and to listen to leaders who promise some panacea. Men have often thought that they were entering into a Kingdom of Heaven on earth and have found only a prison.

It is true that there is inequity and injustice in our Western civilization, and also that it is difficult to describe in terms of a well-thought-out plan. But the Western world has enriched men by making possible for them an immense variety of experiences, and it has evolved what may be more important than a plan. It has evolved a principle of human procedure which is infinitely adaptable and capable of meeting new situations and problems.

It seems to me that the great contribution of our Western society has been its principle that any form of human society is possible and attainable _if its members consent_. Within the political community we have agreed that the majority may adopt any form of economic, political, or social organization, so long as it does not prevent the formation of some future majority which may change its mind. This is the great contract of consent within the single political community.

In the greater world of sovereign states, we still say that these states shall not be bound to anything to which they do not consent. This is our principle, yet leadership in and among such states still wins consent from them. The United Nations and the plans for economic reconstruction display this procedure.

There are imperfections, it is true. But the great advantage of the procedure of consent is that men are more likely to support and work for and believe in that to which they have consented. To win their consent on great and complex problems sometimes far out of the range of vision is an arduous and heartbreaking task of leadership. It may be too slow to save us in an era of catastrophe. Even so, it remains to be seen whether the substitution of force, threats, and trickery for mutual accommodation and agreement is any more likely to save us from the atomic bomb.

In 1880 Europe dominated the world. By 1950 Europe was a trouble spot, war-weary, part of it prey to Communism and the rest threatened, but still enormously productive. While the western remnant of defeated Germany was making a rapid comeback, French cabinets argued and fell, Britain's economy stumbled, and the U.S sought to help her democratic allies. What was the matter?

CHAPTER 15

TROUBLE IN EUROPE*

Chester V. Easum
Department of History

Europe is troubled because it is divided. The reasons for this lie in the history of Europe, which has Germany as its storm center. Germany's central location in continental Europe brought her, historically, great economic advantage in time of peace, and both advantage and disadvantage in time of war. Medieval trade routes from the eastern Mediterranean and the north Italian towns fanned out from Alpine passes to follow German rivers to the North Sea and the Baltic. Especially in the heyday of the Hanseatic League, German merchants prospered as the carriers of much of European trade.

---

* *Reference: Chester V. Easum, Half-Century of Conflict, Harper and Brothers, New York, 1952, especially the middle portion of Chapter 17.*

-178-

Political unification, however, lagged and was retarded in times of greatest German weakness and political fragmentation by intervention from all sides. In the Thirty Years War of the seventeenth century, Hapsburg Austria from beyond the mountains, France from across the Rhine, and Sweden from beyond the Baltic laid waste the German countryside, ravaged German towns, ruined German trade, and left the embers of political and cultural life aglow in only a few of the hardier states or principalities. The hardiest of these was the electorate of Brandenburg-Prussia. The Peace of Westphalia was, nationally speaking, a landmark in a desert.

Under its Great Elector Frederick William, Brandenburg-Prussia emerged from the Thirty Years War with territories scattered from the Rhine to Königsberg. They touched the Baltic in Pomerania but were cut off by Danzig and Pomorze on the lower Vistula from direct contact with its eastern province of East Prussia. About a century and a quarter later King Frederick II of Prussia acquired the land bridge to East Prussia, called it West Prussia, and set his mind on Danzig, which one of his successors soon secured. No German nationalist but a Prussian king, Frederick, challenged Austria for the leadership of the German states. He tried at times to use France, Russia, and Britain against her. But Austria used France, Russia, and Sweden against him.

Neither Austria nor Prussia tried consistently in the eighteenth century to exclude non-German powers from participation in German national affairs. German fought against German in the Napoleonic wars and half a century passed after the Congress of Vienna before Prussia was again ready, under the bold leadership of Bismarck, to challenge Austria for the leadership within Germany. By the "blood and iron" considered necessary to exclude Austria, coerce the other German states, eliminate French opposition, and reconquer the old imperial territories, Alsace and Lorraine, Germany was politically unified during the Franco-Prussian war. The Second Reich, as the Nazis later called it, was arrogantly proclaimed in the Hall of Mirrors in Versailles.

The German fear of being squeezed between East and West in Europe, of being encircled or made the battleground of Europe in a war of others' making, was not a new phenomenon in 1945 or 1952. It was an ancient fear based upon experience, a fear magnified at times by paranoid projection, traded upon at times by war-minded German leaders, and responsible at times--as from 1909 to 1914--for a truculence of tone in the conduct of German foreign relations which made Germany appear to be a more serious menace to world peace than her jittery and apprehensive leaders probably intended.

The encirclement which Bismarck feared but managed by balanced tensions to prevent while he was German chancellor seemed to Kaiser William II and his ersatz Bismarck, Prince Bülow, to have become a threatening reality with the emergence of the Triple Entente in 1907. Thereafter until 1914 Germany turned for safety more and more to shining armor, sabre-rattling, and dependence upon her one ostensibly dependable ally, Austria-Hungary. The Kaiser's notorious "blank check" after Sarajevo was only the last of a long series of assurances that Austria-Hungary might define her own Balkan policy and rely upon Germany's support.

From 1914 to 1918 the Germans fought a two-front war, then surrendered rather than face the prospect of invasion from the south and southeast, although Soviet Russia had by that time made peace. The tenacity of France, the staying power of Britain and the Commonwealth and Empire, together with the war potential of the United States, had worn them down and denied them the conquests they had promised themselves during the war.

Germans were again disappointed by the Allies' refusal at first to rebuild Germany either economically as a source of reparation or militarily as a bulwark against Bolshevism. They resented especially the "war guilt" clause of the Treaty of Versailles which implied unjustly that Germany had been solely responsible for the war. They resented also the "honor clauses" which called for the surrender of the exiled Kaiser as a war criminal, and the trials of lesser criminals for violation of the laws of war and for crimes against humanity. The Kaiser enjoyed immunity in Holland, and the trials of war criminals in a German court were turned into a sorry farce, a humiliation long bitterly resented within Germany and a frustration to be remembered a generation later when the victorious Allies brought German war criminals to book at Nürnberg.

A resurgent German nationalism in a convalescent Germany in a disunited Europe demoralized by widespread economic depression, listened avidly to the promises of Hitler, an atypical new leader, born in Austria, and German only by adoption. He promised to restore order and prosperity, free Germany from the few restrictions still imposed upon her by the Treaty of Versailles, and restore her to her rightful place among the nations. The Western powers, divided in counsel, reluctant to fight a war to keep the peace, and hoping against hope that National Socialist Germany might serve as a bulwark against Russia and aggressive Communism, appeased Hitler and alienated Stalin-- if indeed there had even been any real possibility or probability that he would serve them faithfully as friendly neighbor or ally.

The crucial turning point of 1938 was the signing of the death warrant of Czechoslovakia at Munich. The Union of Soviet Socialist Republics did not sign. Despite numerous previous statements, publicly proclaimed by Foreign Commissar Maxim Litvinov, that the Red Army was ready to defend the principle of collective security and would do so if France and Britain did, the Soviet Union was not invited to the conference. Stalin soon accused the Western powers of strengthening Nazi Germany at Munich, then inciting it to attack Russia. Far from being caught between East and West, Hitler profited momentarily from Germany's central position.

Before proceeding from seizure of territory in Czechoslovakia by threat of force to seizure by use of force in Poland, Hitler made sure that his rear was at least temporarily safe. He agreed with Stalin in August, 1939 to a new partition of Poland, a mutually advantageous war trade agreement, and a division of eastern Europe between Germany and Russia, roughly along the 1919 Curzon line. The uneasy truce between the two totalitarian powers held until June, 1941, when it was broken by the German invasion of Russia.

Fighting virtually alone after the collapse of France in June, 1940, Britain welcomed the Soviet Union as an ally against Nazi Germany. The United States sent Lend-Lease aid in enormous quantities to both. As an active belligerent after Pearl Harbor, December 7, 1941, the United States based its global policy on the hope that the Soviet Union would live up after the war to Stalin's wartime statements of intention to take no territory not previously Russian, to make the U.S.S.R. a member of the United Nations, and to help preserve the peace. Russia signed the Atlantic Charter and the United Nations declaration.

As late as the conference of national leaders at Teheran, November 28 to December 1, 1943, Stalin could be brought to the point of saying publicly that without American Lend-Lease machinery the Allies could not have won the war. Before Teheran, he had promised to enter the war against Japan as soon as possible after Germany surrendered. At Teheran he made known his stated terms: the southern half of Sakhalin and the railway, harbor, and naval base leases lost by imperial Russia to Japan in 1905. After Yalta, Chiang Kai-shek agreed to those concessions and got in return for them a treaty of recognition for his Nationalist government as the government of China, the promise of Soviet assistance in establishing his authority over all of China, and Stalin's assurance that the Chinese Communists would receive no further aid from Russia. The U.S.S.R. withdrew its recognition of the Nationalist government of China in October, 1949, signed a treaty of friendship and alliance with Mao Tse-tung's Communist regime on February 14, 1950, and then at once took up the cudgels for the admission of Red China to the United Nations and the exclusion of Nationalist China from that organization, a controversy which led directly to the invasion of South Korea from

North Korea on June 25, 1950.

The day of Germany's inevitable defeat drew nearer but did not dawn when the Allied expeditionary forces landed in Normandy in June and in southern France in August, 1944. January, 1945, found the Red Army closing up to the right bank of the Oder at Frankfurt-on-the-Oder while United States and British troops continued to climb uphill in Italy and to close up, against stubborn enemy resistance, to the left bank of the Rhine. Anticipating the eventual collapse of Germany, an inter-Allied planning commission sitting in London had already apportioned German territory into separate zones of occupation and arranged that Berlin should be an international zone inside the Russian zone, all Germany to be governed as a unit from Berlin by "agreed decisions" of a conference of the four supreme military commanders.

Thus, in the mind of General Eisenhower, the Supreme Allied Commander, Berlin ceased to be a military objective worth racing the Russians for. The thought of fighting them for it would have been summarily dismissed from the mind of almost anyone then in a responsible Allied position. The United States had another war on, the one against Japan, for which it was already planning to redeploy its troops as rapidly as possible. Britain intended to take what part it could, and both the United States and Britain wanted Russia to participate.

To have quarreled with Stalin then would have been easy; but it would have seemed at that time to be imprudent, unwise, and unprofitable. Allied troops, according to a previous agreement made by their military commander, were therefore stopped short along the Elbe-Mulde-Pilsen line-- short of objectives farther east which they might have reached at the cost of some further casualties--and were subsequently drawn back in compliance with prior international political agreement to occupation zone lines they had crossed in their advance. Neither they nor the people of the areas so evacuated were happy over the withdrawal.

Withdrawal to occupation zones previously indicated and joint occupation of the Berlin zone were effected before the Potsdam Conference, which met from June 17 to August 2, 1945. The four powers, Britain, France, the U.S.S.R., and the United States, were all in Berlin by right of conquest, none by grace of another. Access to Berlin by canal, railway, highway, telegraph, telephone, and air was provided by way of a corridor across a part of the Russian-occupied zone. That corridor was not safeguarded by the occupation of non-Russian troops.

Representatives of powers other than Russian were confronted at Potsdam with certain ominous but accomplished facts. Poland had been heaved westward as if by a Red Army bulldozer, her eastern boundary approximately to the Curzon line, her western to the Oder-Neisse line. The German population of the area east of the Oder Neisse line had been or was being unceremoniously shoveled west of it. Stalin explained blandly that there was really no German population problem in the Russian-occupied areas: the people always ran away at the approach of the Red Army. The Sudeten Germans were being similarly dumped out of Czechoslovakia into western Germany. The population of western Germany, swollen by refugees, was larger than before the war, while its ability to feed its people was materially reduced. The Red Army ruled in Poland, Rumania, Bulgaria, Hungary, and Czechoslovakia. Communist Tito of Yugoslavia was still following Russian lead. The Balkan states--Esthonia, Latvia, and Lithuania--had been taken into the Soviet Union, and Finland had been forced to cede territory and pay reparation. Yet the Western powers dared not quarrel then with Russia. They thought they needed her as a participant in the war against Japan and knew they needed and wanted her as a partner in the peace.

Peacetime partnership with Soviet Russia was not achieved. Russia no longer needed the help of the Western powers as they thought they needed hers. Stalin took full advantage of his favorable bargaining position. The poison of the Marxist doctrine of the irreconcilable incompatibility of communism and capitalism, and of the irrepressible conflict between the two, was again openly at work, as was the companion unethical attitude that there is no obligation to keep faith with an enemy who, because he is inevitably an enemy, must and will break faith. The territorial imperialism of Czarist Russia also came into the open in the form of a demand for control of the Dardanelles. The inherent aggressiveness of communism and the expansionist activity of Russian nationalism were obstacles to partnership and peace between the imperial Soviets and the Western powers.

The emergence of a two-world situation in place of the one-world peace basis which it had sought was recognized by the United States in the statement of the Truman Doctrine on March 12, 1947. The doctrine held that in defense of its national interest the United States would prevent the extension of Soviet influence into Greece or Turkey. The Marshall Plan, European Recovery Plan (ERP), Economic Co-operation Administration (ECA), and Organization for European Economic Co-operation (OEEC) followed. These sought to give substance to the Truman plan by offering economic blood transfusions to those who would accept them, hoping by strengthening these countries to make them less susceptible to the viruses of Communism and Russian influence. Russia herself was offered further aid if she would co-operate, but she fought the plan. Czechoslovakia accepted an invitation to an economic planning conference but was compelled by Russia to withdraw her notification of acceptance.

Russia's real answer to the Marshall Plan and ECA was the formation at Belgrade in September, 1947 of the Communist Information Bureau, or Cominform, essentially a revival of the old Communist International, or Comintern, which had been formally abolished as a gesture to conciliate Western opinion in May, 1943. The Cominform was so used to tighten Russian control over the eastern and southeastern European states, including Czechoslovakia but excepting Greece, that eventually Yugoslavia objected and was expelled from it.

In Germany a power vacuum developed as a result of

the refusal of the Russian commander to agree to any of
the "agreed decisions" necessary for governing Germany
as a unit under the original occupation agreement of 1945.
Marshal Zhukov, as commander of the Red Army occupation forces and governor of the Russian zone, showed at
first a personal disposition to be as friendly as his instructions permitted him to be. Zhukov, however, was soon
sent into limbo and replaced by Marshal Sokolovsky, who
was less co-operative.

Unable to induce the Russians to work with them in governing all Germany as a unit, the Western powers proposed
in March, 1948, that the British, French, and United States
occupation zones be formed into a West German Federation,
and that a new currency be issued to replace the fantastically inflated mark. Marshal Sokolovsky walked out of the control council in Berlin, declared that the Western powers had
forfeited their right to be in Berlin, and imposed restrictions
on railway traffic between the Western zones and Berlin,
which were soon tightened into a blockade denying all access
except by air.

Negotiation in Moscow failed to bring about the lifting of
the Berlin blockade, so the Western powers imposed a counter blockade upon trade between Western and Eastern zones,
and the "iron curtain" closed. Western Berlin, still occupied
by the Western powers, was supplied at great cost through
the winter of 1948-49 by air. The Air Lift served as a striking demonstration of the Western powers' will to stay in Berlin, in Germany, and in Europe. The case was laid before
the United Nations in September, 1948, and was discussed
during the winter by the Security Council and Assembly.
The blockade was not lifted, however, until after the signature in Washington on April 4, 1949 of the North Atlantic
Treaty of mutual defense.

The federalization of that part of Germany west of the
Russian zone was effected by the adoption of a democratic
republican constitution at Bonn on May 8, 1949. The new
state was permitted gradually to take over from the occupation authorities the legislative and administrative powers

usually exercised by free and sovereign nations. France offered a form of economic union under the Schuman plan. The question of the rearmament of western Germany and the incorporation of west German units in a western European army arose. It was considered with misgiving since there was always in the background the fear of Russian aggression using East German Communist "police forces" as its spearhead.

Thoughtful Germans viewed with alarm and understandable foreboding the possibility that their land might again be made the battleground of a general East-West war. Such a war, fought largely by non-Germans but more or less on German soil, would inevitably ruin Germany. Would west-German, then, fight east-German? What assurance could the Western powers give that as a consequence of victory Germany would be re-unified? Would a reconstructed Germany regain the former German territory east of the Oder-Neisse line, occupied since 1945 by Poland? What guarantee of victory was there to weigh against the certainty of Russian retribution if defeat instead of victory should result?

Would Germany again be able, as in 1938, to draw advantage from her middle position between East and West; or would she again be crushed between East and West, as in 1945; again be trampled underfoot, as in the wars of three hundred years ago or as by the armies of Napoleon and his nemesis, the Russian Czar? Would there evolve one Germany or two? One world or two? With or without a reconstructed Germany, there could not exist indefinitely at the storm center of a divided Europe, in a world of tension and conflicting pressures, a power vacuum such as that of 1945-48.

Asia, like Europe, is a trouble spot, but for different reasons. The same war that exhausted Europe aroused Asia. Hope and impatience and the prospect of national independence and better living are creating new problems for the world and new opportunities for Asia's millions.

CHAPTER 16

ASIA EMERGES

Eugene P. Boardman
Department of History

Asian peoples now are on the move. They are insisting that they furnish their own leadership, arrange for their own economic betterment, make their own mistakes, and earn the right to be treated as equals. No longer are they content with things as they have been. They demand some kind of a better life.

These general common aims are accompanied by common economic problems. Efforts are in daily evidence to deal with overpopulation, to improve agricultural methods, to utilize natural resources wisely, and to improve local industrial and transportation systems.

The economic problems are matched by political ones of equal difficulty. There is overwhelming need to train efficient administrators, to persuade populations to participate in the determination of their own affairs, the development of a standard of public morality, and the maturing of political judgment. With their energies fully occupied at home, Asian leaders could well be spared the distractions of international concerns. It is not their good fortune, however, to be thus undisturbed.

In the presence of common aims and problems the East Asian area possesses a certain unity. Yet at the same time each nation manifests individuality in its style of development and its pace of progress. Events in Japan, Korea, and China bear this out.

It is natural to consider the Japanese first because they were the first Asian nation to win freedom from Western control, to evolve a modern political system, and to become a great industrial power. Following the Western example, the Japanese even set about the erection of their own imperialism, a program that culminated in the late attempt to realize the Greater East Asia Co-Prosperity Sphere. But the Great Pacific War--as East Asians call it--put an end to this phase of their national life.

With the end of this war, the United States, chief among Japan's former enemies, took the leadership in devising a process of postwar re-education and reform designed to make Japan both unwilling and unable again to threaten the peace of the world. Institutions which had aided the old order, like the army, the great family businesses, and State Shinto, were greatly altered or eliminated. Those which might make possible an increased amount of self-government were encouraged.

For the first time women received the right to vote. The press was unshackled. Labor unions were presented with opportunities for growth and influence that they had never enjoyed before. A far-reaching redistribution of land ownership occurred. Japan was presented with a new constitution vesting sovereignty in the people. Of the prewar institutions of government, only the Emperor (who renounced his divinity) and the civil service were kept, largely because it was necessary to have someone to help the Americans keep Japanese life going.

For the first years of the occupation the aim was evidently to require the enactment of sweeping measures of reform while allowing the Japanese to be responsible for the functioning of their economic system. The state of the Japanese economy after two years of this policy made it apparent that Japanese leaders could not or in some cases would not accomplish what was expected of them. The American task was then enlarged to include responsibility for the economic health of the nation.

In response to this new requirement, American leaders conceived the ideal of "Japan, the Workshop of Asia" in the hope that, with fifteen million more people than in 1941 and without the China market or the products of important former possessions (Manchuria, Korea, and Formosa), Japan might develop the industry to live by its export trade. American raw materials, technical assistance, and credits were made available. A series of economic surveys and monetary reforms were followed by the reappearance of the yen on the world market, the beginnings of a Japanese export trade, and a merchant marine.

Whether it will be possible to support the present Japanese population with the resources of postwar Japan is an open question. The Japanese people themselves have gone about the rebuilding of their industry and trade as though it were possible. For the moment, the Korean war has provided an unexpected boost in demands upon Japan for goods and services. Meanwhile, the American taxpayer has been making good the Japanese food deficit. At the same time, the virtual cessation of trade with China constitutes a serious blow to Japan's economy. Japan has relied in the past on China as a main source of raw materials and fuel and as a market for her manufacturers. It may be necessary to facilitate Sino-Japanese relations in order to achieve a self-supporting Japan.

Korea today is the same sort of victim of a strategic international position that she was fifty or sixty years ago. At that time, Japanese fought the Chinese and then the Russians for control of this key area, but for the most part the fighting was done on Manchurian rather than Korean soil. The Koreans did not themselves fight. Today the fighting has been on Korean soil, the Koreans have been major participants, and the outcome has global, not merely Far Eastern, implications.

The conclusion of the Russo-Japanese War in 1905 put an end to the first period of international rivalry and delivered Korea to the Japanese. A colonial government was organized on a highly centralized basis, denying Koreans experience in the more responsible posts of government. The effort was made to Japanize Koreans through educational, social, and religious controls. Korea's entire economy was oriented to serve Japanese uses with the result that Korea became an important source of food, manpower, raw materials, and semifinished goods. But the Japanese could not destroy Korean nationalism; the Koreans were able to maintain their own national mores and national entity.

During the years of Japanese control the Korean population almost doubled. The excess population, a shortage of arable land, antiquated methods of production, and an oppressive tenure system produced deepening poverty. The Japanese, nevertheless, had conferred a degree of industrialization. Transport and communication facilities had been expanded. Simple homecrafts were being replaced by modern factory methods.

Heavy industries had been established for the exploitation and primary processing of iron and steel, copper, the light metals, and chemicals. A number of large hydroelectric installations were built in the Yalu River area, whence came quantities of manufactured fertilizer for Japanese farms. Industry and agriculture were carried on in both north and south Korea. South and north complemented each other in the sense that consumer-goods industries of the south received electric power and semifinished raw materials from the north, and the north depended on the southern industries for its consumer wants.

At the time of Korea's liberation from Japan in 1945 the task of reorienting the country's economy away from Japan was added to the older typically East Asian issues of too many people, too little land, and inadequate productivity. Korean leaders had high hopes of complete independence in working out their own future.

But the postwar difficulties of Koreans were to be magnified, not lessened, by the end of hostilities. The 38th parallel, a line originally created as a boundary between Russian and American forces receiving the Japanese surrender, became the dividing line between two different types of leadership, the Soviet and the American. Unable to co-operate in completing trusteeship arrangements which were to have produced a self-governing country, each went ahead to influence the creation of its own style of Korean state, the Republic of Korea in the south, the People's Republic of Korea in the north. The barrier solidified and friction between the north and south developed, widening both the economic and the political breach between the north and the south. Without unity, the prospects for a sound and stable Korean nation grew dim.

The unilateral attempt of North Korea to unite Korea by force began on June 25, 1950. It was also the first trial-by-force of postwar arrangements on the part of the Soviet bloc of nations. Touching off the most serious international crisis since 1941, the war in Korea confronted the United Nations with a crucial test of its ability to maintain international security. The 30 million odd Koreans furnished the land and much of the personnel involved in this military decision, but the decision itself had largely to be determined by forces from outside the peninsula.

The entrance of the Chinese Peoples' Republic into the struggle in November, 1950 represented a resumption of traditional Chinese interest in Korea just as the Russian support of North Korea amounted to a resumption of the Russian interest that was interrupted in 1904. These two Asian powers faced a newcomer to armed struggle and leadership on the Asiatic continent: The United States, leader of the United Nations forces. Enormous problems of unity, independence, and rehabilitation rest upon the outcome of the appeal to arms. Meanwhile, the Koreans themselves have had all they can do to survive.

China, the largest East Asian nation, is neither the scene of arrested development nor yet of industrial leadership. Instead, China presents a picture of a Communist experiment in adjusting the traditional center of Far Eastern civilization to the demands of twentieth-century life.

Unlike the Japanese reaction, the Chinese response to the West was at first a refusal to admit the foreigner or to change until forced to. It took the impairment of China's sovereignty by the construction of a treaty system, the stinging defeat at the hands of Japan in the years 1894-95, the wholesale granting of foreign concessions, and the humiliations of the settlement following the Boxer Uprising to finally bring Chinese leaders to the conviction by the turn of the century that serious reform was imperative. It was evident that China had to recover her sovereignty and discard the old Manchu absolute monarchy for a political form of government suited both to her people and to the demands made upon it. She also had to evolve a more adequate economy.

These tasks have confronted a number of different regimes since 1901. The Manchu monarchy in its declining years tried to create a constitutional monarchy on the Japanese pattern but failed. Sun Yat-sen's efforts to form a Chinese Republic following the Revolution of 1911-12 came to grief quickly, and the country suffered the chaos of warlordism from 1916 to 1927. It was Sun's effort to construct an army independent of warlord connections and a dependable party that led to the formation of the Kuomintang-Communist alliance of 1923-27. The Nationalist regime that emerged under Chiang Kai-shek's leadership cast off its Communist collaborators, unified the country, and gave China a period of party tutelage with certain accomplishments to its credit. China recovered her sovereignty. First came the elimination of the treaty tariff, followed finally by the ending of the foreign settlements and of extraterritoriality. China achieved a managed currency. Her businessmen and capitalists began to supplant foreign leadership. A beginning was made in the training of scientists and technical leaders, and plans were worked out for economic development. But these activities were cut short by the challenge to national existence of the second Sino-Japanese War. At this point Chiang Kai-shek and his Kuomintang led the resistance and helped China to survive. This contribution may become Chiang's most lasting claim to fame.

The end of the war brought victory to China, but the leadership available within Kuomintang ranks after the years of war was incapable of coping with postwar problems. A paternalistic party government based essentially upon personal relationships and quasi-Confucian notions of morality did not trust the peasantry and could not attract fresh leadership or harness the latent energies of the Chinese people. Aided by American support, its postwar opportunities were great but perishable.

What had happened to Communism in China? A vigorous Chinese Communist elite had been driven out of Chinese cities in 1927 and had learned to depend on the peasantry. The long years of the suppression campaigns of Chiang Kai-shek gave way to more years of fighting against the Japanese and produced a veteran army. Where the Kuomintang failed, after World War II, Mao Tse-tung's Communist leadership succeeded. American hopes of reconciling these inveterate enemies seem now to have been illusory. In the appeal to arms that succeeded the truce of 1947 the Kuomintang armies, whether for lack of morale, popular backing, leadership, or foreign support, succumbed. The Chinese people seem to have denied allegiance to Chiang Kai-shek in favor of the new alternative.

The Chinese Communist leaders took up their enlarged tasks, professing a blend of orthodox Marxism-Leninism and ideas based upon thirty years of native experience with Chinese problems. The regime began its formal existence as the Chinese Peoples' Republic in October, 1949. At the time it called for a union of all sympathetic groups in the realization of the People's Democratic Dictatorship, a pre-Marxian stage of development. In the few years since that time the leaders of the Chinese Peoples' Republic have done more to change the face of Chinese society than any other government of China since the founding of the Chinese Empire by the First Emperor of the Ch'in in the third century B.C. Indeed, the two regimes possess many points of similarity. Acting through the threefold network of government, party, and army, the Chinese Communist leadership has organized the Chinese people and enforced a uniformity of thought to a degree hitherto unknown. A type of Chinese official has appeared that is hard to match for zeal, energy, and incorruptibility. Since 1949 these officials have real triumphs to their credit in the control of inflation and in the harnessing of Chinese manpower for great projects of water conservation and railway and port construction. Their style of land reform has been applied to south China.

At the same time, Communist leaders have taken steps to seal the Chinese off from the Western influences that were once responsible for the Christian missionary movement and the training of most of China's educated leadership. When the Sino-Soviet Pact was signed in 1950, the decision was made to depend upon the Soviet bloc of nations for outside capital, trade, and technical assistance.

The fateful decision to enter the Korean conflict in the fall of 1950 may have been planned to serve as many Chinese as Russian uses. For example, a firmer grip on southern Manchuria may have resulted. Certainly the prestige value of the initial Chinese successes was exploited to the full. For the first time in modern history a Chinese army turned back the best that the West could offer. China was again-- as she used to be long ago--a power in Eastern Asia. But the cost of jet planes and other modern armament forced the Peoples' Republic to rely less upon the forces of consent and even more upon arbitrary authority. Priorities for capital expenditure and the "Resist America--Aid Korea" campaign caused the Chinese people to lower rather than raise an already low standard of living.

Despite impressive achievements, Mao Tse-tung's new government was not government of the people any more than the Kuomintang had been. Further, it had only begun the fulfillment of an extensive program of industrialization and economic betterment. It was handicapped by limited resources (except of manpower) and by limited possibilities of outside help. Mao and his clique had done a better job than their predecessors, but at a terrific cost. And because of the fact that throughout their history the Chinese have shown considerable residual capacity to reject unsatisfactory regimes, the Communists can be regarded as still on trial.

* * * * *

The countries of Southeast Asia and Indonesia could be placed along a scale that progresses from those enjoying purely colonial status to those that have achieved full national sovereignty.

To begin with, one finds colonies like Portuguese Timor and the tiny peninsula of Macao, the latter approaching the 400th anniversary of its establishment on the coast of China. The British have long ruled the three states of British Borneo, presently the scene of promising oil production, and the colonies of Singapore and Hongkong. In these regions the colonial power still provides the leadership and makes the decisions.

Two areas in transition were the Federation of Malaya, a major dollar earner for the British Empire, and French Indo-China. The Malayan Federation was plagued with a troublesome mixture of Chinese, Indians, and native Malays. Of the three, the Chinese were economically the most capable and aggressive and the Indians the most alert politically. Both were better organized than the Malays, who tended to depend on the British. Efforts at self-government were dependent for their success on some form of intercommunal co-operation enjoying the thoroughgoing support of the British government. In the meantime, the British were in the midst of a major effort to combat Communist guerrillas, most of whom were Chinese.

Indo-China, or Vietnam, was the scene of a native and authentic nationalistic revolt against the political control of France. The leaders in this struggle were Annamese, who inhabit the three territories of Vietnam: Tonkin, Annam, and Cochin-China. In the other states of Indo-China, Laos and Cambodia, the urge for independence was still slight. This nationalist revolt was combined with a social revolutionary movement that had its basis in overcrowding in the north and unequal distribution of the cultivated land in the south.

The revolt was most strongly pressed by the Viet Minh, the League for the Independence of Annam, led by Ho Chi Minh, a veteran Communist. Communists controlled the government of the insurgent Democratic Republic of Vietnam, which was confronted by the unpromising French-sponsored regime of Bao Dai. A major portion of the French military budget continued to be devoted to an inconclusive struggle against the Communist-led Vietnamese who enjoyed access to China. The economic recovery of Indo-China awaited in large part the outcome of the struggle.

The basic issue in Indo-China could be framed as a question: Was it possible to free the movements for national independence and social revolution from Communist leadership? At the time the only choice for Indo-Chinese was between a government founded on French or other foreign arms and a government based on popular support but under Communist control.

Three of the four independent nations of the area obtained full sovereignty between 1945 and 1952. The independent federal republic of Burma struggled with disorder and rebellion on the part of several minority groups. The recovery of the Burmese rice export trade and Burmese industry awaited the attainment of political stability. The Philippine Republic was handicapped by an unhealthy land-tenure situation and embarrassed by a Communist-led group of Huk rebels who were a threat to public order. Nevertheless, the

Republic was making progress in using its abundant natural resources. It was one of the few major regions of the Far East that did not suffer from excess population.

Recently freed from Dutch control, the Indonesian Republic presented perhaps the most conspicuous spectacle of national leadership in the area. A Javanese-led federation for the most part, Indonesia possessed a middle class which seemed to be making progress in dealing with manifold economic and political problems. Thailand, the only country of the Far East besides Japan to retain its independence during the era of colonialism, enjoyed a favorable economic situation. Bangkok retained more of its prewar flavor than any other country of Southeast Asia. More fortunate than Indo-China or Burma, Thailand continued to be a major exporter of rice.

* * * * *

United States policy since World War II has been to devote an increasing amount of attention to Southeast Asia and Indonesia, giving military advice and supplies where needed against the Communists, implementing a program of technical and economic assistance, and maintaining in the Philippines a center for the spread of information. United States efforts to improve national economies were matched by British Empire leadership in the development of the Colombo Plan. This activity was motivated by the desire to provide an alternative to Communist leadership of movements for political and economic improvement as well as by concern for the countries involved.

While disliking the anti-Communist commitment implied in the acceptance of American economic aid, many Asian leaders under the stress of internal necessities have found themselves unable to do without it. Caught between the tug and haul of Russian and American policies at the same time that its own peoples are restless with their present condition, emergent Asia is on the move toward what it hopes will be a better world.

Before we turn from this scene of nations in turmoil, we pause to remember that our attitudes can add to the turmoil if we are not careful. Some misconceptions we would do well to beware and some fresh views we would be wise to adopt are noted here.

CHAPTER 17

COLONIAL PEOPLES IN TRANSITION

Charles W. M. Hart
Department of Sociology and Anthropology

Recent events throughout the world, but notably in Asia, have brought colonial questions forcibly to American attention. In the midst of their worries over the atomic bomb, the American people are being forced to give some thought to those older problems which concern backward areas, dependent peoples, and the issues of self-government versus foreign control.

Despite the oldness of these problems the average person today still finds it difficult to think realistically about them or to find a modern answer to them. Americans, however, are prone to see the present colonial issue as merely a repetition of their own historical situation in 1776 and are somewhat puzzled that revolutionary situations of Asia do not fit neatly into the patterns of American revolutionary history.

In his tour of the United States in 1951, Prime Minister Nehru disappointed many of his eager listeners by his conspicuous failure to act the role of the George Washington of

India. Chiang Kai-shek has been even less capable of sustaining that role, though enjoying the advantage of a wife who is a Wellesley graduate. In Indo-China the ghostly figures lurking behind the French-supported Emperor Bao Dai can easily be identified with George III and his redcoats, but the opposition forces behind Ho Minh are very difficult to equate with anything of 1776. They seem to be wearing high leather boots and heavy black mustaches.

Much of the uneasiness and confusion on colonial questions that is so marked in the American press and in public opinion can be linked to this failure of the backward areas of the present-day world to conform neatly to the clear black and white categories of our own history which we have all learned in high school. This uneasiness and confusion at times seem to penetrate even the State Department and have been painfully obvious in the Congressional turnabouts on such questions as aid to Formosa and South Korea. Uneasiness and confusion might diminish if Americans were a little better informed about the colonial facts of life.

The issues in the dependent areas and in the colonial empires of today are not the same issues that came to the fore in the original 13 colonies in the eighteenth century. There are, of course, certain respects in which all colonial systems and imperialistic exploitations are alike, but there are other respects--and more important ones--in which the colonial problems of 1776 are as unlike those of the present as George Washington is unlike Chiang Kai-shek.

What is the modern colonial pattern?

The great areas of Asia, Africa, and Oceania, in which nationalistic forces and independence movements are stirring at present, are notably similar among themselves in some four or five important respects.

The first of these similarities is the existence of a color line of some sort. In every dependent territory and in those like India, Burma, Indonesia, and Ceylon, which achieved their independence but yesterday, there is or was a sharp caste line between the white rulers and the native masses. Such a race barrier was the foundation of the whole colonial system and of its local social, political, and economic structure. The reason for its existence, of course, is that a few hundred years ago the so-called "white" races--first the Spanish and Portuguese, then the English, Dutch, and French, and somewhat later the Italians and the Americans --began to extend political control over the entire "native" world. Their success needs no subtle explanation. It was due to their superior armaments. Even Kipling, the great apostle of colonialism and the white man's burden, admitted that

> "Whatever happens, we have got
> The Gatling gun and they have not."

Their universal success made it very easy for some of them to believe that they must be the possessors of some sort of racial or inborn superiority. They were white-skinned, and the lesser breeds without the law were always brown or yellow or black. Their success as political conquerors must somehow be linked with color. Not only were the guns on their side, but so somehow must be God and biology also.

This very gratifying idea passed into the cultural heritage of western Europe and the United States and influenced colonial policies, whether British or Dutch or French or Portuguese or American.

As a result the natives had little or no share in the government of their countries. The administration was centered in the "mother" country and all the important local governing positions were held by whites. Some colonial powers, notably the British and Dutch, have experimented with some forms of local self-government and have produced in many areas what is frequently labeled "indirect rule." It retains local rulers and local authorities in their hereditary positions and allows them to go through the motions of administration. But indirect rule, though not quite such a hypocritical system as many Americans have painted it, nevertheless is little more than a façade of native self-government.

As a result of this political control by the "mother country," there existed a particular type of economic relationship between the colony and the controlling power. There are variations here of course, but by and large no colonial area, not even India, has been allowed by its white rulers to become highly industrialized. The colonial areas are exploited as hinterlands of raw materials; their products are exported for the mother country's industrial processing. Hence the wealth of the colonies remains wealth derived from mineral or agricultural products.

The colonial populations, therefore, are populations of peasants, coolies, and servants. At the top there is a small group of resident white businessmen, the local managers and overseers of the big companies of the mother lands. At the bottom there is the great mass of native peasantry, and in between there is no middle class. Where the middle economic levels exist at all, they are occupied by other outlanders like the Chinese in Malaya, or the Hindus in Burma or Fiji, or the Arab traders and storekeepers in Negro Africa. If it is possible at all for the native to step out of the coolie class into wage or salary occupations, his pay is fantastically low. There are no steps by which he may ascend the economic ladder. In fact there is no ladder.

This situation is found not only in colonial or recently colonial areas, but also in countries like Iran, Egypt, and China, which have never been outright colonies of any European power. Instead of a group of white managers there is a small coterie of feudal potentates and landlords. Again we find the same exploited peasantry, the same absence of a middle class, the same lack of mobility in the social system.

A third common feature of all colonial systems, which is part cause, part effect of the other two, is the very low development of education. Social services in the colonies are sometimes quite extensive, as for example the public health programs in Indonesia under the Dutch and the elaborate agricultural and animal husbandry services for the natives in many parts of British Africa. But ordinary elementary education is typically a very small item on any colonial budget. About this weakness of native education endless argument is possible.

Many colonial administrators take the position that there is no sense in giving European-style education to the natives. What can they do with it? There is no middle class, therefore there is no call for the type of knowledge that middle-class people in the Western nations are expected to have.

This line of argument, though contrary to our American view of education as an end in itself, is not necessarily wrong. On the other hand, there is some truth in the argument advanced by critics of the colonial system who say that the western pioneers dare not educate the natives because if they do the natives will realize how exploited they are and rise in revolt against their rulers. But hard-headed and quite sincere British and Dutch officials have a case when they meet it with the answer that until there are plenty of white-collar jobs available locally, it is wasteful and foolish to create a large white-collar class.

Nobody is more frustrated or personally more unhappy than the out-of-work intellectual or the professional man who has to dig ditches. Why not then leave the masses as relatively contented peasants rather than seek to create a class of "unemployed Ph.D.'s" or technicians without factories or journalists without readers? In this connection it is worth noting that it was precisely this type of people-- the clientless lawyers, the "failed B.A.'s" and the young men returned from abroad with college diplomas--who were most ready to line up with the Japanese and become the Quislings of the Asiatic countries during World War II.

The argument that natives should not get higher education or Western "liberal" education is sound only if it can be carried to its logical conclusion. And no colonial power, not even the Portuguese, has ever dared to carry out such a policy to the point of denying all education to all the natives. Even if some colonial administration did push this policy so far as to appropriate no money at all for native education or build no schools whatever, there are always the Christian missionaries who, often in the teeth of governmental opposition, convey at least a little Western education to at least a few natives. Whether it be China or India or Africa or the Dutch islands, it is from mission schools that the educated native, such few of them as there are, has been produced.

The color line, the lack of any native middle class, and the weakness of educational services are the three bases of the social structure of any colonial or backward area. In recent years a fourth factor has entered the picture and made the local tensions more acute. This factor is the ever-increasing menace of overpopulation. The European masters have everywhere reduced, often in spectacular fashion, the native death rates.

This result was achieved in two ways. Under the law and order introduced by the white rulers, the tribal wars and famines of the East Indies or of the West African Coast, headhunting in Borneo and Burma, Hindu-Moslem strife in India, were checked and controlled. Life was much safer under white control than it ever was under the old native authorities whom the white imperialists displaced. In addition, health has been enormously improved by modern medical services. The stamping out of local bloodshed and disorder and the improvement of public health and sanitation have combined to produce an enormous fall in the local death rates since tribal days and a consequent enormous increase in native populations. Java, for example, contains something like 10 times the population it had when the Dutch took it over. Whatever sins may be charged against the colonial powers, at least they drastically increased the expectation of life of many millions of people. To what extent this is an unmixed good remains for the future to tell.

The pressure upon the local food resources in the colonial areas has thus become intensified and must continue to increase, whether the colonial peoples remain under the foreigner or achieve independence. This population pressure is perhaps the factor which Americans are most likely to overlook, since the land-people ratio in their own revolutionary period was so different. Viewing all colonial questions through the rosy glasses of their own history, they may forget that when their own ancestors threw off the British yoke they had an almost empty continent in which to expand. Only in Canada and Australia were there land-people conditions similar to the American opportunity. Everywhere else, in India, China, Java, Nigeria, Uganda, Indo-China, Burma, or the Philippines, there are no empty western plains for the constantly increasing populations to expand into. "Go west, young man," is completely useless advice to give a young Hindu or young Burmese or Filipino striving to better himself in the overcrowded city or village in which he was born.

The crowds of Puerto Ricans pouring into New York City in the last decade should be enough to direct our attention to the constantly increasing numbers and lack of local outlets for colonial peoples. We should ask what is the situation on the other Caribbean islands, such as Jamaica or Cuba, where the excess population is not permitted free entry into the United States.

The present ferment in the colonial or near-colonial areas can thus be traced to the interplay of these factors: the existence of a color line, economic backwardness, the predominance of a peasant class, the weakness of education and the enormous overpopulation. The failure of American public opinion to understand the ferment is mainly due to the chronic tendency of Americans to project into the picture the cherished but quite irrelevant idea that somehow or other political independence will cure everything. If the whites will only get out, everything will be wonderful. It is true that very rapid expansion and prosperity followed fast upon achievement of independence by the United States, but our history would surely have been different if America north of the Rio Grande had contained in 1776 a dense, illiterate, backward population of native peasants instead of being a virtually empty continent.

When we see the appalling anarchy that has prevailed in Burma since the British left, it is easy to feel hurt and disappointed and quickly stop thinking about such incomprehensible areas anyway. Instead of blindly and idealistically sympathizing with independence movements everywhere, we should give more attention to the likely and immediate results of independence in those areas which are heavily overpopulated with illiterate peasants and which must exist, nevertheless, in the modern world situation.

If we are willing to give some new thought to these matters the question that confronts us immediately is the one often asked by spokesmen for the colonial powers, namely, when is a backward people to be considered ready to run its own affairs? Within the British Empire alone can be found countries at all possible degrees of readiness or unreadiness for independence. In the last few years Britain has conceded that India, Burma and Ceylon were ready and has withdrawn from those countries for better or--as notably in the case of Burma--for worse.

But there still remain large sections of the British possessions which are very primitive. Americans who served on Guadalcanal during the war will hardly contend that the Solomon Islanders are ready to become an independent nation or that the natives of the Owen Stanley mountains in New Guinea should be admitted to the United Nations or invited to send their ambassador to Washington. Yet already the natives of Samoa, a small Pacific island group governed partly by New Zealand and partly by the United States, have sent representatives to Lake Success seeking their independence and asking for United Nations help in obtaining it. If the Samoans are ready to run their own affairs can the Solomon Islanders be far behind?

Between India, already independent, at one extreme and the Melanesians at the other, there are all conceivable gradations of readiness for independence. When confronted with many of these cases, liberal sentiment in the United States has to take some sort of compromise position and say in effect that such people as the Nigerians, for example, or the Malays should be given their independence "as soon as they are ready for it," which is of course exactly what the imperial powers say they intend to do anyway. But what the yardstick or criterion of "readiness" is to be we leave beautifully vague. That is too difficult a question to expect Americans to answer.

The remaining factor--omitted only in the calculations of the most head-in-the-clouds idealists--is the current international situation. The old eighteenth- and nineteenth-century type of imperialism is as dead as the dodo. The British Empire is steadily shrinking. France and Holland are following the example of the British and offering all sorts of new constitutions to their restive colonies. But meanwhile two new types of imperialism have appeared, that represented by Russia and that represented by the United States. As the old-style colonial governors move out, the commissars from Moscow and the promoters from New York move in, and the beautiful vision of independence bringing Utopia becomes sadly tarnished. Of all those weak and generally small countries or peoples demanding independence, shouting at their white masters, "Let us run our own affairs," a perfectly legitimate question to ask is "Where do you think independence is going to get you?" The tragic joke on the newly independent Republic of South Korea is too striking a case to need any elaboration. What has happened to that unhappy country since it achieved independence is much worse than anything that happened to it as a colonial area, however much we may disguise it with high-sounding phrases about liberty and freedom.

Realistically considered, there is no place in the present-day world for small independent nations, yet every little colony is vigorously agitating for the right to become a new babe in the international woods. India, a large and wealthy country, has achieved independence. The British Army has moved out. However, if the Russians should show signs of moving into India, the British Army would be back tomorrow, but only as the advance guard for the American Army that would be there the day after tomorrow.

Whenever the Russians show signs of moving into an independent area, a race develops. In Czechoslovakia the Russians arrived first; in Greece, the Americans. The whole colonial picture has altered with the appearance of the new-style imperialisms, but far too many Americans fail to realize it. They are still fighting the Battle of Bunker Hill and declaring that American troops had no business being in Korea at all.

In view of the international anarchy that prevails, it is dangerous for small countries to aspire to national sovereignty. Why, then, are we faced by a hundred new nationalisms or would-be nationalisms? The answer, of course, lies in the rise of the educated native. Few natives have learned to read and write. Fewer still have anything like the equivalent of an American high school education. But some have achieved it and these are the leaders of and spokesmen for the nationalist movements. No colonial power has been able to cut off its subject peoples entirely from Western-style education, and the few individuals that get it become restless and dissatisfied with colonial status. They get a white-collar education and they want white-collar jobs. But they find all the high-prestige jobs filled by people with white skins. Violent nationalism and hatred of their white bosses are the inevitable result.

There can be no criticism of such a reaction. Logically and in justice, their demand to be allowed to run their own countries is unchallengeable. But there are qualifications which must be made to the self-government argument and it is precisely because these qualifications are not stated often enough that we are apt to be confused or upset by what we read in the papers about the dependent areas.

The number of natives capable of running their own countries is far too small. Placing the blame for this condition upon the mother country which failed to educate any more than a handful to the point where they can handle technical or responsible jobs, does not alter the fact of the smallness of the handful. The number of literates in India or Java is less than 10 per cent of the native populations. There is no literate middle class from which the new independent governments can recruit technicians or administrators or managers or even minor bureaucrats. What passes for a native middle class is a small group of intellectuals itching for power and prestige and completely inadequate both in numbers and in training for the job that remains to be done when the empire builders move out.

Hence everywhere, when a dependent area achieves independence and native administrations take over, there is bound to be a sharp deterioration of the internal situation in every conceivable respect. The old joke about the Liberian navy, which contained 25 admirals, a hundred captains and one fireman, is having now and will continue to have its tragic parallels throughout the colonial world.

On the short-term view, then, whenever the new nationalistic groups achieve their objectives of independence and national sovereignty, there is a high likelihood of a quick degeneration into something approaching anarchy. The Olympian Englishmen or stolid Dutchmen may have been open to much criticism as colonial administrators. But at least they were usually efficient and exceptionally honest bureaucrats who, within the limits of the system in which they operated, gave their districts as much value per tax dollar in roads, law and order, and public health as most cities or counties in the United States receive from their local administrators.

Yet with the efficient and personally honest foreigners removed, countries like India or Burma or Java face a prospect like that of the Spanish colonies in America after they achieved freedom from Spain. Cuba, for example, with American encouragement and aid, achieved its independence in 1898. Its history since that time, as an allegedly free sovereign independent nation, is quite sufficient to show that independence of itself solves nothing.

The inherent defects of backward areas still remain. Overpopulation and poverty increase rather than diminish. The problem of how to obtain from a population of peasants and coolies sufficient revenue to support adequate governmental services is almost insoluble for such countries. Once free, they can not turn to a mother country for niggardly handouts when in distress, nor can their leaders use the mother country as an alibi to conceal their own inadequacies.

A solution often suggested is sharply increased industrialization, but this is a very expensive process and the difficulty in most of the backward areas is to find the capital necessary for industrialization programs. Under the colonial system, industrial progress was painfully slow, but some feeble efforts were made here and there by the imperialistic masters.

When the stage of independence is reached, however, there is no longer any imperial master to look to. In consequence, small, backward, newly independent states, plagued by overpopulation, debt, and ignorance and ruled by a tiny elite of intellectuals with Western ideas and Western tastes, are apt to fall an easy prey to a new type of exploiter, the American promoter (usually disguised as the something-or-other development company). It is not a disparagement of the American businessman with overseas interests to say that he likes nothing better than to see some hitherto backward and colonial area achieve its glorious independence and sail into the heady sea of freedom.

Among other things, such news means that the agents of development companies are now free to move in and seek "concessions" in the new nation, and such concessions have now to be negotiated, not with a tough-minded and personally honest English or Dutch governor, but with members of the tiny ruling clique of natives. These native leaders are usually hard up for ready cash, riddled by petty personal rivalries, and solely interested in either getting themselves in power or keeping themselves in office. Indonesia, for example, had only been a free sovereign state a few months when our State Department had to force the cancellation of an agreement that the Indonesian leaders had entered into with a New York public-relations firm granting them a virtual monopoly of all Indonesia's overseas trade in return for financial help in the struggle against the Dutch.

Little was said by any of the parties about the ethics of this interference by the United States Government in the treaty-making powers of what was being hailed in the press as the new sovereign republic of Indonesia. Yet in principle it seems to differ little from those American interventions in the Caribbean republics and in Central America that aroused so much attention and criticism in the early part of the present century. The Indonesian leaders were babes in the woods of international finance and had to be prevented from making foolish agreements. Since the Dutch were no longer in charge the United States had to act as the vigilant guardian or stern parent.

What becomes of independence and sovereignty under such circumstances? Yet this is a situation which is likely to be repeated as more backward nations receive independence with American help and encouragement. And it is moreover a situation which we cannot blame on the Russians or the cold war, but must attribute to the inexperience in government and lack of knowledge of the world which is characteristic of native rulers just released from colonial status.

This rather pessimistic view of the future of the newly freed colonial areas is of course a short-run view. The South American pattern shows that time, if nothing else, brings gradual improvements and a substantial increase in such things as literacy rates, standards of living, stability of administration--in other words, the bourgeois virtues. As a true middle class emerges, some approximation to a stable democratic state must appear. This is now occurring in at least some of the sovereign nations of Latin America. It has taken them a long time and they still leave much to be desired, judged by the democratic ideal, but they are much closer to it than they were. We can expect with some confidence that time alone will achieve something similar in the newly freed or about-to-be-freed colonial areas of Asia and Africa.

In the present international situation, however, nobody is willing to let time and natural social evolution take its course. All sorts of plans are being made to speed up the process and help the backward areas lose their backwardness and become "modernized." Among such plans are various ideas of international trusteeship and President Truman's Point Four Plan. Trusteeship under the United Nations or any other body is just as insulting to its alleged beneficiaries as is colonialism. To suggest to a backward people that they be put under trusteeship to "more" civilized nations emphasizes their inability to run their own affairs. Actually such inability exists in most of the backward areas.

Already in Indonesia it is obvious even to casual American visitors that life is less safe, government less stable, and the peasant less well off under the native rulers than was the case under the Dutch. But having forced out the Dutch in order to let the Indonesians run their own affairs, we can scarcely advocate sending in an international team to tidy up the consequent disorder.

The Point Four Program does not seem to differ substantially from the trusteeship schemes, except that it would attend to disorder and economic backwardness by employing not international technical missions but missions controlled entirely by the United States. How can the United States give aid without seeming to impose its will?

Symptomatic of this problem was the reluctance of Congress to send wheat to India because Mr. Nehru had dared to take a position on world peace and the Korean War different from ours. No foreign aid program--however altruistic it claims to be--can succeed if the motive behind it is to force American policies down the throats of those it would help. Indeed it might be suggested that the "you do things our way, or else" attitude is equally offensive to Asiatics whether it comes from Americans, Englishmen, Frenchmen, or Dutchmen.

On the other side of the picture, the oil policies of Iran, and the Bell Report, which exposed the corruption and inefficiency of the native government of the Philippines, emphasize again the difficulty of finding a group of responsible and able native leaders who can use wisely the benefits that should accrue from industrialization and modernization. Point Four may build dams and hydraulic plants, even little T.V.A.'s in the desert, but it will still have to solve the human and social problems that peasant and coolie mass populations present.

Prosperity, stability, and progress will not come to the dependent or recently freed areas without the development of a large literate and reliable middle class. Even the overpopulation problem would be closely affected since middle classes have much lower birth rates than peasant populations. The development of a middle class is a sociological and cultural problem. Unfortunately, American "know how" is more skilled and experienced in dealing with technological problems.

* * * * *

The over-all picture, then, is and probably will continue to be a series of interlocking vicious circles. American public opinion will continue to think that political independence is somehow a solution to the problem of backwardness. The State Department may have learned better from its experiences with China and the independent republic of South Korea, but it may be unable or unwilling to stand against the tide of public opinion. More backward areas will undoubtedly achieve their independence (for what it is worth) in the immediate future.

Under independence the poverty and lawlessness will probably become worse than under colonial status. This increase of poverty and disorder will of course provide fruitful breeding grounds for Communist agitation and organization directed by Russia. On the other side it will be necessary to send to these troubled areas more and more Point Four funds, United Nations missions, and American experts to attempt to remedy their political and financial weaknesses.

   Most of these plans and projects of the free world will be technological or financial in character but--under the Russian threat--will in most parts of the world be constantly shaped and dictated by military consideration and directed by military minds. It is sad, but none the less fairly certain, that in the present state of the world backward and dependent areas will not soon be independent in fact. They can only hope at best to exchange their present or recent rulers for either a Russian controllership, as in China, or an American military mission, as in Indo-China. The old-fashioned British colonel of the Kipling era has passed from the colonial scene. His successor is the American Air Force general. But the social problems of the backward areas remain. All we can do is hope that the American generals will deal with those problems a little more successfully than their predecessors.

PART THREE

Our World Community

> *Our troubled world is also a peace-seeking one. In the same decade that nations went to war they created the United Nations--the most recent of men's efforts to replace force with co-operation.*

CHAPTER 18

COLLECTIVE SECURITY — PATH TO PEACE

Llewellyn Pfankuchen

The United Nations was formally created by a charter written at an international conference of 51 nations at San Francisco in 1945. In form the charter is a treaty, stating the principles, organization, and procedures by which the member states propose to maintain world peace. As a duly ratified treaty, the charter is international law, binding (by 1953) upon 60 member nations.

Since the maintenance of peace is a many-sided job, the charter is many-sided. It provides procedures for the improvement of long-run conditions favorable to peace, as in the activities of the Economic and Social Council and the Trusteeship Council, and the many international organizations "related to" the U.N. organization. On the other hand --and herein lie the most spectacular activities of the U.N.-- the charter provides procedures for the peaceful settlement of international disputes and for the enforcement of sanctions against an aggressor.

These latter provisions establish, though in imperfect form, a system of what is called "collective security."

"Collective security" is one of the three main conceptions by which many sovereign states may organize themselves to maintain peace and their own independence, the other two conceptions being the balance of power and world government. Under "collective security" the nations unite themselves in a general organization to protect the independence of each member. If an aggressor attacks any member nation, all the other members are expected to defend the member which is attacked. If the conception works in practice, a nation contemplating aggression, knowing in advance of this united defense, will not carry out its design.

The United Nations Charter, like the League of Nations Covenant, embodies the collective-security conception, though in imperfect form. Certain basic principles are laid down, and organs with limited powers and prescribed procedures are established to give effect to these principles. The principles are (1) that each Member State is sovereign and equal within the organization, (2) that the organization may not intervene in matters essentially within the domestic jurisdiction of any Member, (3) that Members refrain from the threat or use of force against the territorial integrity or political independence of any state, (4) that Members will settle their international disputes by peaceful means, (5) that Members will assist the United Nations and refrain from assisting any state against which the organization is taking preventive or enforcement action.

Six separate organs are created, as shown in the diagram. The General Assembly is made up of representatives of all Member States, each Member State having one vote. It can discuss any question, but its strongest power is the making of recommendations, the most important of which require a two-thirds vote. In reaching such recommendations for the Member States, the General Assembly is assisted on certain types of questions by two subsidiary organs, the Economic and Social Council and the Trusteeship Council.

The Security Council of eleven Member States is actually a great-power organ. The Security Council alone has the power to order enforcement action against an aggressor, and

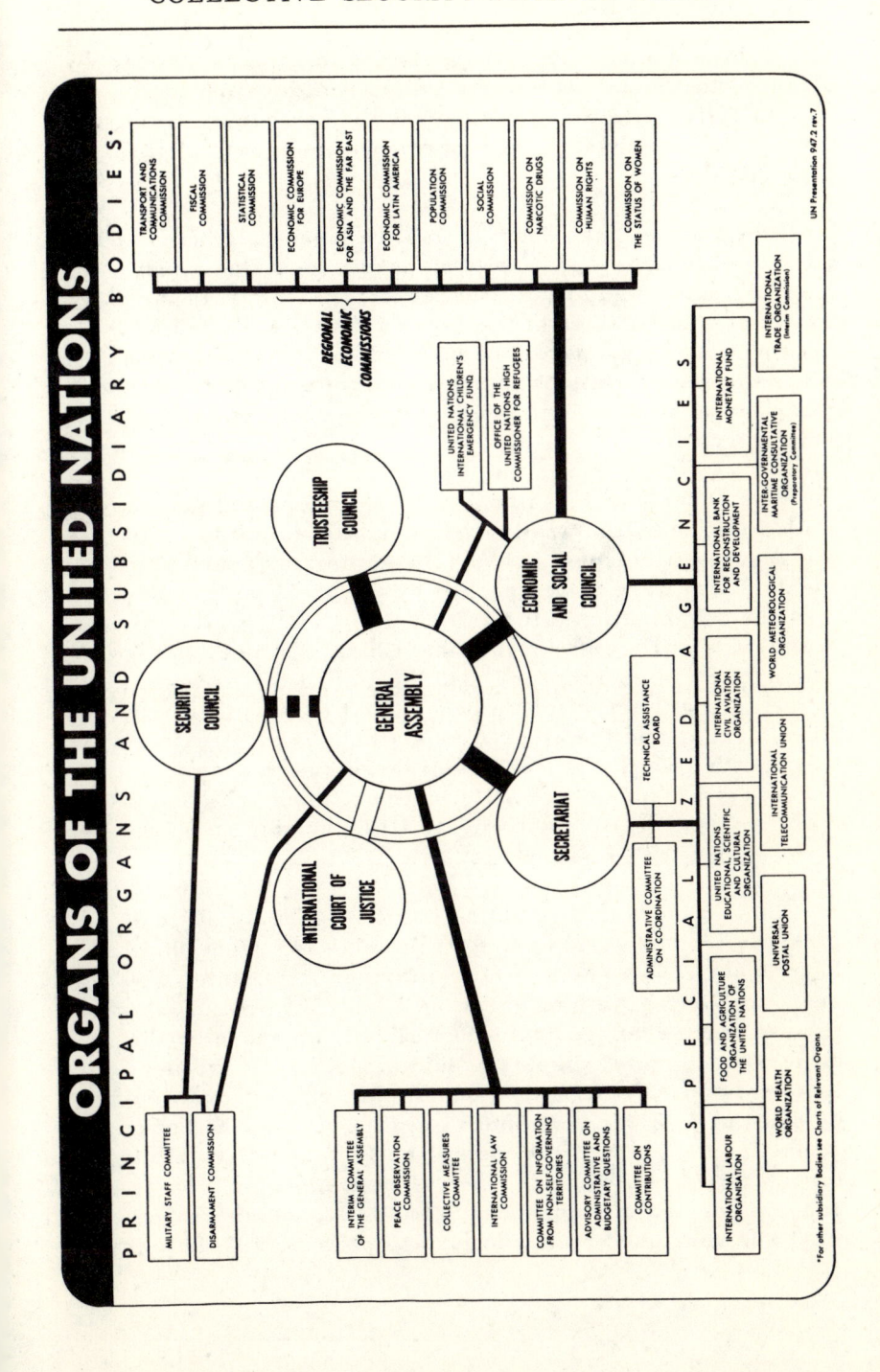

COLLECTIVE SECURITY—PATH TO PEACE 219

it can do this only if its five permanent members (China, France, the Soviet Union, the United Kingdom and the United States) are all in agreement and can secure two more votes from the changing non-permanent members of the Council.

The International Court of Justice gives judgments and advisory opinions--primarily on purely legal questions--on disputes submitted to it. The Secretary General is the chief administrative officer of the organization. Assisted by the Secretariat, he prepares the business of the other organs. Since the United Nations is not a government with power to make laws, he does not have the enforcement powers of a chief executive.

It is of the greatest importance to understand that the United Nations Organization was established not to create the peace settlements, but to help administer peace settlements which were to be reached by the great powers outside the organization. It was thought in 1945, while World War II was still being fought, that China, France, the Soviet Union, the United Kingdom, and the United States would agree among themselves on peace treaties with Germany, Italy, Japan, and the other Axis states. These treaties would establish the boundaries of these states and make the necessary arrangements as to their economy and government and for their disarmament, all by unanimous agreement among the great powers.

This action would establish the new general political structure of the world arising from the war. Once this had been done, it was envisaged, the former Axis states would enter the United Nations, making it truly a world organization. Future changes could then be recommended by the General Assembly, disputes could be settled by the General Assembly and the Security Council, and aggressors would be dealt with by the unanimous great powers in the Security Council, employing if necessary the United Nations armed forces called for in the charter. The achievement by dependent peoples of independence and U.N. membership would be nourished by the Trusteeship Council. The General Assembly would recommend, and the members would progressively adopt, measures freeing trade and raising standards of living. The U.N. would gradually build world disarmament on the disarmament of the Axis powers.

The subsequent failure to achieve world peace was due primarily not to the United Nations Organization, but to the failure of the great powers to reach agreement on the peace treaties establishing the basic political structure of the world. While treaties with Italy and some of the eastern European countries were reached, the treaty with Japan did not obtain the consent of the Soviet Union and Communist China, and there was no treaty for Austria or, most important of all, for Germany. There was even continuing disagreement as to whether Nationalist China or Communist China should cast a great-power vote in the United Nations.

Germany is the long-run center of political gravity in Europe, just as China is the long-run center of political gravity in the Far East. Domination over Germany and China constitutes political prizes of such magnitude that there is no basic political structure in Europe while Germany is unsettled, and there will be none in the Far East until China is settled. It is the position of these questions that has led to the Russian emphasis on its system of alliances in eastern Europe and with China and to the United States' emphasis on the North Atlantic Pact and alliances with Japan, the Philippines, Australia, and New Zealand.

While the organization of such regional power blocs can be squared legally with the text of the U.N. Charter, politically they represent an effort to achieve a balance of power on ancient patterns rather than collective security under a universal United Nations system. So long as these conditions exist there is only a partial basic political structure for the United Nations to help administer. The U.N. is constantly being called on to take sides on questions which the great powers were supposed to have settled and which, because of the fact of their power, only they can settle.

It is small wonder that under this burden the United Nations creaks and groans; that in the Security Council, intended as the benevolent organization of power in the service of justice, great-power unanimity becomes instead the obstructive use of the great-power veto in the service of aggression; and that while the greatest questions remain unsettled the United Nations finds it difficult to deal even with the smallest ones.

The responsibility lies, however, not with the United Nations Organization but with the great powers. The central problem of peace is still the reaching of agreements by the great powers, after which the U.N. can function. Until this happens the United Nations is like an automobile with a magnificent chassis but no engine.

With this perspective we may examine some of the principal failures of the United Nations--failures that on analysis turn out to be failures of the great powers to agree through the United Nations. First, of course, there is the failure to settle the cold war. This has already been dealt with. Next there is a failure to achieve universality of membership. This too reflects the great-power conflict.

The Soviet Union has vetoed, while the West has supported, the applications for membership of Portugal, Jordan, Italy, Finland, Ireland, Austria, and Nepal. The Soviet Union has supported, without securing the necessary votes in the Security Council, the applications for membership of Albania, the Mongolian People's Republic, Bulgaria, Rumania, and Hungary, and the seating of Communist instead of Nationalist China. While this situation continues the U.N. represents only most of the world, not all of it. The exclusion of Communist China, justifiable as it is, leaves outside the United Nations a de facto great power representing one sixth of the world's people. In the long run a world organization for collective security cannot function unless it represents the fact, and not merely the fiction, of power.

A third failure of the great powers to agree through the United Nations is the failure to establish an international police force and to begin reducing armaments, including atomic armaments. Instead of disarmament there began the world's most desperate race for superiority in national armaments--the kind of race that has usually ended in war.

The questions of an international police force, reduction of "conventional" armaments, and international control of atomic armaments are all parts of the same problem, and all these questions are stalemated. In the effort to establish a United Nations force under the Charter, the great powers could agree on neither the nature of this force nor the principles on which it should be set up. They agreed only that since a great power could always veto the use of the U.N. force against itself, the U.N. force should not be big enough to deal with a great power. Consequently, in general each great power proposed a total U.N. force which was smaller than its own existing armed force.

Again, efforts to secure international administration of atomic energy, including atomic armaments, bogged down because of the refusal of the Soviet Union to permit effective outside administration or inspection within its territory. This question is essentially the same one that plagued members of the League of Nations in their work on disarmament between the wars: how can each nation asked to reduce its own arms be confident that the others are not cheating?

Effective international inspection, if not administration, is crucial to the success of both atomic and nonatomic disarmament. And nonatomic disarmament without atomic disarmament would be a farce. But the great powers cannot even agree on how to take a census of existing armaments, and thus the work on "conventional" disarmaments is at a virtual standstill.

It seems certain that these disagreements are so deep because of the unsettled power situation in the world. If the great powers could agree on basic settlements of territorial questions, particularly in Europe and the Far East, there could be much less preoccupation with national armaments, much more willingness to accept well-inspected national disarmament, and much readier acceptance of a real United Nations armed force.

In the settlement of international disputes the U.N. has had both failures and successes. Of course, it has not been able to end the cold war, for reasons already indicated, nor could it prevent the cold war from becoming hot in Korea, Malaya, and Indo-China. Still, the U.N. has been of help even on the fringes of the cold war. It was pressure of the member nations through the U.N. which induced the Soviet Union to withdraw its troops from Iran in 1946, though Iran had granted important treaty concessions while the troops were still there.

In Greece, while Communist guerrillas were driven out by Greek armed forces armed and advised by the United States, the U.N. Commission helped convince the world that this was not Western imperialism. The Russian blockade of Berlin was settled outside the U.N., but the contacts between the great powers leading to the settlement came informally in the U.N. While the U.N. waged de facto war in Korea, other U.N. agencies labored ceaselessly to bring about a cease-fire and a permanent settlement.

The U.N. has been more successful in bringing about the end of hostilities in disputes not immediately connected with the cold war. Thus in 1946 France and Britain withdrew troops from Syria and Lebanon in accordance with the wishes of the Security Council. In Indonesia, though American pressure on the Dutch was important, the activity of the U.N. helped bring about the cessation of hostilities, the recognition by the Dutch of Indonesian independence, and the admission of the Republic of Indonesia to the United Nations. In Palestine and in Kashmir the work of the United Nations resulted in cessations of hostilities, though firm peace settlements were not reached.

Where the great powers agree, the U.N. can act effectively. This was illustrated by the disposition of the Italian colonies in Africa. The great powers could not agree on a substantive solution themselves, but they could and did agree in advance to accept a U.N. solution. As one result of the General Assembly's proposals, Libya became an independent state in 1952.

Despite the cold war the U.N. has shown real progress in formulating what may be called a blueprint for a freer world. More than a blueprint is the fact that one fourth of the world's population has gained political independence since 1945, that the members have used the U.N. to help bring about the independence of Indonesia, Israel, and Libya, and that the Trusteeship Council is actively encouraging the development of non-self-governing peoples toward self-government.

The freedom of the individual has been proclaimed in detail in the Universal Declaration of Human Rights, the most authoritative and one of the noblest statements of the aspirations of humankind. Parts of this Declaration are being written into national constitutions, while civil rights in some countries are upheld by references to it. The programs of the United States for international economic recovery have overshadowed those of the U.N., yet the latter is becoming the main center for international planning and action towards a freer world economy. Most of the economic problems of the world have been subject to regional and functional analysis through the Economic and Social Council and the 11 related organizations like the International Labor Organization and the World Health Organization.

Though progress towards freer trade is not so great as has been hoped, general agreements on tariffs and trade are now provisionally in force among many nations. The technical assistance programs of the U.N. organizations parallel the Point Four activity of the United States. They include programs for economic development, agriculture, health, educational and vocational training, social welfare, and the improvement of public administration. These help people to help themselves by giving them skills and organizational techniques necessary for the most effective use of their own resources, personnel, and traditions. "Indeed," said Secretary-General Trygve Lie, "apart from urgent political questions, there is perhaps no area of the work of the United Nations that should attract more support from all Members than this program, and which is more important to the future of the Organization."

These are largely blueprints, but all great social construction was once largely blueprints. The speed with which they may be translated into reality depends largely on how rapidly the great powers can agree on the basic structure of a peaceful world.

The U.N. action in Korea, beginning in 1950, was the first actual use of armed force by a world collective security organization to preserve the independence of a state. As such it is a step beyond the failures of the League of Nations in Manchuria and Ethiopia and a landmark in modern history. The experience in Korea has already led to the "Uniting for Peace" Resolutions of 1950, which may revolutionize the U.N. by releasing it from its dependence on great-power unanimity. As this is written, the Korean chapter is unfinished, but it contains important lessons about the nature of collective security.

First, the U.N. action against North Korea, the original aggressor, was successful. The result was only thrown in doubt when Communist China, a de facto great power, intervened.

Secondly, the Security Council was able to act in Korea only because the Soviet Union had absented itself and did not exercise its veto. The action of the Security Council was legal. Nevertheless, in terms of reality and of power, unanimity of the great powers about Korea did not exist.

Thirdly, Communist China, the only de facto Chinese great power, was not represented on the Security Council. In fact, it opposed the U.N. action, ultimately with armed force. Thus instead of great-power unanimity in Korea there is a line-up of three great powers against two. This resembles a balance of power and a potential world war situation much more closely than a true collective security action of all against one.

Fourthly, because U.N. armed forces under the Charter had not been organized in advance, the organization of such forces for Korean action had to be improvised. This threw the main burden of action on U.N. members having forces in or near Korea, principally the United States.

Fifthly, Communist China and the Soviet Union were in a geographic position to be immediately much more effective in the military sense in Korea, than the United States and the European great powers. The latter were already heavily committed by North Atlantic Treaty obligations and by existing military operations in Malaya and French Indo-China.

Sixthly, both the Soviet Union and the United States acted outside the United Nations: the Soviet Union by supplying arms and technical assistance to the North Koreans and Communist Chinese, and the United States by placing its Seventh Fleet between Formosa and the Chinese mainland.

In summary, the U.N. collective security action in Korea lacked great-power unanimity, became an action of three great powers against two, and required a military organization to be improvised in a geographic situation favoring those opposing the collective security action. Power politics had not been eliminated from collective security, and the real question was whether there was more power in fact supporting collective security or more against it.

None of the foregoing is intended as an argument that the U.N. should not have acted in Korea. If they had not acted, and the independence of Korea had been sacrificed, the U.N. would probably have been as dead as the League was after Ethiopia. The U.N. has already demonstrated, whatever happens to Korea, that it can do more than the League could do.

The lessons of Korea are registered in the "Uniting for Peace" Resolutions of the General Assembly passed November 2, 1950, by a vote of 52-5, with two abstentions. This resolution nullifies the effect of the great-power veto by providing that if the Security Council cannot act because of lack of unanimity of the permanent members, the General Assembly may consider the matter and recommend measures, including the use of armed forces, to the members.

The resolution also recommends the establishment by the members of national armed contingents for service as recommended by the Security Council or by the General Assembly. If these resolutions are implemented, the United Nations will be transformed into a new and different system of collective security. The use of armed forces of the United Nations can be directed by a two-thirds majority of the General Assembly, not subject to a great-power veto, against an aggressor or aggressors. This means that legally at least the concept of the necessary unanimity of the great powers will have been abandoned. The process has already begun, as the General Assembly declared Communist China an aggressor and recommended an embargo on shipment of war materials.

This endeavor to shift power to the General Assembly is a faithful reflection of the lessons of Korea. Whether it is a workable general principle of collective security in future cases remains to be seen. Collective security on any system of voting cannot function unless it is supported in fact by more power at the scene of action than that opposed to it. Conceivably, a two-thirds vote in the General Assembly might lack the support of all the great powers. It might easily represent a minority of power at the points where power has to be applied. Nevertheless, by circumventing the veto as a means of preventing enforcement action, it makes possible action against one or more of the great powers.

This new collective security is constitutionally very flexible, but it involves great hazards. It can succeed only if it is administered with wisdom. The vote in an organization to punish aggressors must always be supported in fact by enough power to do the job. Even so, the result may be world war in the name of collective security: a far cry from the theory of all against one! If such a war should

COLLECTIVE SECURITY-PATH TO PEACE 229

end in defeat, the conception of collective security among sovereign nations as a means of preserving peace would itself be the principal casualty.

Nevertheless, the test of a system of institutions lies in its ability pragmatically to meet its problems. The U.N. system of collective security was in concept superior to the League system. In practice it has been applied in Korea, while the League system was never applied. The realities of collective security in Korea, so different from the concept of the Charter, produced responses which kept collective security alive and now have produced new concepts which pose new problems.

It is true that we can not now see very far along the road. But we are farther along than we were before Korea, and the U.N. is stronger than it was. If we meet each turning and chasm with similar intelligence and faith, we may yet come to a world in which experience has taught us how to administer collective security as a means to the achievement of peace.

> *Collective security is a halfway step to world government. Such a government, endorsed by its peoples, would be a true community. But such a community would ask of its citizens an allegiance that we are perhaps unwilling yet to give--or are we?*

CHAPTER 19

WORLD GOVERNMENT

Llewellyn Pfankuchen

The whole concept of peace based on national sovereignty was thrown into question by the appearance of atomic bombs. Earlier the League of Nations and the United Nations had both been based on the idea that the security and peace of every nation could be secured if all nations would mutually protect each other's existing political independence and territorial integrity. Collective security was seen as a system in which the sovereignty of each state was the ultimate value to be conserved, through agreed collaboration of sovereign states. When the United Nations Organization was created at San Francisco in 1945--before Hiroshima and Nagasaki--it was thought that this system, with renewed emphasis on the unanimity of the great powers whose continuance was assumed, would be sufficient to preserve the peace once a new status quo had been established.

But in the first official announcements on atomic energy it was recognized that national control constituted a new and hideous menace to international peace and security. Unremitting efforts in the ensuing years produced a United Nations plan of international control that in effect would transfer many of the aspects of sovereignty over atomic energy to world institutions, but this plan was rejected by the Soviet Union. Meanwhile, the fear of uncontrolled national exploitation of atomic weapons has led to widespread discussion of world government in which sovereignty over matters other than atomic energy would be transferred from national to world authorities.

Many varieties of world government have been proposed. So far, the United Nations' plan of atomic energy control is the only one which has the sponsorship of governments. The others are sponsored by enthusiasts and private organizations. The idea of world government is not new as a topic of speculation and suggestion by social philosophers. What is new is its entry into general public discussion as the result of Hiroshima and Nagasaki.

Just what do we mean by "world government?" First, it seems clear that world government must be a system of political organization including all of the present national states: otherwise it could not be world government. This excludes certain existing federations of a limited number of states for limited purposes, like the Council of Europe, the Schuman Plan, and the North Atlantic Treaty Organization. It also excludes the Communist system in which satellite states are subjected to Russian control by a mixture of armed force and internal subversion. These smaller systems might in time become world government, but they would have to go a long way. The same is true of plans of federal union embracing only some of the national states, like the "Federal Union" proposals of Clarence Streit. Nevertheless, any of these federations or systems may be regarded as the first steps on the road to world government --though we would regard the expansion of the Soviet system with something less than enthusiasm.

Secondly, world government must be a system of government. That is, it must have the authority to make and administer policies and laws everywhere in the world. Such authority need not extend to all matters. It might be limited to one or more specified fields, leaving other fields to the control of the national states. The United Nations plan for atomic energy limits international control (or "sovereignty") to atomic energy, leaving all other matters to the control ("sovereignty") of the national states. Other plans of world government would extend international control to armaments generally. A highly developed scheme might extend it also to international migration, international trade and finance, civil liberties, propaganda, and education. Or, a world government might begin with only atomic energy control and by progressive agreement of the national states, through time, come gradually to cover other matters. The essential point is that international authority must supplant the authority of the national states.

Thirdly, within the fields or functions allotted to it, the world government must have the means necessary to make its policies effective. It must be able to make and administer, within the territories of all the national states, laws and rules directly governing individuals, groups, and the use of the necessary land, property, resources, and physical facilities. Practically, this would require some kind of a legislature to make policies and laws. It would require executive administrative institutions and personnel to give effect to those policies and laws. And it would require courts to decide disputes involving them. Since the personnel of the world government would operate almost wholly within the territories of the national states, some means would have to be found to prevent the national states from interfering with such personnel engaged in this legitimate activity.

The power and ability of the world government to make and administer laws binding on individual persons within each of the national states, even though only in a limited field, such as atomic energy, is the key feature of all plans that really propose world government. Plans that do not include this feature must rely on each national state to enforce the "world government's" laws and policies within its territories. This would not be true world government, but only a confederation of states.

Fourthly, most proponents of world government in the Western world agree that it must be brought about by voluntary agreement of the national states and not through conquest or subversion.

* * * * *

It was said above that the majority plan of the United Nations for atomic energy control was the only proposal for even limited world government now being put forward by the national states. Let us see why this is true, taking all our quotations from the Third Report of the United Nations Atomic Energy Commission. (All underscoring emphasis is the author's.)

This report called for "a strong and _comprehensive_ system of international control, defined _by treaty_." The treaty "should embrace the entire programme for putting the international control system into effect, and should provide a schedule for the completion of the transitional process over a period of time, step by step, in an orderly and agreed sequence leading to the _full_ _and_ _effective_ control of atomic energy."

Since a system of international control could not be "comprehensive," "full," or "effective" if any national state remained outside it free to make atomic bombs, it is clear that what is proposed is truly a _world_ system. The fact that the abstention of the Soviet _Union_ is considered to make the system unworkable is clinching proof of this fact. Nor is there any doubt that it is a system of _governing_ atomic energy that is proposed--that is, the authority to make and enforce laws anywhere, though only atomic energy would be subjected to the system.

The system "should be administered by an international control agency, the staff of which would be selected on an international basis...." "Decisions concerning production and use of atomic energy must not be left in the hands of individual nations." "Decisions of the agency should govern the operations of national agencies for atomic energy."

Thus in effect national sovereignty over atomic energy is transferred to the international agency of control.

This limited atomic government is not to lack the means necessary to enable it to operate throughout the territories of every national state. "All activities in this field must either be carried on by the agency itself under powers of operation and management and under rights of ownership, or by nations only under license from the agency." While mines, mills, and dumps might be so operated under license, "the agency would acquire ownership of all source material from the moment it is removed from its place of deposit in nature." "The agency would... determine in each case, whether it would own, operate and manage any source material refinery or whether it would license the operation. The agency would own, operate, and manage all chemical and metallurgical plants for treating key substances and all facilities capable of producing nuclear fuel."

In operations under license, which the agency might revoke or suspend while still retaining control, the agency might "make inspections, conduct accountings, require certain operating procedures, and maintain guards." "Nations must undertake in the treaty to grant to the agency 'rights' of inspection in any part of their territory. The exclusive right to carry on research in the destructive properties of atomic energy should be vested in the agency." The treaty would "prohibit the manufacture and use of atomic weapons by all nations party thereto and by all persons subject to their jurisdiction," and "provide for the disposal of any existing stocks of atomic weapons...." No government would have the power to "obstruct the course of control or inspection." "The Treaty should include provisions specifying the means and methods of determining violations of its terms, setting forth such violations as would constitute international crimes, and establishing the nature of the measures of enforcement and punishment to be imposed upon persons and upon nations guilty of violating the terms of the treaty." "There would be no legal right by which a willful violator of the terms of the treaty could be protected from the consequences."

Such are the proposals for a world agency. They are supported by most members of the United Nations. This agency would have authority to govern atomic energy and the means to execute its authority within the territory of all national states.

There has been a bewildering variety of groups supporting the idea of world government or federation, particularly in the United States; but the leading ones seem to be United World Federalists, the Committee to Frame a World Constitution (headed by former President Hutchins of Chicago University), and Federal Union, which advocates the ideas of Clarence Streit. Outside the United States the British Crusade for World Government seems to be the most important group. In 1946 a world meeting of world government groups was held at Montreaux, France. The meeting established a World Movement for World Federal Government, which endeavored to co-ordinate the activities of some 60 groups in 29 countries.

A second meeting in Luxembourg in 1948 resulted in the most comprehensive statement of the objectives of the movement supported by groups in more than one country. This is described in detail below. A third meeting in Rome in 1951 had hoped to draft a proposed world constitution. This was not done, because the attendance was less than at the Luxembourg meeting; and a conservative policy statement (calling for an all-inclusive world federal government with powers limited to armaments control) represented a very considerable recession from the ideas of the <u>Luxembourg Declaration</u>. The high light of this meeting was a qualified endorsement of the movement by the Pope.

Unfortunately, the world movement for world government is itself divided. A second group, the Peoples' World Convention for World Government, met in Geneva early in 1951. It had been hoped that enough officially elected delegates to its Constituent Assembly would be chosen to frame a world constitution for submission to the governments.

However, only three official delegates appeared: two from the State of Tennessee, elected in an official election provided by the state legislature, and a professor from Nigeria, who was not elected but was able to present credentials from a number of tribal chiefs. No constitution was drafted, but the organization continues and hopes to draft one at a later meeting.

Probably the highest point in the ideology of world government was reached in the Luxembourg Declaration of 1948. This Declaration, calling for a world government with very broad powers, was subscribed to by groups from 22 countries, including the United World Federalists of the United States.

The Declaration calls for a world government which "should be a federation open to all peoples and nations which subscribe to the world constitution." "No government and no political entity shall have the right to secede from the World Federal Government once it has joined." A Federal World Constitution is to be drafted by a world convention, which is to submit it to the United Nations and to the national governments for implementation. Thus a truly world government is envisaged, though until all nations have joined, including presumably the Soviet Union, the organization would be less than a world government.

The institutions proposed would have the power to govern and on a wide scale. "The World Constitution shall provide for a legislature empowered to enact world law, which is to be carried out and administered by an Executive agency and applied and interpreted by a Judiciary." While "all powers not constitutionally granted to the World Federal Government should be reserved to its component parts," the list of powers granted is both extensive and important. Thus, while "the World Government should maintain armed forces sufficient to preserve the peace and enforce world law," the "member nations may maintain only such forces as are necessary for the preservation of domestic order."

The world government "should control atomic energy

and other scientific and technological development easily diverted to mass destruction." It shall guarantee individual and group rights specified in the World Constitution, promote the development of human rights, and plan "for the education of all peoples in the duties and responsibilities of world citizenship." Existing international organizations for human welfare are to be transformed into agencies of the world government. Finally, in a principle which might ultimately mean the control by the world government of world migration, trade, and finance, it is declared that "those powers should be delegated to the World Federal Government which, when exercised by sovereign states, directly affect international relations in such a way as to cause crises or provoke conflict."

Moreover, the world government is to possess the means to accomplish these objectives. Its possession of legislative, executive, and judicial organs and its practical monopoly of effective armaments have already been mentioned. In addition, it is made very clear that "the World Constitution and world law enacted thereunder should be binding not only upon governments but directly upon individuals." A probable power to tax is foreshadowed in the provision that "The World Constitution should grant to the World Federal Government sources of revenue adequate to ensure its financial independence."

It is not strange that proposals of world government have gained more adherents in the United States than in any other country. This is true because citizens of the United States, under our Constitution, have become accustomed to living under many governments at the same time: national, state, county, municipal, and others. All of these make and administer laws through their own officials and have developed methods of mutual noninterference and collaboration. We are accustomed to a constitutional division of power in which certain specified authority is granted to the national government and the rest is reserved to the states, so that the idea of granting authority over atomic energy to a world agency, while reserving all other authority to the United States, does not seem strange to us.

Citizens of Wisconsin, for example, pay income taxes to a distant government in Washington and are drafted to serve in the armed forces of that government. Although as citizens of Wisconsin they are represented by only 1/48 of the members of the United States Senate and only 1/43 of the members of the House of Representatives, they take the policies, laws, and bureaucrats of the national government in stride. We are accustomed to the activities of the many federal civil servants living and working among us. The postoffice and other buildings in which their activities go on do not need special police protection, and we do not regard their operations, directed from Washington, as the machinations of a distant foreign tyranny.

At the same time, Americans should ask themselves whether they are ready for world government. Are we ready for world law? In a world government such laws would be made by a legislature and administered and applied within the United States by a world executive. Neither the legislature nor the executive would be controlled by the United States. This would mean that a considerable body of world civil servants, technicians, and judges would live and work among us. Many of these would be foreigners; some would be Russians; and all, even the Americans among them, would necessarily give their first allegiance to the world government, not to the United States. The Soviet Union has refused such a system for the limited purpose of controlling atomic energy. The Russians say in effect that they do not want foreigners within the Soviet Union, administering laws laid down from the outside. It is easy to criticize the Soviet Union for this; but are we, as Americans, sure that we are ready to accept such a system?

Are we Americans ready to accept only a share in the control of world government? Or would we insist on our own control, or at least an American veto on world government action? This raises a question crucial in all constitutional organization: how is representation to be organized in the law-making and policy-determining body? If each sovereign nation cast an equal vote we should have only one vote in about 70. If population were the basis, we should still have only six to seven percent of the votes in the world legislature. If these two bases were used jointly as in our own Senate and House of Representatives, the share of the United States would still be very small, considering the immense productivity, wealth, power, and influence of the United States among the nations of the world.

On the other hand, nations of lesser achievement in these respects would be very loath to accept a system of representation based on productivity, wealth, and power. Perhaps this can be worked out, though as yet it has not even been in the United Nations proposals for atomic energy control. The Soviet Union insists in effect that this control be subject to the great-power veto, while we wish to abandon the veto in this respect. Would we take the same position if the world government had other powers, for example, if it could tax us and draft our sons for military service?

Would we in fact obey the world government if its policies and laws conflicted with our desires as Americans? This is the "Sixty-four Dollar question," for it asks whether there is in the minds and hearts of Americans the real sense of a world community on which world government can be based.

Historically, voluntary efforts to combine existing political units in larger ones have usually failed when they were not bottomed on some pre-existing sense of community.

The 13 American states which formed the Constitution had a common language and traditions, similar economies, and similar problems of future development. They had fought their War of Independence in common, and they had common problems of resistance not only to Great Britain, but to France and Spain, which still occupied large parts of the Americas. Even among Americans, two secession movements, one from New England and one from the South, almost destroyed the Union. Do we as Americans now have sufficient conviction of our common problems with Africans,

Chinese, Europeans, Russians, and others to enable us to join with them in world political institutions in which we would all truly share a common destiny?

Suppose the world legislature should decide, against the vote of the United States, that existing atomic energy facilities should be distributed among all the nations of the world. If the world government technicians and civil servants began to dismantle Hanford and Oak Ridge, what would the attitude of Americans be? Would their loyalty to the world government cause them to insist that their governments, national, state, and local, aid the world government in this work? Or would feelings of national patriotism be so great that Americans would demand resistance and insist that their own governments prevent this unpopular action of a "distant" and "foreign" authority? If we as a people cannot answer this question in the right way, are we truly ready for world government?

These same problems exist for peoples everywhere in the world who still prize their increasingly hollow national sovereignties. Because of them, progress towards world government will be slow. Particularly while the Soviet Union objects to a world government limited to atomic energy and reached by consent and promotes its own world government conceptions through Communist parties, prospects for a truly world government are dim. Nor are they improved perceptibly by ideas of "world" federation without Russia and China, which would not be world government at all.

Indeed, in the state of the world in 1953, there is danger that too much attention to a goal still over the horizon may take our eyes from our immediate and very dangerous problems. We still must establish the stable conditions of immediate peace by some resolution of the issues dividing the Eastern and Western worlds. For the time being, this requires the organizing of collective defensive armed force, which we hope may bring a settlement without war; learning to administer collective security through the United Nations; and organizing a system of world economy and welfare.

Yet while this goes on we may rejoice that ideas of world government have emerged from the philosopher's study into the market place and have become the subject not only of public discussion in many countries but of official United Nations proposals for atomic energy control. This is real progress, and we should welcome wider discussion of world government everywhere in the world as well as better understanding of the problems of establishing and underpinning the peace so needed in our time.

If inconsistency is charged between ideas of world government on the one side and a peace settlement administered with the help of the United Nations on the other, a very human reply is ready. In most periods of rapid change inconsistent ideas have struggled for possession of the minds of men. Mankind has had to operate with traditional ideas and institutions while newer ones were being born. World government may be born too late to save us from atomic world war, but this is not necessarily so. Men genuinely bent on averting war can find ways to do so through existing institutions; while men bent on making war, if they control national governments, could find ways to do so even under a world government.

Buying and selling spell prosperity when they are widespread and balanced, but competing nations still erect trade barriers and sign preferential treaties. A prosperous world community, on the other hand, would seek more customers from everywhere. Although scarcely a unified community, the world is growing more prosperous. This chapter tells us some reasons why.

CHAPTER 20

WHY TRADE?

Theodore Morgan
Department of Economics

The world as a whole is more productive if it trades. Trade implies specialization: one region produces more than it consumes of Commodity A and swaps the surplus for imports of Commodity B, which another region produces in excess of its consumption. Specialization can increase production because regions, like peoples, can do some things better than others: Wyoming can provide cattle cheaply; Ceylon, tea; Switzerland, watches.

The sensible person (and the sensible region) does not produce at home what can be bought more cheaply elsewhere. A given amount of resources, labor, and equipment in the United States can obtain more sugar if it is first devoted to making automobiles in Detroit, exporting them to Cuba, and buying sugar with the proceeds, than if it were devoted directly to producing sugar. As specialization increases and total production grows, each area normally gains through obtaining a larger slice from the bigger pie.

The possible gains from effective specialization, or of losses from self-sufficiency, are large. There are plenty of areas where people would promptly starve to death without trade, but in fact live relatively well by specializing on and exporting minerals or manufactured products (England, for example).

This is the basic truth: increased production is made possible by specializing in the lines of greatest relative efficiency. It is for this reason that economists have almost without exception, during the past century and a half, preached the virtues of international specialization and free trade. Under free trade, they have pointed out, goods are produced where their money costs are lowest. And this means that in general resources go into the products that consumers regard as most valuable.

Yet governments have almost as regularly continued policies of interference with trade. The means are tariffs, quotas, embargoes, bilateral treaties, exchange control, discriminatory legislation, subsidies to home producers, campaigns to "buy at home" and the like. The interference of governments has been due partly to the pressures of special interests, partly to simple confusion of thought.

Pressure from special interests is often successful because the gain resulting from tariffs is concentrated and obvious, while the loss is spread thin. Although the loss is larger, it is not obvious. For example, a shoe manufacturer may be saved from bankruptcy if he can lobby a tariff increase on imports of shoes from abroad. His gain and that of his employees, stockholders, and home locality are large. The loss is spread thin over the whole country when all of us pay a little more for shoes and other products because an inefficient producer has been kept in business.

The confusions of thought that support trade restriction make up a long list of plausible fallacies in which the literature of international trade is remarkably rich. Among these protectionist fallacies are assertions that tariff duties are a good source of revenue to the government because "the foreigner pays the tariff." And that "if I buy a good from a foreigner with a dollar, I get the good and he gets the dollar; but if I buy at home, both the good and the dollar stay at home." Or that a "scientific tariff" is one that just raises the foreigner's total costs to equality with domestic costs, after which "let them compete on even terms and the best man win." Or that the high standard of living of the American workingman requires protection from imports of low-wage countries. All these plausible statements are wrong. It is a useful exercise to reason out where their errors lie.

Yet there are sometimes valid reasons for interfering with free trade. Free trade will increase world production to the maximum only if three conditions are fulfilled.

The first condition is that prices of products should be proportional to the social cost of production. As examples of divergence, monopolistic selling tends to raise prices above the costs of production. Products of factories that cause deterioration of neighborhoods and incite social hatreds are priced below this level; their money costs of production are less than total social costs. Again, if labor is paid less than the going market price, money cost of production and presumably selling price for product are less than the true social cost of production. In general, this first condition is not of major importance.

The second condition is that the regular exchange of goods will not be seriously interrupted by war, depression, shifts of consumer tastes, and changes of commercial policy. This is a possibility of considerable importance especially for "underdeveloped" economies that export one or a few products and so are peculiarly dependent on the market for that product or those products. Such economies often import much of their food and other essentials and so are equally dependent on continued supplies of these goods.

WHY TRADE? 245

The possibility of interruptions to trade justifies taking out an insurance policy against them--that is, diversifying production and accepting the resulting lower average standard of living as the price of avoiding occasional sharp drops in production or consumption.

The third condition is that economic progress will not be speeded up by interference with trade. This is sometimes a completely valid qualification. A country may be able, through a policy of trade restrictions or subsidy, to speed up technical progress and encourage investment in industries that will eventually be efficient.

These are special-case arguments. They are valid only if their particular conditions are met. But in a field where special interests have so strong an incentive to push for advantage, and where political discussions tend to be so immersed in error, we should do well to retain our general presumption that free trade will make a poor world less poor and that restrictions will deepen its poverty--unless we have very clear proof to the contrary.

We may, with careful reasoning, conclude that in this or that particular case a tariff or other protection would be desirable. There are a few duties here and there that reflect a prudent balancing of apparent gains and losses. But most protectionist measures have little or no justification: they reflect successful pressure of local interests at the expense of the general interest; or they give evidence of the persuasive power of fallacious protectionist doctrines, or a combination. Most duties are too high. Most are kept on the books too long: seldom are they reconsidered often enough in the light of changing conditions.

* * * * *

Has the United States been making grants and loans abroad, since the war, because of "dollar scarcity" among friendly nations? Or is this explanation spurious?

Any country can lower the exchange value of its currency. And almost every country, during most situations and times, could lower the exchange value of its currency rate <u>enough</u> (causing demand for foreign currency to slump off and supply of foreign currency to rise) to bring about equilibrium in the exchanges. But this means that domestic products are priced in terms of a cheaper currency and hence that more domestic products must be exported in order to bring in a given amount of foreign products. A fall in the standard of living is forced on the nation whose currency is cheapened.

Hence at the exchange rate that would put the balance of payments into equilibrium (at which the demand for dollars equals the supply of them), the standard of living might be lower than is consistent with political stability of the existing government, or than the United States would want to see on humane or on political grounds. Then the United States would still give grants or loans. Balance of payments deficits abroad are not the real reason why the United States makes grants and loans. Such an explanation is a fraud and a hoax.

Since prices and incomes in a country are changing as the months and years go by, an exchange rate initially in equilibrium may not be so a few months or years later. Relatively rapid economic progress in a country (read here the United States), unbroken by the scourge of war with its disruption of the economy and destruction of capital, means that the equilibrium value of its currency will rise (i.e., it means scarcity of its currency at current exchange rates). On the other hand, relatively rapid inflation of prices and incomes in a country means that the equilibrium of its currency will fall (i.e., it means surplus of its currency at current exchange rates).

This leads straight to a fairly safe prophecy: that in fact in the next several decades--barring drastic alteration of the world economic pattern by general war--United States technical progress and productivity will increase faster than that of the rest of the world, and that inflation elsewhere will rise faster than in the United States, so that "dollar scarcity" will repeatedly recur, even if exchange rates are repeatedly fixed at current equilibrium levels.

But nothing we have said here is more than a qualification to the basic fact that the world is made less poor by specialization and trade; and that, in general, interference with the free flow of trade deepens poverty.

PART FOUR

What the United States Can Do

What makes a first-rank industrial power? Men, materials, machines, management, scientific research. These the United States has abundantly, in a world that is only just learning how to use them. Their expert use raises standards of living and health--and, surprisingly, raises problems of population pressure.

CHAPTER 21

THE UNITED STATES — PRODUCTIVE GIANT

Theodore Morgan

Two thirds of the world's people live in impoverished areas. Their economies are obsolete and stagnant. Their average incomes are about $41 a year (1936-40 data)-- about one tenth that of developed areas. They have about one twentieth of the mechanical energy per person. They possess one tenth of the equipment per worker of the developed areas. Their life expectancy at birth averages about 30 years, less than half that of the developed areas. Over three quarters of them are illiterate. They live in most of Latin America and Africa and in nearly all of the Near East and of Southern and Eastern Asia.

Areas	Population	Per cent of world population	Annual Income
Low-productivity	1,565 million	66.9	$ 41 per person
Transitional	389 "	16.7	$154 " "
High-productivity	384 "	16.4	$389 " "

The contrast between the incomes of the most and the least productive areas is more emphatic when we look at specific countries. In 1948 the average income per member of the work force was in the United States about $81 per week. We do not have trustworthy postwar data for many other countries. But weekly incomes, put on a comparable basis, for the four other most populous countries of the world were before World War II about $6 for India, $3 for China, $11 for Soviet Russia and $10 for Japan.

Plainly, the world is a poor place. Prosperous areas are the exception in the sea of general poverty. This poverty has been the rule over thousands of years, back into the uncertain dawn of history.

In sharp contrast with economic stagnation in most of the world is the remarkable advance in productivity and in standard of living of the United States. Improvement has been taking place in every aspect of living standards. In housing, for example: While in colonial days the fireplace gave heat for the house and for cooking, by the 1860's most houses were heated by kitchen or living-room stoves, and by the late 1940's the majority of homes had central heating.

Or in clothing: The coarse and home-made linen, and wool that most people wore in Colonial days has been increasingly replaced by ready-made clothing showing little difference in appearance between well-off people and those of little means. Food has improved in variety and quality.

Advances in public health, in part correlated with our growing productivity, have raised life expectancy from between 30 and 40 years at the time of the Revolution to 67 years in 1948. Enrollment in secondary schools rose about 90 times and in colleges about 30 times between 1870 and 1940, while the population of the United States was rising three times. We have taken part of our increased productivity in decreased hours of work: average hours of work (outside of agriculture) have fallen by nearly one third since 1900.

The goods and services that an hour's work by the average employee produces rose over the first 50 years of this century by about 2 1/2% per year. During the past several years the rise has been greater--up to a remarkable 6% between 1949 and 1950.

Why is it that United States' experience has been so favorable, in contrast with that of most of the world?

The basic limitations on producing more of everything are simple: the resources that go into production are scarce. Human labor and natural resources (like fertile land, mineral deposits, water power, and forests) are the resources necessary for production. But labor is, beyond a moderate amount, unpleasant to human beings. And natural resources, though present in varying degrees of quantity and quality in different parts of the world, are never available in the quantities and qualities we should ideally desire. We could always produce more if we had more resources available.

How then has the United States been able to get ahead of the game? Even the 2 1/2%-per-man-hour-per-year improvement we have been averaging, though it appears modest, has been possible only through a favorable combination of a number of causes of increased production.

First, we probably do not "work harder" now than did our ancestors of the eighteenth century and before. Nevertheless our work is inherently of better quality because of advances in health and skill. The percentage of unskilled workers has been falling--from 36 per cent of the work force in 1910 to 26 per cent in 1940. The increasing percentage of the population that attends high school and college is further indication of a rise in the level of skills. Between 1870 and 1940, for example, the number of technically trained engineers increased over 13 times as fast as that of all the gainfully employed. And presumably our increasing life span has been correlated with less day-by-day sickness and with more energy and vitality per person.

Secondly, we have added to our known natural resources and to our machines, equipment, buildings, and stocks of goods being worked on. The more of these that we have, per person of the work force, the more productive we can be. An hour's work is more productive because labor has more to co-operate with: more things to work on, and more aids in the working.

Part of our production of capital goods has gone into replacing those that were wearing out. Another substantial part has gone to outfit the increasing numbers of the work force, as time has gone on and the work force has grown. But the remainder is substantial. Between 1900 and 1950, produced capital per worker in the United States (equipment, stocks of goods, and real estate improvements, but excluding natural resources) has increased about 37 per cent, reaching a level of $10,000 per worker in 1950. If we had not, in past years, been producing factory buildings, Diesel locomotives, drill presses, copper smelters, stocks of wool and sheet lead, bridges, and trucks, we should be less productive today.

Third, improvement in methods of production and trends of equipment are of prime importance. Many kinds of products simply can not be made by primitive methods -- for example, jet engines and electronic calculators. Most products have been produced more quickly and in better quality as better methods and improved kinds of tools and equipment have come into general use. We are accustomed to take improvement for granted, hardly conscious of how fortunate we are that examples of improvement are so abundant.

Finally, the critical importance of another factor, effective management, is often not realized. It is easy to be inefficient and to lag wastefully behind in ways of utilizing materials and machines and of organizing and encouraging men. The managers of 1850 just could not handle, with their methods of administration and cost control, the problems of larger sized enterprises of today.

Where the possibilities of waste--and, as historically proved, the possibilities of improvement--are so great, it is urgently desirable that a society train people in its work force to be effective business managers and encourage them to the utmost economy in consumption of resources and to maximum alertness and initiative in trying out better possibilities of production. During World War II the worst shipyards had three times the cost and required four times as long to build a standard-sized Liberty ship as did the best yards. Management was a major explanation for the difference.

There is every prospect that recent increases in U.S. productivity will continue. In the first place, an increasing proportion of young people are completing high school and college training. The "G.I. Bill" gave advanced general and technical training to several millions of young people who otherwise would have stopped sooner. The numbers enrolled in apprenticeship programs have been growing more numerous, and training in industry is being extended to people who are already executives. The effect of all this toward higher productivity will be gradual but significant.

In the second place, during the years 1946 to 1950, 203 billion dollars' worth (1950 prices) of new capital goods were bought by American industry. This is about double the investment of the best previous five-year period in our history. It implies we shall have more tools and raw materials to work with. Just as important, it implies that our industry is rapidly modernizing its equipment. And as new and more efficient equipment becomes a larger proportion of total capital, average efficiency of production should rise.

Expenditures on research have been increasing rapidly. The United States government has been spending about a billion dollars a year on research, of which about three quarters goes for natural science and military research. In American industry generally, expenditures for research have roughly doubled every 10 years from 1900 to 1939--

twice the rate of increase of the national income. The results are a long line of spectacular achievements: radar, rocket and jet propulsion, guided missiles, atomic energy, special purpose steels and other metals, improved abrasives, resistance welding, hybrid plants, chemical weed and insect pest killers, antibiotic drugs, and electronic calculators.

Hardly any other conclusion is possible than that under normal conditions of reasonable peace in the world, U.S. productivity is going to increase much more rapidly in the future than it has in the past.

Is the rest of the world also going to increase its productivity--that is, its production per work hour? Once again we have to look at the four influences we have already discussed: (1) the skill and the effort applied by the average member of the work force; (2) the natural resources and produced capital (machines, equipment, and stocks of goods) available per member of the work force; (3) the kinds of processes and of equipment used in production; and (4) efficiency of management.

The rest of the world is a heterogeneous place. Nevertheless, we can make a few generalizations. The changes to be expected in workers' skills and efforts and in the processes and equipments used in production should, over the course of the next several decades, be entirely favorable. This assumes, naturally, that no major war or equal catastrophe occurs.

The skills (not the effort) of the work force of the rest of the world will gradually improve, mainly because of the effects of long-run improvement in communication. Significant factors here will be special campaigns such as domestic development programs, United Nations and intergovernmental assistances, private lending, and United States loans, grants, and technical assistance. Through the same influences, there will be improvement in processes and in kinds of equipment.

The critical problem is: will improvement in workers' skills and in processes of production be aided, retarded, or more than offset by changes in natural resources and produced capital available? We are concerned with a ratio between the quantity of natural and produced capital on the one hand and with the numbers of the work force on the other.

Of course, many natural resources are constantly being depleted through use. We are using up iron ore, coal, oil, tungsten, tin, and the like. But to offset this, new deposits of resources are discovered from time to time. And more important, the growth of technical knowledge is constantly revaluing resources, often making previously worthless minerals useful. Low-grade deposits of gold, of iron ore, of tin, and of bauxite become valuable when practicable techniques are devised for smelting them. Uranium and thorium ores are not sought after until it becomes technically possible to produce radiations, explosions, and power from them. Likewise, growing chemical knowledge makes it easier to substitute abundant for scarce commodities--plastics, impregnated wood and plywoods, and special kinds of glass for particular kinds of metals.

It is by no means certain that the "quantity" of natural resources to be available limits the increase possible in productivity. And of course, most countries are adding to their produced capital: they are producing more machines, tools, buildings, stocks of goods, and the like than they are using up.

But any advantage obtainable here can be overwhelmed by population increase. The Malthusian problem is the crucial economic problem for a large part of the world--usually met by evasion and hope, rather than by significant policy.

Not all the impoverished areas of the world are overpopulated. Iraq and Syria suffer from too few people compared to arable land and other resources. These and other such areas would have higher productivity with more people because of the opportunities for increased specialization by skills, processes, and kinds of enterprises that would be made possible by a denser population.

But South and East Asia, Egypt, and parts of Latin America--over half the population of the earth--face the classic Malthusian situation. It is illustrated best from India, which has good population and birth- and death-rate data over the past eighty years. The population has been increasing over this period. But the increase has been checked for periods of a year or several years by drastic rises in the death rate, correlated to some extent with moderate declines in the birth rate. The explanation is plain. Improved methods have on the average been increasing food supply and enabling more people to survive. But the trend is interrupted repeatedly by bad harvests or crop failures, whose main effect, in a population on the margin of subsistence, has been to enfeeble and debilitate people, making them easy victims to the diseases of malnutrition.

If this is the pattern, then any increase in production will be promptly swallowed up by multitudes of new backs to clothe and new mouths to feed. If we want to raise the standard of living, we must check the population increase. Birth-control clinics and supplies can be provided by government action. Cultural attitudes, often now hostile, can be altered by intensive publicity so that the need and the objective are understood.

If such a population policy is successful, replacing the current policy of drift, then population will be kept in check by fewer births rather than by disease, debility and early death. The average individual will live a healthier, more vigorous and longer life.

The productive giant that is the United States knows when it is sick and when it is well, but it is uncertain how to live healthily. This chapter considers symptoms, causes, and suggested cures and goes out on a limb about the future.

CHAPTER 22

DEPRESSION AND INFLATION

Theodore Morgan

The late 1920's were notable in the United States for the easy confidence with which professional economists and the public viewed the economic future. President Hoover's Committee on Economic Trends reported in 1929, just before the stock market crash, that nothing but the rolling uplands of increasing economic prosperity were to be anticipated.

Even after the downswing was well under way, optimism continued. At the meetings of the American Economic Association in December, 1930, a group of well-known economists were asked when the depression would be over. All but two agreed that it was in fact already over--though the man in the street, who didn't understand economics very well, hadn't yet realized the fact! Of the two mavericks, one thought the depression would be over by spring, the other, that it would be over by fall.

The U.S. came into the depression, plainly, with a heavy backlog of assumptions that prosperity and high employment would be the normal economic state and any deviation temporary. This frame of mind persisted while incomes and employment were collapsing. The net national income dropped, between 1929 and 1933, from 87 billion dollars to 40 billion dollars. The fall in volume of goods and services produced was of course less, since prices were also declining. The numbers of employed in this same period dropped from 47.9 millions to 39.0 millions. Unemployment rose from 3 per cent to 25 per cent of the civilian work force.

How was the United States to meet this problem of depression and unemployment? Two main weapons were adopted: monetary policy and fiscal policy.

Monetary policy is concerned with the supply of money. In the 1920's rather general confidence had prevailed among most economists and government officials that monetary policy was sufficient to control the business cycle. Attention was centered mainly on the movement of prices. If prices should rise unduly in a time of business boom, it was argued that the Treasury and Federal Reserve should use their powers to raise interest rates. These would be felt as higher costs by businessmen and would discourage them from borrowing and investing. In other words: "To avoid a depression, slice the top off the boom."

In time of depression or threatened depression, it was argued conversely, the interest rate should be lowered to encourage investment.

The Federal Reserve followed this reputable prescription. As the recession deepened, the interest rate charged to commercial banks was lowered sharply--from 6 per cent in 1929 to below 2 per cent in 1931.

The quantity of money dropped sharply, despite Federal Reserve measures. But after 1933, it rose and during the late 1930's a huge increase occurred in the quantity of money available for lending. At the same time the demand for loans was shrivelled because businessmen were gloomy and consumers were apprehensive. This supply-demand relationship was the cause of a continued fall in interest rates.

The swollen supply of money available for lending flowed only partly from actions of the monetary authorities. It resulted in part also from a huge inflow of gold into the United States, in part from an increased volume of silver certificates, and finally, in part from the funds supplied by lending agencies of the Federal Government, especially the Reconstruction Finance Corporation.

All these together amounted to a test of an "easy money" policy against depression. The test was extravagantly thorough. If the recovery record of the economy can be looked on as the result of that policy, then the policy was a failure. It is true that there was a rapid recovery from 1933 up to 1937. But in that year, when interest rates were much lower than in 1932, there was a sharp setback. From then until the defense expenditures of 1941, the economy bumped along with 8 to 10 millions of unemployed. Low interest rates did not bring the economy back to any adequate prosperity.

* * * * *

We turn to the second major antidepression weapon, fiscal policy. It aims at stabilizing the economy through use of the government's revenues and expenditures. Its basic logic is simple: taxes are depressing--no one likes to pay them. Taxes shrink current income available for spending and restrain prospective income from being invested in business ventures. Expenditure, on the other hand, whether from government or any other source, is expansive. It may directly buy goods and services, it puts money available for further spending into the pockets of people, and in general it leads to optimistic expectations.

Hence too much taxing with too little spending by government forces falling incomes, depression, and unemployment on the economy. Cutting taxes and raising spending tend toward higher incomes, higher business sales and production, and rising employment.

Fiscal policy is not a weapon against depression that economists and officials first thought out carefully, then applied. The Government did not plan it that way.

The Hoover administration, in office until March of 1933, wanted to balance the budget, that is, to have tax and other revenues at least equal to expenditure. It made serious efforts to economize on its expenditures. But as the national income dropped by more than half between 1929 and 1932, the revenue of the Federal government dropped also, by about the same proportion.

In addition, there was an unavoidable increase in expenditures for relief of individuals in distress and for shoring up shaky banks and other businesses. It is curious to remember, in view of later expenditures from the Federal treasury, that the main charge of the Democratic campaign of 1932 against the Republican administration was extravagance. The Democrats were particularly critical of budget deficits and the loans of the Reconstruction Finance Corporation in support of large banks.

After the Roosevelt administration came into office in 1933, the deficits continued. Influential administrators, research economists, and legislators viewed these deficits as an unfortunate necessity, not as desirable. No one really thought that recovery might be effected by higher government spending and lower taxes. The deficits continued-- and grew in size--because of apparent necessity, not because of policy. Tax yields continued low while relief and other emergency expenditures grew.

Official views continued to be dominated by the emphasis on monetary policy and price level that had characterized the 1920's. Officials announced repeatedly that the Government intended to raise prices to their 1926 level. One means was devaluation of the dollar from the old level of $20.67 for an ounce of gold to $35.

Curiously enough again, this latter policy was not undertaken--as we might reason now--on the plain grounds that a cheapened dollar would encourage foreign buying in the United States. Instead, it followed a much more roundabout and uncertain theory propounded to President Roosevelt by Professors G. F. Warren and F. A. Pearson, who had found historical cause for believing that a cheapened dollar in terms of gold (that is, a higher price for gold) would stimulate gold production, which would expand the money supply and in turn raise prices.

In the summer of 1934, J. M. Keynes visited the United States and achieved some attention with his claim that if the Federal Government spent in excess of tax revenue only $200 millions a month, the country would slump back to the trough of the depression as in 1932; but that if spent $400 millions, complete recovery would ensue. Many government economists and administrators agreed in general with this prognosis (even if they were not impressed by its precision). But the official government policy continued to aim at a balanced budget, hopeful that once this elusive goal was attained, businessmen and consumers would be so encouraged by the plain evidence of judgment and fiscal morality as to expand their own expenditures sufficiently to bring about high employment and production. The annual budget messages sent to Congress by the President regularly promised that the budget would soon be balanced.

There was also considerable unofficial talk, from 1933 to 1935, of the possibility and merits of "pump priming." If a well pump has no suction, one can generally get it to work by pouring a little water into it, wetting and swelling the leather valve. So with the economy. A little added spending by the government, it was reasoned, would expand consumer buying, encourage more investment spending, and increase confidence in the future. Soon the economy would find itself well on the road to recovery. Government deficits would disappear as tax revenues swelled out of the rising national income, and as relief and salvaging needs declined.

In the spring of 1938 came the shift of official policy from balancing the budget to stimulating the economy through higher government spending. Just before the sharp downswing of 1937-1938, the budget had temporarily come into balance, partly because regular Federal revenues were increasing with better business conditions, and partly because a social security reserve was now being built up. At the request of the President, and for the purpose of offsetting the downswing, a new spending program was put together hurriedly in the spring of 1938 and was passed by Congress.

Once again the pattern of economic discussions followed --with a long-time lag-- the course of economic events. Talk of pump priming died out after 1937. It was obvious that the pump had not been primed: the deficits of government had not initiated an upward movement of private consumption and investment spending that kept going on its own momentum. It was best to let the matter drop in an embarrassed silence.

Instead, discussions grew, after the recession of 1937-1938, as to whether the U.S. economy was not in for "secular stagnation"--a persisting, decade-after-decade era of inadequate private investment and consumption. There would, as a result, be persisting heavy unemployment unless government spending compensated for the deficiency in private spending. If, for this purpose, the government should tax less than it spent, its debt would continue to rise--and many people were already worried by the growth of federal debt from 14.8 billion dollars in 1930 to 31.4 billion dollars by 1937. The debt increase was a favorite target of Republican orators viewing with alarm the policies of the Democratic administration.

But soon any preoccupation with the possibility of secular stagnation became academic. First defense and then war expenditures of the Federal government swelled national income and production to levels that no economist had seriously thought possible. A favorite catch phrase of the early months of the war period was Goering's "Guns or Butter"--the choice before the U.S. economy was said to be more armaments or more consumer goods and services. You couldn't have both.

But it turned out that it was possible to have more of both. Production expanded so hugely that not only did the government, from 1939 to 1944, increase greatly its take of goods and services mainly for war purposes (up by 444 per cent), but consumers at the same time did a little better (by 20 per cent). Consumers did suffer a bit through reduced supplies of "durable" consumer goods (mostly those containing metal), but they more than made up for this through increased supplies of nondurable goods and services.

Total national income in this period, of all goods and services together, rose by 89 per cent. Under pressure, the U.S. economy proved its ability to produce phenomenally. How was such an increase in production possible within five short years? We can cite three reasons.

First, more people went to work. There occurred a major reduction in unemployment, from 9.15 million to 0.7 million. Also, the work force was growing (from 55.6 million to 65.9 million), because more people were coming into the work force than were retiring from it. Part of this reflected the normal growth of population, and part reflected an unusual addition to the work force. Servicemen's wives took jobs when their husbands were away. Some people took jobs because they were easy to get, well-paid, and attractive in other respects.

Secondly, hours of work increased. In manufacturing they rose from 37.7 hours a week in 1939 to 45.2 hours a week in 1944.

Thirdly, productivity per employed person rose (by about 26 per cent) for a number of reasons. To some degree, the increased hours of work were a factor. Another factor was increased use of mass-production methods, often more than compensating for the lesser skills of a considerable proportion of the larger work force. A reduction in development work in some areas, better "load" factors in others, favorable growing seasons in agriculture, the spread of superior techniques, and--probably not least--a sense of co-operation and the high morale that comes from united purpose--these were all influences toward higher productivity.

Meanwhile, the national debt was expanding vastly, passing 263 billion dollars by the end of World War II. But during the war little was heard about the menace of a huge public debt. The preoccupations of economists and the public were elsewhere.

The question that was asked more and more by businessmen and economists during the war years was: "What will happen to the economy when peace comes again?" We can see clearly in retrospect that a depression neurosis afflicted both groups, a hangover from the bleak experience of the 1930's. It just did not seem possible either to businessmen or to economists that the 200 odd billion dollars of gross production that the economy would produce at full employment could be absorbed. Where was the purchasing power to come from? During no year of the 1930's did the economy buy half so much. During each of four years of the 1930's it bought less than 75 billion dollars' worth.

The clearest indications of this depression neurosis are the forecasts made by government agencies and by private economists and businessmen. The Office of Price Administration differed from its sister agencies only in the depth of the pessimism with which it viewed business conditions six months or a year after the end of the war. Private businessmen, according to a survey made by Fortune Magazine, were on the average even more pessimistic than the New Deal economists in Washington. One of the large mail order houses geared its postwar policies explicitly to the expectation of deep depression.

Only very slowly did this depression frame of mind wear off, as year after year the economy remained at full employment levels of production. Between the years 1944 and 1950, the fall in government purchases of goods and services (by 54 billion dollars) was more than made up by increased purchases of goods and services by consumers (up by 82 billion dollars) and by businesses for investment (up by 41 billion dollars). A minor recession in 1949 was already over by the first quarter of 1950, so that even before the Korean outbreak in June, the persisting postwar problem, creeping inflation, was again upon the economy.

In the fall of 1951, it appeared that the main weight of the post-Korea rearmament drive of the United States would be felt during 1952. In that year inflationary pressures would be heaviest, and consumers would put up with some moderate cuts in goods and services available to them. But by 1953, barring all-out-war, the rearmament program would be tapering off. That, together with increased productivity and production in the economy, would enable consumer supplies to return again to their pre-Korea level. Beyond that--who could say?

* * * * *

What caused the Great Depression?

There are many doubtful or wrong explanations floating about. One of the common erroneous theories is that of "crime and punishment"--that in the 1920's the U.S. people were spending wildly on night clubs and silk shirts instead of being thrifty and prudent. This theory forgets that, whatever his moral status, the prodigal son evidently stimulates business activity by his spending.

Another erroneous view is that the U.S. economy produced more goods than its public wanted. "It is a glorious thing to contemplate," said a banker in 1932, "that we can at long last produce more than we care to consume." But the average per-capita weekly money income in 1929 was $13.40 and in 1932, $6.20--not princely amounts that could buy all one fancied. The limitation on what the U.S. public consumed in both years was not that they had run out of wants but that they had run out of money.

A third wrong theory argues that the U.S. suffers from chronic deficiency of purchasing power. Some commentators have suggested that the existence of savings inevitably causes purchasing power to be less than the total value of goods coming on the market. Marx has added his thesis that consumers under capitalism cannot buy as much as the capitalist machine can produce. But those who complain that "Labor gets paid too little to buy what it produces" forget that profits, rent and royalties, and interest are also purchasing power, that not all the products of labor are consumed by labor (try to consume a drill press or a turret lathe), and that money for spending can be dis-hoarded by individuals or created by banks.

A fourth common error holds export demand to be crucial. Thus, a famous mathematician and scientist has asserted in a published article: "The United States cannot succeed in keeping the purchasing power of the people in balance with the productive capacity of the country. The United States is compelled to emphasize her export trade. Without it she could not keep her total productive machinery fully utilized." But alas, the professor, out of his field, did not know the relevant facts.

Since World War I, net exports from the U.S.--that is, the excess of the value of exports over imports--contributed at the most 8.9 billion dollars, or 3.8 per cent, to gross national income. This happened in 1947, when the economy was already suffering from excess spending, and foreign buying was decidedly unwelcome from a domestic point of view. In ordinary peacetime years, the effect is much less. In 23 of the 32 years, 1919 through 1950, net exports were less than 1 billion dollars. Over the whole period, they contributed six tenths of 1 per cent to gross national income --a negligible fraction that could have only negligible influence towards sustaining income.

The overwhelmingly large proportion of total purchasing power in the U.S. economy therefore comes from <u>domestic</u> sources: consumer, business, and government spending. It is here that one should look to explain past variations, and it is here that policy proposals for the future should be focused.

DEPRESSION AND INFLATION

A fifth wrong explanation of unemployment and depression in the United States is that wages were too high and should have been lowered. The basic reasoning of this argument goes: a surplus of labor is to be explained just as one would explain a surplus of unsold goods of any kind, namely, the price is too high. To avoid an oncoming depression, the argument suggests, cut the wage rate. If this reasoning is sound we could expect also to raise wages in time of inflation. Although some businessmen (and classical economists) have often urged a drop in wage rates as a cure for depression, they never in time of inflation urge that a rise in wage rates is a cure for rising prices.

We are inclined to ask: is a selfish interest involved? Since businessmen are inclined to regard lower wages as a blessing, perhaps the catastrophe of depression is an excuse to them for emphasizing what is their normal preference.

Side by side with such a view we should put the contrasting labor argument that "money in the pocket is money to spend." This view would seem to urge that the way to get out of depression is to raise wage rates. But suppose that the higher wage rates cause employers to hire fewer men. Then total wages and total spendings of labor would decline.

The businessmen's view is correct as far as it goes. Wages are costs. But the labor view is also right. Wages are income and purchasing power as well. Any wage-rate change has a two-edged effect, both on costs and on spending.

To give briefly the conclusion of much discussion among economists: the net effect on income and employment of a wage-rate change is uncertain. Changing the wage rates does not necessarily cure depression.

What then were the causes of the U.S. depression?

They can be grouped under four headings: First come the speculative fevers of 1927-1929, both in the stock market and in real estate. These markets were sustained, beyond a moderate point, by buyers who expected to unload their purchases onto someone else at a higher price. They did not buy because they had any faith in the long-run value of what they bought. Prices under such conditions are bound to collapse, once people come to doubt whether they will move upward forever. Once the collapse began, investments, farms, and homes were jeopardized or lost. Few experiences unsettle one more than the loss of a roof over his head. Despair was piled upon distress.

Second, the banking system was weak. As the depression deepened, three waves of bank failures spread economic paralysis and intensified the growing conviction that all was lost. Almost as solid a body blow as to lose the roof over one's head is to lose the money one has in the bank. The banking failures were probably in the main avoidable, had government operations to sustain the banks been prompt and energetic enough.

There was a third possible cause of depression. Several major industries, like housing or automobiles, may have come, for the time being, to their limit of expansion; that is, they could not sell their output at anything like existing prices. Of course, once the collapse began, industries capable of rapid growth, like chemicals and electrical supplies, faced the general shrinkage of demand and were influenced by the pessimism that prevailed.

Fourth, there were foreign events and policies that had a depressing influence on the United States. After the middle 1920's, the raising of tariffs by a number of European producers forced several raw-material-producing countries off the gold standard. The gathering collapse of the gold standard undermined confidence everywhere, reduced lending abroad, and diminished business activity throughout the world.

These four items indicate that the cause of the great depression was a fall in domestic spending. The road out of depression, therefore, is a rise in domestic spending.

When central policy--that is, government--is called on to devise means of accomplishing this aim, it should seek to stimulate consumer spending, to encourage and support business investment, and to choose the most socially desirable channels in which to increase public spending.

* * * * *

From the end of World War II into 1953, the United States has faced the problem of creeping inflation. The most rapid rise was in 1946, when wholesale prices rose about 31 per cent. In 1947 the rise was 16 per cent, and by 1952 the total price rise since V-J day was about 62 per cent. Since 1939 the total rise amounted to 122 per cent.

Inflation is a persistent tendency for prices to rise. It indicates too much spending just as plainly and simply as depression indicates too little spending.

The cause of inflation in the United States and other countries after World War II lay in the financial phenomena of the war. The Government taxed heavily, but it spent still more heavily. The result was that the total money available for purchases rose, but the volume of goods and services did not rise proportionally. Consequently, competition for the scarce items caused prices to rise.

If the cause of inflation is too much spending, what is the cure?

A plausible and frequent recommendation is: "Put legal ceilings on prices!" Since rising prices are the evil, make it illegal to raise them.

But price controls are not necessarily of much use. When ceilings are placed on basic consumer goods, the incentive to produce them is reduced and demand is encouraged by relatively low prices. They grow scarce and hard to find. Scarce consumer goods can of course be rationed in the interest of fair distribution. But then ration tickets, which are shared equally, become the real money and people lack incentive to earn more money than they are entitled to spend under the ration system. Effort languishes, absenteeism grows, production may fall and inflationary pressure can be greater than ever.

Luxury goods are often exempted from price controls or rationing. Then people spend on these luxury goods the money they cannot spend on the basic goods whose prices are kept down and whose quantities are rationed. As prices rise in these uncontrolled areas, labor and other resources are attracted into production there, and output of basic necessities sags further. If in consequence controls are extended to all goods, then enforcement, always a problem, becomes much more difficult. The growing complexity of the system means growing opportunities for evasion. The laws are more and more disregarded. Enforcement becomes spasmodic and ineffective.

These hard lessons of experience have been taught in many countries of the world. The evils of such "repressed inflation" can be greater than the evils of open inflation.

What then is the cure for inflation? First, there is always the happy possibility that it will end of itself. Business investment may decline as business-equipment needs are met. Consumer buying may ease off as the demands for cars, washing machines, radios, and the like are gradually satisfied. Government spending may dwindle for a variety of political reasons. This can happen.

But suppose the inflation does not end of itself. Then Government policy should seek to reduce demand by such devices as heavier taxes, decreases in government spending, and encouragement of citizens' savings. Direct controls--price ceilings, consumer rationing, and allocations of scarce industrial goods--are useful only if they are undertaken as a supplement to a policy that accomplishes the fundamental task of cutting down demand.

No one of these policies is painless or without a social cost. There is no easy road out of inflation.

* * * * *

What generalizations can we draw out of these remarkable decades of economic history since 1930? Three things stand out. First is the variability of production, income, and employment. Real national income fell 40 per cent from 1929 to the depression bottom of 1933. From this low it rose 190 per cent by the late 1940's. The increase in total productivity through these years has been remarkable. No one had the foresight to predict it.

Production per employed person rose 51 per cent between 1929 and 1951. An understanding of the causes of this productivity advance is vital: the urgent economic need of the world is increased production.

Second--and this is a prediction growing out of recent history rather than found in it--it is unlikely that within the visible future the U.S. or other like economies will again experience deep depression. Entirely aside from any conceivable defense or war expenditures, there will probably be a decade-after-decade tendency toward excessive demand for goods. One reason for this is that any tendency for employment and prices to fall will be seized on gladly by legislatures as an excuse for increased government spending. Legislatures have always liked to spend (politically popular) without taxing (politically unpopular). Now out of the post-Keynesian discussions, they have a rationalization for what has always been their desire. Also, errors are more likely on the side of too much rather than too little spending. The political cost of deflation and unemployment is severe, and no sensible politician will want to face it if he can avoid it. In contrast, the political cost of the inflation and over-full employment that accompany too much spending is light. There may, in fact, be net public sentiment--and votes--in favor of inflation as opposed to stability of prices when individual decisions are made on welfare schemes, economic improvements, and defense. Finally, there is the growth of state enterprises found in many countries. These will often be inefficient and lose money. But they will not be closed down. Instead, the state will finance the deficit and in so doing will persistently expand the money supply.

In these factors we have a central explanation of continuing high employment and inflation in a number of fascist and communist countries (notably in Russia, which since 1929 has been undergoing one of the major inflations of history). It is the result not so much of "economic planning," as the logic of political decisions on economic matters. The same influences exist in varying degree for less centralized economies throughout the world.

Third, there is the persistence of attitudes after their causes have disappeared. We are always looking at today's events with minds filled with the habits and presuppositions of yesterday. In the late 1920's economists assumed permanent prosperity. In the late 1930's they were inclined to take seriously the possibility of permanent depression. In the defense and early war period they could not imagine, against the background of the depression decade, how huge a flow of production the economy would be capable of when pressed. Toward the end of the war, they could not imagine how an economy proved so productive could possibly sell to its citizens the abundance it could produce.

The facts of the current day stared them in the face. But their interpretations of those facts assumed repeatedly--and wrongly--that the experience of previous months and years was typical and normal. As one economist put it, "Economists are dogs who bark after the retreating chariot of progress." But we probably should not pick out economists for special distinction. The charge holds for most of us, in every occupation.

> *If we want the world to become a more peaceful, stable community, we can scarcely expect to live in relative luxury while two thirds of the world goes to bed hungry. Nor can we support the world. But we can share our productive skills with those who need them, by helping others help themselves. This the United States has already begun to do.*

CHAPTER 23

HELPING THE WORLD

Theodore Morgan

The concept of economic progress is fairly new in the world. It is new even in the area of Western civilization. Medieval Europe assumed that repetition of the old social and economic routine was normal: There are records of contracts that were to run for over 400 years!

It is much newer in the East and in other low-productivity parts of the world. There, until recent decades, the indefinite continuation of the round of grinding poverty, broken by occasional famine or pestilence, was taken for granted. The most conspicuous religion of the Orient can be viewed as a rationalization of this prospect: if one cannot obtain more of the goods of this world, then he should reduce his desires and through renunciation achieve the contentment that he cannot hope to obtain through acquisition.

The cause of the new-found hope of low-productivity parts of the world in economic progress lies mainly in improved communications, which present the example of vastly higher standards of living and the fascination of modern gadgets. World War II, like other wars before in history, has been an unsettling influence. Millions of soldiers from societies at different technological levels were shifted about the world and saw for themselves how others live. The fine promises of politicians competing for popular favor have had some influence in arousing hopes that are not easily put down. It is rather likely that the historian of the future will find that the effort of low-productivity areas of the world to increase their productivity is the most significant economic phenomenon of the twentieth century.

Over the world a wide range of specific policies and institutions is relied on for economic development. Usually there is a much stronger element of government action than in the United States. Government planning, government assistance to private enterprises, and government ownership are conspicuous in the programs of other lands.

There is also a strong emphasis on the development of manufacturing industries. Argentina has adopted the policy of expanding iron and steel production and fabrication, Ceylon has undertaken a chemical project, India is expanding the production of chemicals and electronic equipment, China and Russia have a high priority on the expansion of metals production.

The general trend toward industrialization seems to go squarely against arguments given in Chapter 20 for free world trade based upon national specialization. Every nation wants to industrialize, whether or not it can have efficient industry. But there are reasons. They are found in the economic position of these countries and in the international economic weather of the past half century.

Specialization carries with it an economic risk. The specialist depends on a continued good market for his product and on a continued adequate source of supply for the things he does not himself produce.

The low-productivity countries are in general highly specialized--much more so than high-productivity countries like the United States, England, or Sweden. (Just before World War II, of the twenty Latin American republics, eighteen found over half the value of their exports arising from three or fewer export products.) Hence they are more vulnerable to shifts in world demand and supply: they are more subject to boom or depression abroad and more susceptible to shifts in foreign trade policies.

Furthermore, the products in which they specialize are largely agricultural: wool, beef, coffee, rubber, tea, sugar. Now agricultural output depends on unpredictable year-to-year changes in the weather. Agricultural production, from thousands and tens of thousands of farms and plantations, is not able to protect itself against falling demand and prices by cutting volume of output. Further, agriculture is peculiarly subject to technological obsolescence because of the new synthetics that compete with, for example, natural rubber and wool and cotton. All the more reason for these less industrialized countries to feel that they are peculiarly exposed to the risks of specialization!

Three times in the past generation--during World War I, the Great Depression, and World War II--these countries have faced drastic economic readjustments as their markets abroad and their sources of supplies were radically disrupted. Small wonder that they should be willing to endure appreciable lowering of their already low standards of living in order to diversify production and protect themselves against occasional drastic declines in their standards of living.

But never does any government official in low-productivity areas confess to his public that a policy of diversification (or "self-sufficiency" or "industrialization") will lower the standard of living or check its rise. Instead he is emphatic in explaining that the policy will make everyone better off.

The hard-pressed public in many of these countries is being misled. "Economic development" policies will raise the standard of living <u>only</u> if they expand the kinds of production whose comparative costs are low. A country will benefit economically from the expansion of any given industry if it has or will have a relative abundance of the resources predominantly used in that industry--the minerals, power, equipment, and skills. A steel mill in Argentina, where both coal and iron ore are lacking, is an expensive luxury to the country. Argentina is getting steel by a high-cost and extravagant route when it could get it cheaper by growing, say, beef, in which it has relative advantage, exporting it, and importing steel in exchange.

The "relative advantage" on which economic policy should be based is a long-run concept. As time goes on, particular resources may grow less available or more available, and there is likely to be technical change, or changes in consumers' tastes. In consequence there is a wide intermediate region of uncertainty between the clear cases of economically sensible expansion (tea in Ceylon) and economically foolish expansion (steel in Argentina).

* * * * *

The development programs of low-productivity countries, like the reconstruction efforts of war-injured countries after 1945, have been helped to an appreciable degree by aid from abroad.

The obvious kinds of aid given by the United States to other countries in past decades have been mainly gifts by charitable organizations, like the Friends' Service Committee and the Red Cross, and funds sent back to relatives and friends by immigrants. Both of these items have become relatively small compared to other forms of aid.

In the 1920's there was also much private capital flowing abroad. United States residents bought foreign bonds and stocks and other property. In general, although there were abuses, these purchases of foreign credit and property benefited both him that gave and him that took: people in the United States received interest and dividends while foreigners increased their production by more than the amount of interest and dividends paid.

During the depression these gifts and flows of capital abroad dwindled off. Their place has been taken increasingly--especially since World War II--by government and international gifts and loans. From 1946 through 1952 the United States exported 43.0 billions of dollars more goods and services than it imported. Of these exports 35.1 billion dollars worth were made available to foreigners by a remarkable variety of United States Government gifts and loans. Some were made under UNRRA, some through civilian supplies distributed abroad by the armed forces, some through direct aid to the Philippines, China, Korea, Greece, and Turkey. Some were made through the International Refugee Organization and through Interim Aid. Others were made through the European Recovery Program and the Mutual Defense Assistance Program, through Export-Import Bank loans, the United Kingdom Loan, surplus property disposal abroad, Lend-Lease credits, and subscriptions to the International Bank and International Monetary Fund.

Also the United Nations organizations have made grants for particular purposes. The International Bank for Reconstruction and Development has made long-term loans and the International Fund, short-term loans. The Colombo Plan has organized aid to countries of south and east Asia from other parts of the British Commonwealth.

Among these programs of aid, whether U.S. or international, the two most conspicuous have been the Marshall Plan (European Recovery Program) and the Point-Four program. The Marshall Plan originated out of facing the economic facts and the political implications of a European economy damaged, run down and disrupted by war. The physical deterioration associated with the war was estimated accurately by economists and statisticians of the United States Government. It was measured by the destruction of factories and machines, by the wearing out and obsolescence of equipment, by shortages of coal and other raw materials of industry, and by populations weakened physically and spiritually by the long disaster.

But the experts underestimated the more intangible yet heavy burden of dislocations between country and town, and between one country and another. Contacts between businesses and between sources of supply and markets had been disrupted and had to be rebuilt.

A special problem arose from urban-rural price dislocations. Agricultural prices after the war were set by law at levels that were low relative to prices of urban products. At the same time, in war-torn countries, urban production for several years was scanty in volume and poor in quality. Farmers had little incentive to produce for urban consumption, and the cities were in desperate need of food. Most of these countries had in addition lost much of their shipping and had used up foreign assets whose interest and dividends previously helped to buy imports.

At the same time, claims on production were much above the prewar level. To the normal demand for consumer goods was added that coming from increase of population-- some seven per cent for western Europe. And there was more need for investment goods--to replace and add to the supply of houses, to replace equipment worn out with war use or destroyed by enemy action, and to fill the pipelines of industry with raw materials and semifinished products.

The United States, with its productive plant uninjured by war and with its high productivity raised still higher by war incentives, was one of the main sources for food and the only important source for industrial equipment and supplies. Between June 30, 1945 and the end of 1947, the United States made grants and loans to its allies totalling $14.6 billion. But much of these were emergency aids of a hand-to-mouth variety that kept people from starving and met some of the most urgent needs for industrial supplies. The help was not sufficient in quantity nor was it rightly directed to get economic expansion under way. Recovery lagged.

Secretary of State Marshall, after prolonged discussions with the Russian leaders about European recovery, concluded in early 1947 that they were in no hurry to see Europe revive, that instead they hoped to make political capital out of Europe's continued prostration. In June, 1947 he made an informal proposal.

"It is logical," said Marshall, "that the United States should do whatever it is able to do to assist in the return of normal economic health in the world, without which there can be no political stability and no assured peace....Such assistance...should provide a cure rather than a mere palliative. Any government that is willing to assist in the task of recovery will find full co-operation, I am sure, on the part of the United States Government. Any government that meneuvers to block the recovery of other countries cannot expect help from us....It would be neither fitting nor efficacious for this government to undertake to draw up unilaterally a program designed to place Europe on its feet economically. This is the business of the Europeans.... The role of this country should consist of friendly aid in the drafting of a European program and of later support of such a program so far as it may be practical for us to do."

Marshall's suggestion met with immediate response. Sixteen nations, who with Western Germany had a population of 270 millions, sent their representatives to Paris. Russia decided not to enter the program, kept her satellites out, and later adopted a policy of bitter opposition. Her staying out worked to the advantage of the plan, for decisions in the European Committee were prompter and more effective than they would have been had Russian representatives been sitting in.

The Paris conference considered what resources the assembled nations had, what they could do for themselves, and what they needed from outside to realize minimum recovery goals by mid-1952. The eventual pared-down figure was $21 billion. Of this, $17 billion was to be obtained from the United States in gifts or loans and the remaining $4 billion from other Western Hemisphere countries and from the International Bank. The total was broken down into individual commodities. Food, steel, coal, and transportation equipment were the crucial needs.

During the fall of 1947 three committees in Washington laid the requests from Europe side by side with resources available in the United States. They considered the financial impact of the program on the United States' economy and noted that we were already under an inflationary pressure to which the plan would add further. In the winter 1947-48 the final work of the Paris conference and of these committees was put before Congress and eventually accepted without major change.

The Marshall Plan has been a major success in raising production. The Office of European Economic Co-operation (OEEC), which was the continuing organization set up in Paris by the European countries, estimated in August, 1951 that industrial production in the co-operating countries had by 1950 risen 25 per cent. (These percentage increases are smaller than reported increases during the same period for Russia and its satellite countries of eastern Europe. But it is clear from the work of Naum Jasny, Alexander Gershenkron, Colin Clark, and others, that statistics in Communist countries have been "co-ordinated," and are not worth taking seriously as objective statements of what really happened, without exhaustive critical scrutiny and qualification.)

The OEEC in mid-1951 drew up a new program for action, aiming at raising western Europe's over-all production by 25 per cent during the succeeding five years and, through joint efforts, overcoming the obstacles in the way of production increases.

* * * * *

The Point-Four Program was first suggested in President Truman's inaugural address in 1949. He urged a "bold new program" to help the people of the low-productivity areas of the world raise their standards of living and to give them new hope for the future. A major purpose of Point Four was that it would serve to block the expansion of Soviet power into underdeveloped areas, which had (like eastern Europe and China) shown themselves, because of their primitive agriculture and often feudal forms of land tenure, more susceptible than higher-productivity nations to Communist ideas.

The Plan was proposed to Congress late in the summer of 1949. There was to be a world-wide objective of providing technical assistance in the fields of health, agriculture, forestry, industry, power, and flood control. Other nations would be invited to pool their technological resources in the undertaking, and there would be co-operation with such United Nations organizations as the Food and Agriculture Organization, the World Health Organization, the Educational, Scientific, and Cultural Organization (UNESCO), the International Bank, and the Institute of Inter-American Affairs. Any other like international program, such as the British Commonwealth Colombo Plan, would also be brought in.

Through Point Four and co-operating organizations, technical aid in every field has become far more readily available the world over than it ever was before. No nation that really wants such help has trouble getting it.

Since V-E and V-J days, a major increase of production has occurred throughout the world. This is due, in part, to "natural" forces of recovery and development, but it is also due to the material help and stimulus provided by the international economic programs we have just described. They have been well justified despite waste and a plain spirit abroad of getting all one's nation deserved from Uncle Sam and other sources--and maybe more. There is reason to expect continued increase in production and morale among free nations because they are co-operating together in a constructive cause.

The billions of dollars that the United States has contributed to reconstruction and development since World War II make an impressive total. No nation in the world's history has done so much--either absolutely or relative to its income--to advance the welfare of other nations. Without the threat of Russian expansion facing us, we should probably have done something, but not nearly so much. We have behaved more effectively and creditably for world welfare than we would have in a safer international context. The cost to the United States has been a somewhat smaller volume of goods and services available at home and an increased inflationary problem.

But even the high productivity of the United States does not enable it to do much more than help others to help themselves. The United States can and should continue to act as a catalyst. If it is successful, there will be greater political stability in an unsettled world and greater production in a poor world.

A small country's foreign policy rarely causes the rest of the world to sit up and take notice. But when the United States offers aid to Europe or calls upon the U.N. to send soldiers to Korea, it has to anticipate what the rest of the world will think. No nation wants to be bossed around, nor does it want to become a battleground in the struggle between communism and democracy. This chapter reviews the delicate but necessary task we face of obtaining international co-operation for peace.

CHAPTER 24

OUR FOREIGN POLICY: TOWARD A BETTER WORLD

Fred Harvey Harrington
Department of History

Where are we heading? What are the probable lines of American foreign policy for the future?

Some find the answer in the words, "We must stop Communism." These words, however, pose other questions: "What is the best way to stop Communism?" and "Is an anti-Communist policy enough? Should it not be joined to a program of building a better world?"

As we consider these questions, we realize that the problems ahead are complex. No single, simple answer will take care of all our needs. Such a conclusion, of course, will displease the impatient, who want decisions in a hurry. It should be remembered, though, that oversimplification can be dangerous. In World Wars I and II, many Americans felt that beating Germany would solve all the problems of the age. The tendency, therefore, was to neglect everything except "the German question." This oversimplification and its consequences proved unfortunate and should suggest the importance of taking the broader view today and tomorrow.

Despite complexities, it is possible to make certain generalizations which help explain the past and may provide clues for the future. First, and most important of all, it should never be forgotten that the history of the United States is the history of an expanding nation.

To elaborate: in the agrarian age (from the colonial era down to the mid-nineteenth century) Americans pushed westward, taking territory and settling land until the republic stretched from the Great Lakes to the Rio Grande. As an industrial nation--since the 1870's--the United States has shown less interest in acquiring territory, although we have picked up a few overseas possessions. But expansion has remained the keynote of American foreign relations. American goods have found markets all over the world. Americans have sought and obtained raw materials from many lands. The United States, through its citizens and through the government, has invested enormous sums in foreign countries. Decade by decade, twentieth-century Americans have pushed their strategic horizons, or defense lines, farther and farther from home shores. Every generation has increased its cultural influence overseas.

Given the extent, the natural resources, and the population of the United States, this record of expansion is far from surprising. Moreover, given the same facts, there is little reason to expect the expansion to stop. If anything, the rate of expansion has speeded up in the last decades. One can safely predict that American activity and influence will increase in the generation ahead, in a great many foreign areas--Latin America and the British Empire, western Europe, southeast Asia, the Near and Middle East and Africa.

Many Americans will not subscribe to such an analysis. Overseas enterprises have their drawbacks. They call for great military expenditures, which produce an even heavier tax burden. They lead to uncomfortable commitments far from home, as in Korea and Iran. They produce ties to foreign leaders widely disliked in the United States--Tito, as one example, or Franco. Many, therefore, oppose further expansion and say that the United States should be content to defend the western hemisphere, leaving other tasks to others.

This antiexpansionism is nothing new. In 1803 antiexpansionists opposed purchase of the Louisiana Territory beyond the Mississippi. The antiexpansionists of 1898 were against the annexation of islands in the West Indies and the Pacific. Anti-interventionists in World Wars I and II opposed increased commitments overseas. But in each case the commitments followed, just the same. In each case, the decision (rightly or wrongly) was for the policy that meant expansion of the American economy, extension of the American strategic zone, and a broadening of American influence.

Now, of course, it is sometimes possible to reverse directions. This was done, in a limited way, after World War I. In rejecting the Treaty of Versailles, the United States chose, for a time, to limit its political and military commitments in the eastern hemisphere. There was, however, no economic withdrawal; American commercial and financial expansion continued through the 1920's. And the next major international conflict, in the 1930's and 1940's, saw the establishment and extension of all the political and military commitments spurned in 1919.

From now on, there is not likely to be any turning back. For one thing, many feel that the withdrawal of 1919 was a costly error. For another, many Americans recognize that the aviation-and-atomic-warfare character of our age has made withdrawal far more difficult than before. Closely associated is the feeling of Americans that Soviet Russia and world Communism must be checked, in the interest of the safety and prosperity of the United States and democratic nations generally. And the decline of British strength seems to leave much of the job to the United States ("Britain's heir").

This puts it negatively. It can be put the other way around. Consider the economic picture. While becoming the chief industrial nation, the United States has remained a great agricultural power. American production, in factory and field, tends in peacetime to create surpluses of agricultural goods, manufactured goods, and capital. Full employment, good prices for the farmer and satisfactory returns for the businessman are likely to result if these surpluses are disposed of abroad, either in normal trade or in subsidy programs, such as the Marshall Plan and the current military-aid programs. Business, labor, and agriculture supported the Marshall Plan when it was proposed, not only to fight Communism, but also to assure continued prosperity at home.

It follows that Americans, associated with an expanding economy, would object to any program that would mean restriction of economic opportunities overseas. It seems likely that Americans in the future will be tied more, rather than less, closely to the world economy. That in itself guarantees continuing diplomatic commitments and influence. For, after all, we now live in a world of exchange controls, state trading, and increasing governmental power. American commercial and financial activity abroad therefore inevitably involves political as well as economic relationships.

Or take the military situation. Down through the nineteenth century the United States was satisfied to defend its continental possessions; the near-by West Indies were controlled by British, not by American, naval might. With the extension of trade and influence overseas after the 1870's, Americans adopted the sea-power policies of Captain Alfred T. Mahan and broadened their strategic concepts to cover the West Indies and also the Pacific to the line from Alaska to Hawaii to the Isthmus of Panama, where we were soon to dig a canal. Acquisition of the Philippine Islands in 1898 led some government officials to consider seriously pushing

American control all the way across the Pacific, by securing bases in China and Korea. World War II finally brought realization of this program of dominating the whole Pacific. Meantime, the United States had assumed military responsibility for the entire western hemisphere and had enlarged its security zone to include the north Atlantic, western Europe, and the Mediterranean.

These enormous increases in American military commitments came with dizzying speed, largely in one decade (the 1940's). Many Americans were not happy about the new security pattern. But even the most vigorous antiexpansionists (ex-President Herbert Hoover, for example) have advocated only a very limited withdrawal from these advanced positions. And, considering the continuing Russian threat, commitments seem almost certain to be extended rather than reduced in the years ahead. When Communist activity in the Balkans threatened Anglo-American domination of the Mediterranean, the American government brought forth the Truman Doctrine (aid to Greece and Turkey, 1947), which involved a definite enlargement of American military influence in the eastern Mediterranean. When North Korean Communists invaded South Korea in June, 1950, American military strength was thrown into the balance; and after a year of war with the Russian-backed North Koreans and Chinese, the United States certainly had a permanent military commitment in the south if not in the whole of Korea.

To be sure, the United States did not throw its full military weight into the Chinese situation in the late 1940's, when the Chinese Communists defeated the Chinese Nationalists. The Communist triumph in China, however, convinced both Truman Democrats and their Republican opponents that Communist advances into key areas could not again be permitted without endangering American defenses. Hence it seems likely that future crises may see an increase in American military influence in such regions as Iran, India, and Burma. Even if the crises do not develop, the possibility of a Communist advance is likely to lead to the inclusion of these regions in the American strategic zone. The developing European side of this pattern is seen in the North Atlantic Pact, the Truman Doctrine, and the military agreement with Spain. The fighting in Korea, administration pledges to defend Formosa, and the American military pact with Australia and New Zealand show the trend in the Far East.

* * * * *

Look also at the field of ideas, always important in world politics, and doubly so when an ideological program is linked to economic and military action. American democratic thought has always been a substantial force abroad; and today, American culture is more important than ever before. The world is tremendously interested in American institutions, American ideas and ideals, American technological and scientific accomplishments. So great is this interest that the United States has become, in many ways, the cultural center of the Western world.

Government cultural activity has been particularly prominent during crises. In the World Wars, American democratic ideas were used to combat German ideology (George Creel's Committee on Public Information in World War I; Elmer Davis' Office of War Information in World War II). Since 1945, American ideas have been used as weapons in the conflict with Communism. The United States has worked through such agencies as the Voice of America, the United States Information Service, the Fulbright Awards. A variety of factors, including Congressional suspicion of the Voice of America, has limited the effectiveness of these programs; and, so far, Russian propaganda efforts have in many areas been more effective than ours. The importance of this work is, however, widely recognized in the United States, and sooner or later government activity will be markedly increased. This, and the continuing interest of foreign peoples in America, should guarantee that American ideas will have more and more influence in the world in the years to come.

It is evident, then, that American influence overseas is on the increase. That being the case, the main job for makers of American foreign policy is to see to it that this growing strength is used in an intelligent way. Clearly, it is to our advantage to check the spread of Russian influence. It is likewise to our advantage to adopt policies that will advance the economic interests of peoples in other lands. It is easy to denounce the "Santa Claus" character of such policies. Actually, though, a program which raises living standards abroad helps us as much as it helps others. If, for example, we can increase the productivity and prosperity of the peoples of Greece and the Philippines, Malaya and Latin America, these areas will be more useful allies against Communism than they now are--more useful, too, for the trade which is so important in our own pattern of prosperity.

One of the greatest assets in the years ahead is our commercial and financial strength. The Russians cannot now match the power of our dollars. In France and Italy, our economic strength (as represented in the Marshall Plan) helped turn those countries away from Communism. Since World War II our economic strength has helped support Great Britain, an indispensable ally. Economic strength enables us to finance arms subsidy programs.

But, for all our wealth, we cannot support or finance the world alone. To attempt to do so would be to make our already heavy tax burden intolerable. American economic strength must be used not only to subsidize and arm our allies, but also to strengthen them so that they will be able to carry on alone. The Marshall Plan incorporated this strengthening idea, though it was not always kept in mind during operation of the plan. The Point-Four program of providing technological assistance to economically backward regions aims in the same direction. And the American government, since World War II, has sometimes tried to direct public and private lending overseas toward this goal.

It can hardly be said that the program has as yet succeeded. There are many obstacles. In many parts of the world, there is opposition to new ideas. There is, in addition, suspicion of American motives. The American Congress, while willing to vote huge military budgets, has been reluctant to put up large sums for economic projects overseas. The promising Point-Four program got into politics, opponents of the administration feeling that President Truman desired to make political capital out of this issue.

On the world front, the immediate problem of combatting Communism has made it difficult to concentrate on long-range building. The Communist menace has led the United States to co-operate with virtually every foe of Russia. This has meant working, in Yugoslavia and Spain, with totalitarian leaders basically hostile to the human liberties on which our democracy is based. It has meant trusting a Japan and a west Germany that are far from completely reconstructed in spirit since World War II. And it has meant co-operating, in Greece, Iran, the Philippines, and Latin America, with groups unsympathetic to the land and other reforms desperately needed in those areas.

Though discouraging, the situation is far from hopeless. American efforts have brought limited improvement in some areas, as in western Europe and in Greece. The American Point-Four program has finally got off to a fair start, and a similar and related United Nations program may yield significant results. American companies abroad--United Fruit, for example, and the oil concerns--are coming to the conclusion that old-fashioned exploitation was less efficient than they once believed, and that it is wiser to help the peoples of Latin America and Asia diversify their econqmies, raise their living standards, and obtain educational and other benefits. The years ahead, therefore, are likely to bring increased interest in American policies designed to improve economic conditions abroad. If well-considered, these policies should provide an answer to Russian charges that the United States exploits but does not aid.

For some time to come, economic policies are certain to be tied closely to military considerations. There has been a growing tendency--for a full decade--to rely heavily on military judgments. The military departments are strongly represented on the National Security Council (created in 1947), an agency that has had much to say about national policy. President Franklin D. Roosevelt relied heavily on military advisers, as did President Harry S. Truman. Both used military personnel for vital diplomatic tasks. The public, too, listens with attention to the professional military. This is logical, in view of the current military crisis and the terrible destructive power of the new military weapons. It would be unfortunate, however, if military considerations came to dominate the whole diplomatic pattern. It is wise, surely, to leave the control of atomic energy with a civilian-dominated commission and to make certain that military factors, while they receive full attention, do not exclude from consideration other important factors.

In the economic and military fields the United States has already, and frequently, demonstrated its strength. Our showing in the ideological field is much less impressive. But despite the lost opportunities of the past the American republic can still do much in the future. Already an important force is the large group of foreign students who have enrolled at American universities. The American scholars and technicians sent abroad under Fulbright, Point Four, and other programs have already done significant work. There is need, however, for a much expanded public program, aimed at combatting Communist misinterpretation of the United States and spreading information about American democracy.

There are limiting factors in the field. It is difficult to export ideas. And American democratic ideology will not suit all nations in the near or even distant future. Nor is it likely that we can make all foreign peoples love us; the weak and poor rarely harbor much affection for the rich and powerful. But, by promoting understanding of America, we can win respect and a certain amount of friendship; and we can help build a world that will be better for us as well as for others.

In developing foreign policy, the United States must of course work with other nations. This runs counter to one

American tradition, for in the nineteenth and early twentieth centuries, the American republic carefully avoided permanent political alliances with major foreign countries. Pearl Harbor changed this pattern. And it is clearly changed for all time. It is impossible to imagine a future American foreign policy without alliances.

* * * * *

The American alliance system is two-sided. First, we are allied to many foreign countries by special agreements. Second, we are a leading member of the United Nations.

The ties with individual countries are many and growing. We are allied to western European countries through the North Atlantic Pact, the Truman Doctrine, and other agreements, and there are special ties to Britain, our most important ally. Our New World alliances include a close connection with Canada and alliance agreements with most of the Latin American states. In the Pacific we are allied in one way or another to the Philippines, to Australia and New Zealand, to our former enemy Japan, to the republic of Korea. It seems certain that additional links to the south Asiatic countries will be forthcoming.

The total alliance picture is all the more impressive when one considers that the whole system is less than a decade old. Yet the alliance system is, quite obviously, permanent. At the moment, its main purpose is to check Russia. There is reason to hope, however, that America and her allies can also work together to improve economic and social conditions in the areas under their control (as, indeed, Britain and the United States are already doing in the Caribbean). It may be hoped, further, that direct American relations with the new native governments of old colonial areas will be increasingly important; in the past, our tendency has been to deal almost exclusively through the European overlords.

While building an American alliance system, the United States has also been active in the United Nations. Possibly in its anxiety to have the U.N. launched in satisfactory fashion, the State Department overstated the importance of this world organization, oversold the U.N. to the American people. The result was disappointment and a reaction against the U.N. when it failed to end Russian-American conflict after the war. Fortunately, the Russians were temporarily absent when the Korean conflict began in 1950, and the U.N. was able to back American efforts in Korea.

This meant relatively little in a practical, military sense, but it meant a great deal in the fight for world opinion. It also sold the U.N. to the American people. It would be absurd, of course, to claim that the U.N. can solve the problems of the world in the near future. The organization, however, is of enormous value to the United States, for it provides international support for many of our national policies. And the U.N. is a symbol of dedication to the struggle for world prosperity and world peace. However far away may be this future, it is well to preserve the symbol, so that the goal may be kept constantly in mind.

For success any American foreign policy must weather the storms of domestic politics. These storms are going to be heavier in the future. In the past, American politicians have often ignored international issues, on the ground that these issues did not decide elections. Today the growing importance of diplomacy makes such side-stepping difficult if not impossible.

One result of this new concentration on foreign policy has been the appearance of many irresponsible and uninformed statements on diplomatic questions. But in the long run, public discussion of international issues is desirable from the citizen's point of view. Particularly so in view of the probability that, in the future, diplomatic problems will figure more prominently in political campaigns than they have in the past.

Closely related to this matter of politics is the growing interest of Congress in foreign affairs. If made aware of the significance of foreign-policy decisions, Congress will most certainly interest itself in these decisions in the years to come. In a way, this may seem unfortunate, for it will make the United States seem divided at home. Consider, however, the alternative--complete presidential control of foreign relations. Concentration of authority in one man would not appear to be in line with our democratic traditions. Therefore the increase of Congressional interest in diplomacy may prove desirable as well as inevitable.

During World War II, the Roosevelt administration and the Republican opposition worked out a bipartisan foreign policy. To some degree the bipartisan foreign policy still continues; and certainly Americans are likely to pull together in major crises. By mid-century, though, conflict had become more common than agreement in discussions of foreign policy. Conflict is likely in the future, for, as diplomacy grows in importance, the party not in office cannot politically afford to agree with the incumbents at every point. The resulting bickering is bound to make a dismal impression overseas. Yet there are advantages in the breakdown of the bipartisan approach. When the key politicians agreed, they settled things in private, at the seat of government. Disagreeing, they will carry issues to the public. Often the issues will be badly defined, and the voter will be confused rather than prepared to exercise an intelligent choice. But, in time, public discussion should contribute to public understanding and enable the citizens to take an active part in determining policy.

That, of course, would be in the best democratic tradition. The question is: will there be free discussion? Will Americans be able to speak their minds? There is some tendency now to stifle free discussion in the United States of America. This is an unfortunate trend which we may hope will be arrested. Freedom of speech does not exist in Soviet Russia and other totalitarian states. Its absence is one of the marks of authoritarian rule. Our tradition of civil liberties features the right of the American citizen to speak his mind, freely and without fear. Preservation of this right is essential for the maintenance and continued growth of American democracy.

As we face the troubled years ahead, we should remember that we do not stand alone. In one crisis, over Korea, the United Nations organization has given us assistance. In the future, therefore, we should maintain the closest ties to this world body. It is feeble now, but growing stronger; and it may, in time, be able to make significant contributions to global peace and prosperity. Here is one real source of hope for our troubled world.

The road ahead is not an easy one. Often Americans will become discouraged or angry if goaded by the policies of other powers. At such times, the tendency will be to "do something," to "take decisive steps," to resort to military action. The hope is that the United States will not quickly abandon the quest for peace. It is far from certain that a third world war would provide solutions for the problems of today. And it is certain that a third world war would mean suffering such as the world has never seen. Science has given mankind great blessings but also fantastic powers to destroy, kill, maim, and madden. Americans whose houses have never been bombed may have difficulty appreciating the full significance of this fact. But it is a fact, and one which should never for a moment slip from our minds. Let us hope that our future will be a peaceful one; and let us work as best we can toward that goal.

In closing, it is well to take the long view. For three centuries we have been building America: a nation devoted to democracy, to economic prosperity, and to the rights of man. During the last two generations we have been moving into a new, world phase of American history, likely to last for centuries to come. Our efforts and the efforts of our descendants should be to preserve our heritage and to give the rest of the world the opportunity to take for mankind the best that the United States can offer from our continuing democratic struggle for higher living standards and human rights.

PART FIVE

What We Can Do

So far, we have examined various impersonal factors that affect the peace of the world: especially scientific research and technology, ideologies, and the role the United States is playing. The basic question now is what we as individuals can do. This chapter gives some insight into the way our democracy formulates policies.

CHAPTER 25

MAKING SENSE OUT OF POLITICS AND PRESSURE GROUPS

Ralph K. Huitt
Department of Political Science

The study of politics, writes Harold Lasswell, is the "study of influence and the influential...the art of who gets what, when, how." There are other definitions of politics, of course, but all seem to revolve around the words "power" and "influence." Politics, then, would seem to consist of the struggle of people, through the various groups with which they identify themselves, to influence social decision-making.

The stakes of the struggle are as diverse as the people who engage in it; they include prestige and economic gain and priority for one's values. The struggle assumes many forms, as people employ whatever weapons they can--propaganda, economic sanctions, even violence. The aspect of politics with which we shall deal here is concerned with attempts to influence or control, directly or indirectly, the organized state and to use its authority and prestige to support group goals.

Nice people in this country often look on politics as a dirty business. They like to put in their group constitutions firm pledges to stay out of politics, and to say of important issues that they should be taken out or kept out of politics. But no group which makes claims upon other groups and upon society can stay out of politics. It has only the alternatives of trying or not trying to be effective politically. No group can afford to ignore government, for even in a strictly laissez-faire system--if such were possible-- the government would have to provide the framework of legal norms within which social action takes place. Anyone who doubts this should try making out a list of the minimum of regulations needed by even a simple society. He will find that the list is long and that it impinges upon his life at every point.

Furthermore, attempts to take issues out of politics are foredoomed to failure. Indeed, politics can be avoided only if there is no issue. The question of monogamy in marriage, for instance, virtually is nonpolitical in the United States now because there is a very wide area of social consensus in regard to it. It is not an issue. The same obviously could not be said of public housing. The only way politics could be taken out of the settling of social issues would be for all groups but one to surrender their points of view.

The task of government in any organized state is to mediate the political struggle and somehow achieve the compromises that make it possible for people to go on living together with a reasonable degree of peace and contentment. Government must provide the agencies--legislature, courts, elections--to channel the struggle and insure compliance with decisions which are legally made. A system which purports to give a majority of the people what they want through representatives of their own choosing must provide agencies to shape up alternatives, or the ballot is meaningless.

This is the job of political parties--to present slates of candidates, to make policy promises, to educate through election campaigns, to conduct the government if they win and to criticize the government if they lose. They make democracy workable by presenting the electorate with the simple "yes" or "no" choices which it must have if it is to function at all effectively.

Much depends upon the institutions of the state. England has, for instance, a unitary system, meaning that all power is lodged in the central government and local governments are subordinate to it. The British party system has effectively united the executive and the legislature, so that the "government"--the cabinet and the ministers--controls the Parliament which makes the laws and the administrative agencies which carry them out. The government which cannot control these must resign and turn over the power to a government which can, or else face a general election. Party discipline in Parliament, as a consequence, is nearly perfect. The special-interest group must deal with the party leaders, because the leaders can control their party. The voter's task is reduced to a choice of party, for the party can and will do what it has promised if it wins. The politician's career line is clear: he obeys the party and seeks advancement in it. He can afford to lose an election, but he cannot afford to lose the endorsement of his party. The result is that all attempts to influence the government tend to be channeled into partisan politics.

The American system is organized quite differently. Here we have not one government but forty-nine, each exercising a set of powers guaranteed to it by the Constitution. It is not possible for any party to capture all these governments simultaneously. Even the most sweeping victory at the polls leaves pockets of resistance. Moreover, the makers of the Constitution deliberately erected barriers to the control of the federal government by any one group. They feared the "impulsive" masses. They wanted it to be difficult for a temporary majority to tyrannize over the minority. They provided for a "separation of powers" which institutionalized a conflict between the president and Congress that not even the unifying influence of the political party has been able to overcome. They gave to each branch, as "checks and balances," part of the power of the other, so that obstruction is as easy as co-operation is difficult. They provided a "time check" on democracy by giving senators long, staggered terms. They made the Constitution very hard to amend. It is virtually impossible for the leadership of either party to get that control over the apparatus of government which would be necessary if it were to carry through resolutely a promised program of action.

The result is a fragmented political power. The two great parties are not really national parties. They are loose federations of state and local parties which rally every four years to try to elect a president. Neither party has any genuine national leadership. The President is generally recognized as the leader of his party, but no matter how large a majority his party has in Congress, he has no assurance that he can persuade it to enact his legislative program.

The opposition party is in even worse straits. Its last condidate for the presidency is its titular leader, but no one would seriously argue, for instance, that Mr. Dewey after his 1948 defeat exercised any leadership over his party's members of Congress.

The most striking fact about the operations of the American Congress is that all controversial legislation is passed, or defeated, across party lines. Party lines hold on the organization of the two houses, on patronage questions, and on occasional questions which somehow come to be recognized as "party issues." But on most issues the supporters of a measure must try to build a majority from whatever elements are available, enlisting through compromises and bargains as many interests as they can.

Our system of government does not merely make matters difficult for political leaders. It also provides many opportunities for effective obstructive action by those who are opposed to a particular course of action. Interests that want to preserve the status quo have an enormous defensive advantage, for where the proponent of a measure must guide it through a long and perilous journey, its opponent has repeated opportunities to kill it in its tracks or mutilate it beyond recognition. The measure can die in committee, or in the chairman's pocket. It can find access to the floor of the House of Representatives blocked by the powerful Rules Committee. It must make its way through similar hazards in two houses, and after passage in somewhat different forms by both it may be drastically changed by a conference committee. If it survives it still must get the president's signature. Then, after all this, it may be made impotent by the failure of the Congress to appropriate necessary funds, or an unsympathetic executive agency may not enforce it vigorously.

Interest groups in the United States understand the character of our political system and have adapted their tactics to it. They know the party to be a defective instrument for those who are interested in public policy. To rely on one party exclusively would be folly, for it cannot be depended on even if it wins. Most interest groups therefore try to keep friends in both camps. The political party itself is an interest group, wanting from government the patronage and perquisites of power. To gain them it must control the government, and to control the government it must win elections.

But a party that cannot discipline its members in Congress is equally helpless to give them effective support at the polls. Each candidate for Congress knows this and acts accordingly. He makes alliances with whatever groups he can in his district. If he wins he is loyal to these groups, for it was they, not the party, who elected him. It is the exposed position of the individual congressman that furnishes the best clue to the activities of the great national interest groups of today. These groups have learned that the most effective lobbying is done, not in the corridors of the national capitol, but in the home districts of congressmen, with the people who decide who shall sit in Congress.

Much of the present-day criticism of lobbying is directed at a kind of activity which is obsolescent, to say the least. The term "lobbyist" got its unsavory connotations from the nineteenth-century type of lobbying which often involved bribing legislators with wine, women, and money, and relied primarily upon the influencing of individual lawmakers. The type is not extinct, but it is relatively unimportant. Several large-scale investigations of lobbying in the twentieth century make it clear that really effective modern pressure activities are rarely corrupt, increasingly indirect, and largely group, rather than individual, efforts.

The modern "pressure group" typically is a giant association and, like the party, a federation of state and local groups. It has a Washington office, staffed with experts who appear before congressional committees, but whose chief job is that of intelligence--keeping the organization alert to matters which affect its interests. It promotes massive public-relations campaigns to effect a climate of opinion favorable to it, so that it may rely on a sympathetic public in time of need. It has great financial resources; a congressional committee has called lobbying a "billion dollar industry." But its greatest asset is its "grass-roots" strength, its thousands of local units ready at a word from the national office to bring to bear the kind of political pressure which counts in the American system--pressure on the individual congressman in his home district.

The pressure tactics of interest groups vary with the nature of the organization. A group which has a great mass membership numbering in the millions may concentrate its efforts upon mobilizing its own members for action. A group with large financial resources and relatively few members obviously will make greater use of propaganda through the mass media of communication.

Some activities are designed to reach the congressmen directly. Floods of letters, telegrams, and phone calls are familiar weapons. More subtle and probably more effective are the communications from individuals in the congressman's district, selected by their organization because of their supposed effectiveness with him. To facilitate this kind of pressure, files may be kept of persons loyal to the organization who have influence with individual congressmen. Delegations of persons to appear before committees are carefully "stage-managed" for maximum effectiveness, including, if possible, representatives of groups ordinarily identified with the opposition. In addition, of course, favors to congressmen, such as arranging housing or access to Washington society, or providing remunerative speaking or writing engagements, are standard practices.

Perhaps the most impressive development in the past two decades has been the increased use of the mass media of communication to create or maintain a "climate of opinion" favorable to group goals. The outpouring of materials is statistically overwhelming. As an example, a congressional committee investigating lobbying reported that the Committee for Constitutional Government sent out between 1937 and 1944:

> Eighty-two million pieces of literature--booklets, pamphlets, reprints of editorials and articles, specially addressed letters, and 760,000 books.
>
> More than 10,000 transcriptions, carrying 15-minute radio talks on national issues, besides frequent national hook-ups for representatives of the committee.
>
> Three hundred and fifty thousand telegrams to citizens to arouse them to action on great issues.
>
> Many thousands of releases to daily and weekly newspapers--full-pay advertisements in 536 different newspapers with a combined circulation of nearly 20,000,000.

It is here that the congressional friend of the interest group can be helpful. He can insert the group's material in the Congressional Record, have thousands of copies printed by the Government Printing Office at a fraction of the cost of commercial printing, and lend his frank to the group to eliminate the usual mailing cost. The Committee for Constitutional Government has admitted the distribution of eight to ten million franked releases in a four-year period, two and a half million pieces going under the frank of one member in a single year. Local outlets are used where possible, one group furnishing its local units with "90 key paragraphs" which could be combined as desired for speeches, editorials, and radio broadcasts.

The opinion-molding institutions--schools, churches, press--are natural targets for this barrage. Canned editorials, news releases, "boiler-plate" cartoons are offered to the editors. Texts, courses, teaching aids are available for teachers. The National Association of Manufacturers, to cite only one example, states that it issued 18,640,270 pamphlets in five years, with 53% going to students. In the year 1950 more than half of its output of nearly eight million publications went to students. This is supplemented by the massive advertising in national media that is concerned with political ideas--a form that has been especially intensive since the advent of World War II. These efforts to influence opinion add up to what has been called "government by public relations," in which the race goes not to the swift but to the well-heeled.

What is the relation of interest groups to the general welfare? A hardy perennial in American politics is the demand that the special interests be regulated to safeguard the general welfare. But here the lawmakers face a dilemma: how far can regulation go without impairing the constitutional rights of petition and freedom of speech and press? Regulation by the various states and the nation so far has been limited to requirements that lobbyists and their sponsoring groups identify themselves and furnish information periodically concerning their finances and activities. Attempts to regulate them further will go on, for these attempts are themselves part of the political struggle. Efforts to change the rules to hamper the opposition are standard tactics, and when they succeed they are demonstrations of political strength. But rules only alter tactics and confer advantages. They do not abolish the contest.

It may very well be that there are practices which should be and will be regulated, but this should not be confused with the naive notion that if someone would make the special interests go away something called the general interest would assert itself and all would be harmony. What is the general interest? There is no formula in any society for discovering it except through the pull and haul of groups in the political process. The contest, it is true, is unequal, but neither does any formula yet exist that will enable weakness to prevail over strength.

Closely tied to our insight into practical politics, stressed in the preceding chapter, is our understanding of how opinions are formed and how they affect passing events.

CHAPTER 26

MAKING SENSE OUT OF PROPAGANDA

Ralph O. Nafziger
Director, School of Journalism

Is propaganda important in the making of social decisions? The answer, of course, is yes.

Should it be important? One of the reasons why we are discussing this question is that it represents a vexatious problem to all of us and one which none of us has resolved to his satisfaction. We haven't resolved it because we know few facts about the effects of pressure groups and propaganda. We also believe that our social problem should be concerned not so much with what people can be persuaded to accept, but with what corresponds to the facts and the truth as we see them. Also, we have been unable to determine a means for ridding ourselves of the sinister connotations which have become attached to the words "pressure group" and "propaganda."

This topic is important because of the chronic anxieties that many of us believe are loosening public faith in personal and intellectual freedoms. Yet, for a long time our society has thrived on controversy, and we cannot afford arbitrarily to crack down on free discussion simply because we don't like what some men are saying or because some men and some organizations are abusing their freedom in this country by trying to cripple or to destroy us.

In the meantime we are being bombarded as never before with all kinds of impressions and viewpoints. There are many reasons for this.

In the first place, our social needs change from time to time, and consequently the "ins" and the "outs"--the advocates of the status quo and the advocates of change--will argue about social and political values and will struggle for power. Our society requires understandings of one sort or another, but these understandings are accompanied by sets of misunderstandings, points of real contention, needs for new understandings in the light of new developments. And these changing needs stimulate widespread discussion and argument.

As a result, our society stimulates argument and facilitates special pleading. It likely wouldn't be a democracy if this were not the case. We have come to accept contention among competing groups in our communities as a manifestation of the liberties we enjoy. In other words, we believe that the dangers which lie in a struggle among competing viewpoints and power groups are less sinister than the danger which lies in a centralized or arbitrary control of opinion.

In a democratic society, also, the extent and limits of freedom are determined basically by public opinion. To maintain our freedoms our people must believe in them and, if necessary, be urged and stimulated to believe in them. But there are many interpretations of "freedom" and "freedoms," and the public is subjected to pressure from all kinds of interpreters.

At the same time, leadership in our country depends on public approval and therefore seeks to win and to maintain approval. The same is true of those who seek to assume leadership. Since opinion leadership in the United States is diffused and decentralized (fortunately!), the battle of words goes on and on. This give and take is a safety valve or at least an outlet for the common man who fears what he does not understand and who distrusts leaders that do not prepare him for forthcoming issues and troubles.

In addition, the effectiveness of our society depends in part on the extent to which we get a reasonably correct view of the world. Most of the information which we get of our country and the world comes by way of middlemen--media men--because we cannot observe and know independently of them what goes on. The propagandist knows that too. He hopes to be included among the middlemen.

Meanwhile, we assume that our citizens will, if they are supplied with adequate information, use good judgment and make wise decisions about public affairs. In detail the theory does not always work out well. In the first place, we don't always get a balanced supply of information about public affairs. Moreover, many people do not care to be informed about public affairs, have no particular convictions about public affairs, or are literally impervious to information about the public's business which is brought to their attention through the information channels. On the other hand, pressure groups and propagandists feed on public apathy, for they know that many people must be stimulated to act and to give consent to one side or another on public issues.

It is not surprising if we are inclined to exaggerate at times the power which pressure groups and propaganda exert. Our predispositions based on our environment, our educational background, our standard of living, and other factors have a bearing on the extent to which we approve or disapprove of appeals from special pleaders. In summary, we have in this country fertile soil for the development of pressure groups and special pleaders of all kinds.

To talk about pressure groups and propagandists, however, as something foreign to us or alien to our society is to talk in a vacuum. We do not propose blindly to accept them and their viewpoints. Instead, we must evaluate carefully the evidence they submit to us. We must read and listen to our information channels with care and discrimination. We must retain our confidence in the freedom to discuss, to argue, and to mend our ways. For pressure groups and propagandists apparently are here to stay, the sinister and the public-spirited alike. They require study. We need studies on the social significance of propaganda, or better yet we need studies which will give us better information than we have today on how ideas spread and are spread in this and other countries.

* * * * *

So let us turn briefly to propaganda--the word that means different things to different people. Propaganda is essentially concerned with the propagation or dissemination of ideas. It stems from a desire to influence the minds of others, to seek gains of one sort or another. It applies to various methods used to influence attitudes and public opinion and to stimulate people to action.

The simplest procedure here would be to deal only with the menace of propaganda and pressure groups and to suggest a pat solution. But such an approach would not be realistic. We shall be wiser to discuss propaganda in a broad sense.

"Good" people as well as "bad" people use propaganda. People who profess high standards of ethics and others who care nothing about ethical principles employ propaganda to promote causes in which they are interested. This makes propaganda a troublesome word. To many of us it is all bad, a despised business of hoodwinking other people, involving what someone has called the "dictatorship of palaver." It is busy changing attitudes when it should be clarifying them. It attempts to confuse people and to prepare them for the kill.

But propaganda may also be used sincerely to help society. Most of us believe that propaganda in behalf of vaccination is not bad. Our government believes that the Voice of America is good propaganda. All of us have trouble drawing a line between propaganda which we don't want and propaganda which we do want. Most of us would like perhaps to define the word narrowly and to confine it to the kind of propaganda we don't like. Such narrow interpretations define propaganda as something concealed, emotional in appeal, controversial.

Is it always concealed? Not necessarily.

Is it always based purely on irrational or emotional appeals? Not always.

Is it always connected with controversial matters? Surely not in the case of the Red Cross or any other charity.

Is it all-powerful, as we are sometimes led to believe? Apparently not. It is a question whether any country has ever been won over by propaganda alone. In practice, has Soviet Russia ever won over a country merely by employing propaganda alone? Did the Nazis? No. Propaganda feeds on events which it can exploit. It builds on hopes and desires which it reinforces and accelerates. It is used by governments as one form of weapon against their enemies and opponents. It is not generally a weapon used independently of other means--like force--to win battles. As a matter of fact, propaganda is now a formal branch of government, used to explain government agencies to the home public. In addition it is used by governments to promote national interests abroad. The United States is now heavily engaged in this enterprise.

Our support of the Voice of America has wavered at times, but over a period of years its volume and range have been greatly increased. We contend that our radio Voice follows the "strategy of truth," that we do not propose to deceive or intentionally to mislead our listeners abroad. It is still propaganda, however, which we are carrying on because we believe that we must defend ourselves and explain ourselves on the propaganda front--whether we like the game or not--just as we must sometimes meet artillery on the military front.

Indicative of our purposeful use of propaganda abroad is the record of our activities in one recent year. Some 40 transmitters were used by the Voice of America to send out messages over short wave to other countries. Seventy programs a day in 25 different languages contributed to our Voice. Local relays carried programs beyond the reach of our central Voice. Thousands of foreign newspapers received our press releases, and 75,000 opinion leaders in foreign lands had access to these releases. A wireless bulletin went by radio teletype to more than 60 U.S. missions abroad. Printed letters, pamphlets, and photographs were issued by us, and thousands of subscriptions to American periodicals were given free to key persons. It was reported that 134 information centers attempted to distribute information from America.

It is clear that propaganda is a part of our present-day social and political organization. The question that concerns us ultimately is what various propagandists are doing and what the objectives and consequences of their activities are.

Thus we object particularly to the deceitful forms of propaganda which are personified in our minds by certain evil geniuses like those who have advocated the "big lie." We object to immoral, unethical means for justifying ends, to the strategy of division, the propaganda of fear and defeatism, the honeyed words of appeasement, the play on our emotions, the attempts to hit us in soft and blind spots and all of the sinister forms of misrepresentation which we have observed in recent times in this and other countries.

We object justifiably to these activities. We are inclined to counterattack too. It is important that we try to recognize and to meet propaganda that is hostile to our principles, lest it blot out the evidence of genuine progress toward social justice and other socially useful objectives which we have achieved. We hope also that we can continue to see enemy propagandists fall apart against the weight of opinion, as has happened before, because they cannot justify themselves in the end.

I hope that most of us will agree that we must move strongly against actual sabotage and espionage by Communists or any other ill-wishers who hope through conspiracy to destroy our society. But we must not overestimate the power of propaganda itself. We must be watchful of tendencies to silence by police control freedom of discussion among persons who oppose our views. We must combat alike the conspiracies against our government and those who tell us that we should despair, that we are weak, that the country is in a bad way. For the evidence is overwhelming that we are strong, that we have reason to be confident of ourselves, and that our liberties are not liabilities.

The purposive propagandists don't like to have us think. They like to tell us, as you know, that "this is what you want. Here it is. Act on it. Our food is good for you. So eat it! (Don't think about the merits of the case.) Our view of government is good for you. So join us!"

This is only an example of the vulnerable spots in us that the propagandist hits. He has profited and expanded his effects by taking advantage of the rise in literacy and popular education in this and other countries, the spread of manhood suffrage, the expansion of industry, the rise in our standard of living, the development of new means of communication, and the newly acquired insight into means for getting people to respond to all kinds of appeals.

He has taken advantage also of the fallibility of our language, our inability to comprehend information when it is called to our attention, and our lazy reading and listening habits.

We forget how elusive words can be, and we don't always take time to understand what is being communicated to us. The newspaper items are not always clear and precise. Someone could use a news story, if it were considered important enough to exploit, to spread a completely warped interpretation of events, knowing that few readers would go back to the item or could recall clearly what was actually reported. There are many persons who will take advantage of our apathies by selecting for us or interpreting for us what we get to see and hear, in order to affect our attitudes. The facts in the materials we read and hear don't always speak for themselves. The special pleaders know these failings in us and make the most of them.

What does this imply?

It means that all through our school system we face the task of teaching people how to read and how to appraise reports of events. What evidence we have of people's reading habits seems to show that the reading of articles about public affairs and public ideas tends to increase with the amount of schooling which the readers have. That speaks well for the schools. It suggests, however, that we haven't learned --and the newspapers haven't learned--how to reach effectively much of our public which needs to be stimulated in a democracy to attend to information on public affairs. And we haven't learned how to train most newspaper readers sufficiently to recognize the words of the special pleader.

Our choice is not, however, between propaganda and no propaganda. Our choice lies somewhere between diversity of propaganda--freedom of propaganda, if you wish--and the tendency in the world to impose only one channel of propaganda on the public. For propaganda works best where one channel or one source has a monopoly, where there are no competing propagandas, and where censorship can enforce a concentration on a single stream of ideas. The menace of some forms of propaganda is real, but the right to discuss, to argue, to propagandize, is a privilege which is, as a matter of principle, altogether preferable to regulations that would decide who shall and who shall not have the right to be heard.

The suggestion has sometimes been made by persons who have been irritated and alarmed by the activities of propagandists that the special pleaders in our society be suppressed. But majority opinion for generations in this country has believed it unwise to protect people against propaganda by police action. We haven't been willing to decide who shall determine which propaganda must be suppressed by law and which may be heard. We have believed that suppression of propaganda, short of treason or a conspiracy against our form of government, would fail to solve our problems and would be damaging to our national vitality.

Our ideal for special pleading is the dissemination of <u>conclusions</u> developed after free discussion. If a cause is made attractive to the public, if the object is believed by the public to be sound, it will gain acceptance faster than if it merely is made to <u>seem</u> attractive after the manner of the old-time press agent.

Let us remember also that propaganda alone does not govern public opinion. Factual knowledge governs it too. We can continue to apply critical questions to pleas for our support on social issues. We can ask of special pleaders: What are they saying? Is it true as far as my sources of information go? Does it seem to be soundly based?

For what purpose is he talking? Who really cares? Who benefits? In whose interest? Why are they talking?

Will action on it benefit the sponsors alone or also those to whom it is directed? What is the effect? Who gets what and how as a consequence?

Who opposes it?

Let us admit that truth doesn't always win over falsehood and that freedom of discussion leaves open the gates for selfish and greedy interests. But we can recall a few oft-quoted lines from Walt Whitman:

> We know well enough that the workings of democracy are not always justifiable, in every trivial point. But the great winds that purify the air, without which nature would flag into ruin--are they to be condemned because a tree is prostrated here and there, in their course?

MAKING SENSE OUT OF PROPAGANDA

We can oppose false information because it is false, not simply because someone is concerned about the effect it may produce. It is particularly the authoritarian or the totalitarian government that talks most volubly about the effect of so-called "bad" information. In this connection we may recall the press agreements in the 1930's which were urged and fostered in Europe by dictatorships to control what they called information injurious to their countries and their leaders. We may recall also the inability of the UNESCO subcommittee on freedom of information and the press to reach agreement because of demands of Soviet Russia and other states for more--not fewer--restrictions on free and equal access to information and free distribution of information across national boundaries.

Finally we can find comfort too in the evidence that propaganda ultimately must prove its points: that progress, fulfillment of promises, and victory are the bases of successful propaganda in the long run.

The menace of propaganda can best be met, in summary, by keeping our information channels clear and open.

We must resist the creeping paralysis of censorship that throughout the world has reached far beyond security requirements. Free access to information at the source of information facilitates free discussion of public issues.

Keep open information channels which are independent of direct government control.

Maintain cheap rates for transmitting information within and among countries.

Demand more--not less--information. Demand progressively better performance by press, radio and other mass media of information, performance which will win and maintain the sympathy and loyalty of the public.

Publicize the activities of the hired hands of propaganda sources. Lobbying is now subject to regulation in many of our state capitals and the federal government now requires the registration of propagandists for foreign countries. Reputable newspapers now attribute propaganda statements to the specific sources.

Do whatever we can to see to it that our governmental, social, and economic institutions and our information channels perform in a manner which will win and maintain the sympathy and loyalty of the public.

Freedom of expression and resistance to propaganda dangerous to our institutions are more likely to be maintained, censorship is less likely to increase, and the gulf between our leaders and people is less likely to widen, if the people are not made apathetic to public issues by unpopular performance of our social and political institutions.

There is no known panacea for the problems we have been discussing. If, however, we maintain a spirit of inquiry, tolerance of many viewpoints and a "show me" spirit, we have an excellent chance to solve our problems in the future as we have done in the past.

As this chapter points out, probably ninety-five per cent of the new ideas presented to us are fool ideas. But no one has learned to separate reliably the good ideas from the bad. This is why the intellectual freedom guaranteed by our Bill of Rights is a precious essential to the wise conduct of our public affairs. On the other hand, intellectual freedom is not an absolute. It has its limits, and this chapter suggests some of them.

CHAPTER 27

INTELLECTUAL FREEDOM — ITS SOCIAL USE*

Mark H. Ingraham
Dean, College of Letters and Science

At the outset I wish to make it clear that this discussion is strictly limited to a small portion of the subject of freedom. Obviously, this limitation is necessary if one considers our psychological attitude toward freedom, the history of the struggle for freedom, and the measures we use to guarantee it to our citizens.

---

* *A considerable portion of this chapter has appeared elsewhere, in particular in the BULLETIN of the American Association of University Professors, Vol. XXVI, No. 1, February, 1940; and in the BADGER QUARTERLY (A University of Wisconsin Publication), Vol. 10, No. 2, December, 1947.*

There are few things which seem as essential to the individual as does freedom. It is, along with good health, security, or affection, instinctively desired by almost all. No one can see even a trapped bird without realizing this. The child who instinctively pulls away from the hand that would guide it safely across the street is showing this love of freedom. One of society's most used punitive measures is imprisonment. The final degeneration of personality caused by incarceration is the loss of the love of freedom when the prisoner "regained my freedom with a sigh." The objectives of the Allies were expressed in terms of freedom. The history of freedom is in a certain sense the history of mankind.

We say that freedom is a part of the American atmosphere but freedom is not like air, easily attainable by all. Many persons seem unable to use their own freedom without denying it to others. Property rights are both an assertion and a denial of freedom. So is a dictatorship. It is unshared freedom carried to an evil extreme. Thus the many have had to provide measures to protect their freedom from the powerful few, but no less has society been forced to find means to protect the individuals from the dominance of the many.

This book presents in essence the problems brought upon society by its scholars and technologists and the opportunities afforded to society by the work of these same persons. This chapter therefore deals chiefly with intellectual freedom, the freedom of thought, especially of trained scholars--it is sometimes called academic freedom. It does not deal with this freedom as chiefly the personal right or privilege of the individual but as a means of making the community of scholars useful to society. It also deals with the means of protecting and using this freedom.

What follows is an attempt to answer briefly the following questions:

To what degree has the human intellectual enterprise been worth while?

To what degree does its future value depend upon intellectual freedom?

Since no freedom is absolute, how far should society go in granting intellectual freedom?

What are the means society should use to protect this freedom and, where necessary, to control it?

What are the individual's obligations in the use of his freedom?

What is the relation of intellectual freedom to democratic control on the one hand and orderly progress on the other?

The basic intellectual disciplines are sometimes divided into the natural sciences, the social studies, and the humanities. These overlap and there are also gaps between them. The division, however, is useful to our thought.

The greatest present danger of disaster and the greatest opportunity stem from the same fact, the amazing progress of the scientist in making possible the control of nature. Our greatest fear today is caused by the possible destructive use of atomic energy and of microorganisms. This danger is not only that of war, but also the power for evil that may be concentrated in the hands of individuals or groups of individuals, power of insane destruction, power of military dictatorship. Man can do more to destroy life than ever before and as yet we have little in the way of social controls that we did not have before the last two wars, except fear, and fear has always been a tragically weak reed upon which to lean.

On the other hand, there is a different side to the picture. The conquest of sources of energy has till now been the road of progress. Slavery was doomed as much by the steam engine and the electric turbine as by the moral sentiment of the West. We do little enough to feed the world, but the tragic famines of Europe and Asia would not even be touched by us except for modern transportation. The picture of bacteriological warfare is scarcely more horrible than the plagues of cholera or the Black Death actually have been. The accounts of physics, chemistry, mathematics, and bacteriology with the human race still have a favorable balance.

The opportunities are vast. Controlled use of atomic energy will inevitably be economically valuable, while the medical and scientific use of radioactive isotopes of various elements is already proving to be a marvelous tool. The knowledge that makes biological warfare possible also makes possible the control of disease. Life is being prolonged. If you want to see a glum group, talk with actuaries about their annuity business. Further progress is expected. Life-insurance companies are hedging against how much longer they expect you and I will live after we retire as compared with how long we would live if we had now reached the age for retirement. With proper social controls the human race already knows enough to live in a condition of health and plenty that has been unknown to any previous era.

I must be honest. If you asked me whether I am glad that the physicists were able to produce the chain reaction that makes the atomic bomb possible, I would have to say "No." I hoped that they would find it impossible to do so. Man is a very unreliable psychological animal to be allowed to play with such toys. But also remember the choice we had was not between the bomb and no bomb but between science and no science. Among the forces that created science were human curiosity, human imagination, and human freedom. Those forces could not have come to the threshold of the knowledge of atomic structure and stopped short of that knowledge. Those forces could not have created the science of immunology, of antibiotics, of preventive medicine, and not have known how to produce anthrax, psittacosis, and botulism.

Certainly at no time since Galileo could the progress of science have been checked. If it could have been done, would it have been well? By no means! Even today science taken as a whole must be one of the things for which we are thankful.

There can be very honest doubt whether our social progress has kept pace with our technology. There can be no doubt however that we have made great social progress. Social progress is not, to the same degree as scientific progress, a matter of accretion. Although it is based on the analysis of facts, its expression is behavior and in such behavior there can be long or short periods of retrogression.

The decline of Roman civilization seems to have been one such long period. Whether our last two wars marked a short decline or the beginning of a long one we cannot as yet say. However it would seem clear that even with these setbacks the history of the human race has on the whole been one of an upward climb in its social behavior. We are again trying to reaffirm the great tradition of the unity of Western civilization and, in fact, develop a tradition of the unity of civilization as a whole. We have not given up the development of the religious tradition of the brotherhood of man. The very fact that when we wish to condemn people we speak of them as barbarians indicates that we believe we have risen above the level of our not too remote ancestors.

And in the realm of taste and artistic expression, in spite of the neon light and the juke box, the human race has acquired a marvelous heritage. It is appreciating that heritage and adding to it.

In spite of much that can justify current pessimism we must conclude that we are better off today because of the intellectual leaders of the past and present than we would be without their works. I have perhaps labored this point too much but there is a wave of anti-intellectualism among the abler, but not the ablest, persons which must be faced. The man of push and executive ability does not always have deep understanding and sometimes resents those who have.

* * * * *

To what degree does the future value of the human intellectual enterprise depend upon freedom?

Intellectual freedom gives to the scientist the right to examine whatever topic seems to him to be of interest, to announce whatever facts he finds, and to bring forward whatever hypotheses he believes will best correlate these facts. These are basic elements in the scientific process. Science would have been impoverished if it had not been for those who were determined to satisfy their curiosity whether or not they could forsee the applications of their finding. It is, of course, also true that many basic contributions derive from the work of the applied scientist who clearly foresees at least some of the results which arise from the problems on which he works.

Science is of little use if the scientist is limited in the publication of his data or in his full freedom for development of the theories based thereon. Efforts have frequently been made to deny these freedoms to the scientist. From Galileo to Darwin the road has been a thorny one. Persecution in a violent sense has only been a small part of the limitation placed upon scientists. The lack of support for basic science, the denial of publication facilities, the jeers of one's colleagues, have probably in total amounted to a greater limitation than political or religious bans. Perhaps no value has been more frequently claimed for academic freedom than that it permits the publication of scientific truth.

Also vital and more difficult to obtain is intellectual freedom in the realm of the social studies. Most of us seem to like novelty in small things and seem to resent it in important matters. Perhaps this is wise. Variety is pleasant, but major readjustments are not only difficult; they are often disastrous.

I firmly believe that the new ideas that are called fool notions in ninety-five per cent of the cases are fool notions. I have no sympathy with a new suggestion just because some other idea that worked out well was once new and scoffed at.

I reiterate, at least ninety-five per cent of the so-called fool ideas are just that, but the other five per cent contain the vitamins of our civilization. I do not believe that our intellectual chemistry has reached the point where we can eliminate all the impurities from our food and still leave in the elements of life. I believe it is to our advantage to arouse people to proclaim their faith so that we may use in each generation those new ideas which are necessary for progress and may trust the common sense of the listener and the competition of other doctrines to eliminate whatever is false.

I take this rather uncompromising stand not because I believe the teacher should personally be an extraordinarily privileged character, but because I believe scholarship can be of the maximum use only when it is given the greatest freedom of expression. Frequently I have heard it asked, "You don't really think Professor Jones has a right to make a fool of himself with impunity, do you?" I think the answer is clear: "No. I am not at all interested in Professor Jones' right to make a fool of himself, but I do think I have the right to have Professor Jones permitted to make a fool of himself." It is terribly difficult to distinguish between the 10 persons who because of stupidity, maladjustment, desire for notoriety, or pure cussedness want to change the status quo to something worse, and the one seer who gives us a real glimpse of how to make the world a better home for our race. For the ignorant, freedom of speech is the privilege of the speaker: for the wise it is the privilege of the listener. The world that prosecutes the fool will too often persecute the sage. I would rather live in a world with both the fool and the sage than with neither. We must, therefore, in order to preserve the seeds of progress, also submit the chaff to the process of "winnowing and sifting."

Perhaps equally vital is freedom in the matter of the humanities. Here not only the right to publish the truth and to proclaim one's belief as to how mankind should behave must be preserved, but also the values of diversity. Our cultural heritage is rich largely because it is diverse, expressing as it does not only the differences of peoples and places and times, but also the differences of individuals. My own belief is that far too great emphasis has been placed on the proclamation of truth and the protection of progress in the discussion of matters of academic freedom. And too little emphasis has been given to the enrichment of our culture through differences, and to the dignity of the individual through our recognition of his right to be an individual.

* * * * *

Freedoms are not absolute. They could not be. Absolute freedom is self-contradictory since it implies the right to enslave others. I merely state that in my opinion we are at present in more danger from suppressing freedom, especially intellectual freedom, than we are from its abuse, in spite of the latter danger being very real. I am glad that there are constitutional safeguards to our freedom against even the democratic process.

I believe in democracy. It is part of the framework of opportunity. Yet I do not believe in democracy as strongly as I believe in the fundamental freedoms. The Bill of Rights was enacted not to protect us just from the tyranny of a king, or the monied class, or the military caste, but to protect us against infringement of certain fundamental rights by anyone--even by the majority or their representatives. I have known administrators who believe that membership in a teachers' union is sufficient cause for the dismissal of a professor. I have seen legislators, citizens, and students uphold the expression of certain opinions while advocating the suppression of others. Even the Puritans were unwilling to grant freedom to others. Bigots persecuted Baptists and Quakers: the superstitious in Salem hung men and women as witches. We sing of the "pilgrim feet whose stern, impassioned stress a thoroughfare for freedom beat." We must admit that often there was more sternness and passion and less freedom in those feet.

We must not for a moment assume that everyone favors intellectual freedom, academic or otherwise, yet the trend to intellectual freedom is ever present. No rights are absolute, but the limitations on freedom of speech, for example, should be only those that are clearly necessary. Here I shall remind you of the masterful opinions of those great jurists, Holmes and Brandeis, which held that even speech inciting disorder was not illegal unless there was a "clear and present danger" of such disorder actually being caused by the speech.

It is difficult to answer our fourth question concerning the means society should use to protect this freedom and to control abuses against it. It is particularly difficult because historically the means of protection have been built up to protect against the abuse on the part of powerful individuals. Although this is still needed, society must find a way to protect the individual's freedom from the danger of abuse by democratic action. It should be remembered that it was not Pilate, but the people, who demanded that Jesus be crucified.

As our first line of protection come our constitution and our common law as interpreted by our courts. Second come certain traditional freedoms such as recognized by our strongest universities and colleges in the matter of academic freedom and by our best newspapers in the matter of freedom of the press. In educational institutions, in order to protect academic freedom, the tenure of a scholar in his academic position is recognized. I quote from a statement approved in 1940 by the American Association of University Professors and by the Association of American Colleges:

> Institutions of higher education are conducted for the common good and not to further the interests of either the individual teacher or the institution as a whole. The common good depends upon the free search for truth and free exposition. Academic freedom is essential to these purposes-- purposes which apply to both teaching and research. Freedom in research is fundamental to the protection of the right of the teacher in teaching and of the student to freedom in learning. It carries with these rights duties that are correlative.

Tenure is the means to certain ends. On the one hand it is the means to freedom of teaching and research and extramural activities and on the other hand the means to a sufficient degree of economic security to make the profession attractive to men and women of ability. Freedom and economic security, hence tenure, are indispensable to the success of an institution in fulfilling its obligations to its students and to society.

Thus the universities recognize that the teacher is entitled to full freedom in research and to the publication of results of research, that he is entitled to freedom in the classroom in the discussion of his subject, and that he is entitled in the community to the privileges of a citizen.

Basically, however, we must attain a much higher recognition on the part of the public not only of the individual's rights, but of the value of supporting the work of persons with opinions and tastes different from those of the majority whenever it is clear that this work is being carried out in what the worker believes to be the interest of the public.

If as great freedom is granted to the individual as I believe desirable, the individual should be careful not to abuse these privileges. If the teacher is furnished a platform he should remember that it is more than a soap box, and that a member of a learned profession has special obligations to the community. All of us should remember that the first competition between fact and fancy should be in the scientist's mind, that the first analysis of the effect of a social program should be in the mind of its promulgator, and that the first expression of good taste is the refusal to bring forth trash. Moreover, if the methods of freedom are to produce the greatest good, freedom itself must be used with great courtesy.

Perhaps discourtesy is an even more dangerous abuse of free speech than is evil propaganda. The constant rudeness to which public servants are submitted must dull their sensitivities and discourage many men of the highest qualifications from entering or continuing in public life. We may disagree with our political leaders or even criticize the effectiveness of their work without subjecting them to vilification.

The president of the United States, the United States senators and representatives, the governors and legislators of our states should be accorded the consideration, the courtesy and the respect that both their offices and their services deserve. We also witness with sorrow the discourtesy in our political representatives to our public servants and to our private citizens. This appears to be a growing evil and one that sometimes goes beyond mere discourtesy to protected defamation. American life would have a better tone and in the long run the American people would be better served if courtesy were the rule. However, it is custom, not police power, that must enforce such a rule.

* * * * *

I turn to our last question. Our principles of freedom are accompanied by supporting and in some cases competing principles. Freedom as described above is one of the tools of human progress even if in a certain sense it is also one of the aims. There are other tools for human progress. One of them is the democratic method of government. Another is the process of orderly and legal change.

The world's opportunity for progress depends upon a keener appreciation of methods. Consider these three: the method of democratic control; the method of freedom, especially intellectual freedom; and the method of legal and orderly procedure. This country to a greater extent than most has all three, but not to a great enough extent, and in particular they are not used intelligently enough. The interrelations are not understood and the conflicts between the three are not fully analyzed.

The rule of the people, the rule of the majority, is by and large the best rule we know in practice. It has many drawbacks. It is not swift in making detailed decisions; it is not analytic in considering complex problems; it is frequently abandoned to gain some limited end. It is amazing, however, how effective it is with even a relatively inexperienced people, and in most difficult situations. For instance, in war the democracies seem to bewail their inefficiency, and win the war. And democracies do move forward with the aims of the people in mind in a way that no stratified rule has ever done.

Above both the democratic method and our untrammeled freedom, I place at the present time the necessity for legal and orderly procedure. Let me give two illustrations. I cannot see that the doctrines of socialism and of communism are very different. I do not happen to agree with either. However, as they have developed in this country, I believe that the Socialist Party and the Communist Party are poles apart. The Socialists wish to persuade America to follow an economic course far from that which it has in the past and far from that which the majority now wish to follow. Yet in general they use legitimate means to try for their goal. I happen to disagree with their perennial presidential candidate, Norman Thomas. However, I also believe he is a great American. The means he uses to forward his beliefs are the democratic method of the ballot box, the use of his right to free speech, and respect for the laws of his country and for his fellow citizens.

The difficulty with Communists is not their economic doctrine, which they have a right to hold and proclaim, but their methods of forwarding that doctrine by following the dictates of a foreign power, by party discipline that is the negation of intellectual freedom, and by willingness to use illegal means to forward their ends. Economic radicalism, no matter how we disagree with it, has a right to be debated openly and considered fairly. But I believe it is of utmost importance to distinguish between opposition to economic radicalism and our abhorrence of disloyalty to our country, our contempt for the abdication of intellectual individuality, and our determination to enforce our laws, such as that dealing with perjury. We must insist on orderly and legal

INTELLECTUAL FREEDOM-ITS SOCIAL USE

methods of change. We must also insist on orderly and legal methods of resisting change.

This does not mean that I believe revolution has never been justified. But I do firmly believe that our form of government provides for orderly change to such an extent that here and now there is no possible excuse for the disruption and misery that extralegal means entail.

The second illustration of legal methods that I wish to consider is the method of due process in the administration of justice. It should be remembered that the protection of due process is protection for the innocent, not for the guilty. It must be applied to all in order to protect the innocent. Lynchings are evil whether they arise from the vile motive of race hatred or from the highest moral indignation, or from a combination of these. They are evil not because we would protect the degenerate from summary justice, but because society must be protected from a process that can bring cruel injustice to the innocent.

Consider for a moment the first chapter of Genesis: "In the beginning God created the heaven and the earth, and the earth was without form and void." After the earth was formed and ordered on engineering principles and populated on biological principles, man was created. Chaos presents an opportunity only to the Deity. Man's opportunities arise from an ordered universe. We cannot build the future by wiping clean the slate upon which the past has written.

This is not a judgment for all times and all places. But in America of the present I believe the method of orderly and legal procedure is primary of the three great methods I have discussed; that of intellectual freedom which under our basic law should have complete protection is second; and that of democratic rule, a very important third. All of these methods, however, are valid only if they are infused with moral purpose set in a great moral tradition.

We need knowledge but knowledge must include the knowledge of good and evil; methods must be directed by good will and foresight; culture must be spiritual as well as intellectual. Opportunity arises not just from the traditions we inherit but from a selection of those that should survive and a suppression of those that should perish. There must be a sense of values to inform the whole.

Human values are the basis of human actions and are therefore at the end of this book, although in importance they might well have come first. Their statement here is meant not to close discussion, but to renew it. This chapter brings up to date an idea once stated in these cryptic words: "...whosoever shall lose his life...shall find it." Quite simply: the way for a man to realize the best in himself is to lose himself in his interest in human welfare.

CHAPTER 28

"LIFE, LIBERTY, AND THE PURSUIT OF HAPPINESS"

A. Campbell Garnett
Department of Philosophy

One of the tasks of the philosopher is to discover and state the fundamental principles of human rights and obligations. On the broad issues of man's basic obligations there is a large measure of agreement, that there exist duties of two main kinds: Duties to one's fellows to fulfill the requirements of a generally satisfactory social order; duties to oneself to fulfill the requirements of maintaining integrity of personality and, with it, the basic conditions of true personal happiness. Our enquiry therefore should be directed to the question as to what is involved in each of these.

The principles of social order I wish to point out are so broad and fundamental that they will all be found embodied in the Declaration of Human Rights drawn up by the United Nations.

Social order may be maintained in one of two ways-- by force and authority or by free acceptance and co-operation. Every social order that has ever existed has combined both elements. Every society has to choose to emphasize one or the other. At different stages of development, or in the face of different problems, the emphasis is apt to change. There can be no doubt, however, that the choice of American society, and that of all the democracies, is for an emphasis on free acceptance and co-operation rather than authority. Our problem therefore is to decide what are the rights and duties that must be recognized if we are to maintain as much individual freedom as possible.

A free society must be one in which every person, so far as he is reasonable, accepts the rules as the sort of rules he wants to see generally required of his fellows and which he therefore must agree should be required of himself. But this means it must be a society which guarantees to all its members those rights which are essential to the full development of personality. A free society must be one which removes fear and frustration, prevents exploitation, and secures for each individual the opportunity for the full development of his personality.

Our problem is to consider the fundamental needs of personal development and state the system of rights which it requires. This leads us to see that the social ethic of a free society requires the recognition of the following 12 fundamental human rights:

(1) Security from physical violence. It has long been recognized as the primary duty of the state to protect its citizens from injury to life and limb, and the primary duty of the citizen to refrain from physical injury of his fellows. It includes also, of course, the right to freedom from im-

prisonment or other punishment except for violation of the law. It does not, however, deny to the state the right to call upon its citizens to risk their lives in common defense. It rather implies the duty of the citizen to join in such defense when called upon.

(2) Security from false defamation. Next to life itself, and above almost everything else, a man values his good name. Character assassination is a despicable form of crime. Yet it is something from which it is difficult to protect the individual by law. Our libel laws could probably be strengthened with advantage. Our political life also needs to be guarded carefully against this cruel but often subtle violation of the rights of the individual. We need to cultivate a public opinion which will recognize slander so readily for the revolting thing it is that slander, even when it is not open to action for libel, can no longer be made to pay political dividends.

(3) Security of livelihood. This is the right of access to the means of production and the right to an opportunity to earn a living. A social order which does not secure this right to the citizen cannot survive as a free society. It will inevitably be forced to resort to regimentation and rule by violence to keep those that suffer in idleness in subjection. It will collapse into Fascism or Communism. In our free economy the land and factories become the private property of a limited number of citizens. We preserve this system because of the great capacity it has demonstrated to produce goods in abundance. But it is subject to dislocations and stresses which at most times exclude some from the opportunity to earn a living and sometimes for long periods exclude large numbers. It is surely only just that, out of the abundance the system is able to create, it should provide for these casualties. There is always useful work in society to be done, and when our economy does not, through individual enterprise, provide productive opportunity for all, then we should recognize it as our collective responsibility to provide a livelihood in useful work for those whom the privately controlled economy cannot employ.

(4) Security of property. This right is almost as old and well recognized as the right to security of life and limb. Without it there can be no orderly relation of human activity to the material things by which we live. To fail to uphold it is to invite chaos. Property, of course, may be held by private individuals and groups or by public bodies, and the conditions under which it is held and protected must be defined by law and are subject to change by law. Property is not above the law. It is an institution created and sustained by collective action for the common good and can be changed by the same means for the same purpose. But violent and revolutionary change would constitute a moral violation of the implicit contract of the state with the individual, a contract which sets up the conditions under which the individual may acquire property and is promised security in possession of it. This is the moral wrong of such revolutionary action as is proposed by Communism. The state has a right to transfer property to collective ownership, but if it does so it must do it by constitutional processes and must recognize the right of the citizen to compensation.

(5) Security from want in time of misfortune. The relieving of want due to misfortune has long been looked upon as an act of charity, a gratuitous expression of human good will and sympathy. It may be charity from the standpoint of the individual, Gradually we are coming to recognize, however, that from the standpoint of the community it is simply an act of justice. The individual has a right to expect that the community will come to his aid in time of misfortune. This is implicit in the very idea of a free society as one of the principles which all freely accept as most conducive to the welfare of all. It is impossible for all to acquire sufficient property, or to obtain sufficient income, to insure themselves against all the accidents of life. If, therefore, a free society does not guarantee such protection to its members we can expect that those who are unable to protect themselves will be ready to purchase such security at the cost of some limitation of their own social freedom and that of those who deny it to them.

(6) Freedom in pursuit of employment and choice of avocation. This is simply the rejection of slavery in all its forms, a freedom which this country has established at terrible cost.

(7) Freedom to marry and raise a family. This is a right which is rarely denied, though it is rightly hedged with some restrictions seeking to ensure that it shall not be exercised without due sense of the social responsibilities involved. It is also restricted in some countries which have a caste system and by some countries, such as South Africa, and some American states which are afflicted with race prejudice. The most serious barriers to exercise of this right, however, are not political or social, but economic. It is a bitter joke to say that men and women are free to marry and raise a family if their earnings are not sufficient to keep in health and strength the children that are born to them.

(8) Freedom of religion and conscience. Whatever a man believes to be his duty, to God or man, he ought to do. There is no principle upon which ethical reflection is clearer than this. It is quite compatible with a recognition that one's ethical and religious views may be mistaken and that one should constantly subject them to open-minded and critical reflection. But in these matters one must be true to one's own convictions or moral degeneration sets in. To force a person to violate his conscience is to force an injury to his moral life. Conscience is violated when a person is required to do what he believes is wrong (as when a pacifist is required to go to war). It is violated when he is required to refrain from doing what he believes he ought to do--as when restrictions are placed on "heretical" forms of worship. Such violations of freedom of conscience are only justifiable when to allow that freedom would involve a more important violation of the rights of others.

(9) Freedom of speech and of assembly. These rights are corollaries of the right of freedom of conscience. There is no freedom of conscience if a man may not speak the truth as he sees it, and if those who wish to hear him may not

assemble to do so and to discuss and formulate any plans of action within the law. Further, no one can be expected to give his free consent and support to a social order which forbids him to use the methods of human communication and peaceful persuasion in pursuit of his own interests. These rights have therefore long been recognized as fundamental to the structure of a free society. They can only be justifiably restricted when used to incite some to invade the rights of others.

(10) Equality before the law.

(11) Equality of basic political rights. These two principles of equality have long been recognized as essentials of a free society. No one can be expected freely to accept and co-operate in a social order which arbitrarily discriminates against him.

(12) Adequate educational opportunity. This is a right which every man who loves his children will demand for them. And it is clearly in the interests of society as a whole to see that it is granted. Good brains are the most precious possession of any community, and society is the loser if they are not given adequate opportunity to develop their resources to the full.

If these 12 rights are guaranteed, a social order will be strong in the free acceptance of its members and their willing co-operation in its maintenance. These 12 rights include all that is necessary for the full development of personality. Where they are lacking there is social weakness, stimulus to discontent and revolt. They do not of themselves guarantee a perfect society but they remove evils which many would find intolerable and they put in people's hands the instruments to use in remedying evils without overthrowing the social order.

For the most part, though not altogether, we can congratulate ourselves that these rights are fairly well established in our country. It is this that gives our society its comparatively high stability in this age of social turmoil.

But we can not rest secure until these rights are completely established. The world around us will not be secure, and therefore we will not be secure, until they are well established in most of the rest of the world. The peoples of the world are today too closely related for their social orders to maintain stability one-half authoritarian and one-half free. It may be a long time before we can hope that freedom will spread behind the iron curtain. But in those countries which now have a large measure of freedom there can be no security unless all these rights which constitute the conditions of a free social order can be progressively attained.

This fact places upon all the people of the free countries, and particularly upon us Americans, the duty of working to ensure the maintenance and expansion of these basic human rights in all those countries where we can make our influence felt.

The fulfillment of this task is obviously in the interest of the American community. It must be admitted, however, that to work for, uphold, and respect these rights of others is not always obviously in the interest of every person at every time. It will often appear to an individual that he can better promote the satisfaction of his own private interests by violating some one of the rights of others, or at least by neglecting to give them needed support at times when such support is apt to be troublesome or costly. This raises the question as to whether there may not sometimes be a conflict between the two generally recognized types of duty referred to earlier, that is, duties to one's fellows to fulfill the requirements of a generally satisfactory social order, and duties to oneself to fulfill the requirements of maintaining integrity of personality and, with it, the basic conditions of true personal happiness.

This problem must be squarely faced. We must not hide from ourselves the fact that there is often a conflict between private interest and public interest. The crucial mistake of the Liberalism of the eighteenth and nineteenth centuries was that it failed to recognize this fact. It assumed that all interest is self-interest, that therefore an enlightened self-interest (interpreted as an enlightened selfishness modified only by sympathetic concern for family and friends and some compassion for human suffering) is the best that can be expected from human motivation.

From this same view of human nature Thomas Hobbes drew the conclusion that only authoritarian regimentation by the sovereign power of the state could save society from a war of all against all. But the Liberals put their trust in democracy, hoping that the free clash of private interests, expressed through popularly elected legislatures, would issue in a highest common denominator of public interest. They also were encouraged by the laissez-faire economic theory to believe that free competition for private wealth was the surest way to bring about that abundant production and broad distribution of material goods which would best serve the public interest.

In its application to politics, however, the theory proved wrong because large and well-organized groups, pursuing their own interest without thought of the public welfare, are able to exploit and oppress smaller and unorganized groups. In its application to economics the theory failed because accumulated wealth gives power and power corrupts. It led to the horrors of the industrial revolution, and this in turn led to reaction in the totalitarianisms of left and right which have repudiated Liberalism and all its works. Clearly, Liberalism, so far as it has relied on the sufficiency of enlightened self-interest, has failed. It has only succeeded, or indeed survived, in so far as there has found expression within it another motivation, an interest in the public welfare, organized and directed by individuals who manifest a high degree of devotion to the common good.

Enlightened self-interest fails to realize the common good for two reasons: first, because the profits of selfishness can often be reaped quickly and safely while the social damage it causes works slowly and spreads widely, not falling severely on the one who initiated it; secondly, because the promotion of movements for the common good needs the devoted leadership of people who get more criticism than gratitude for their pains and reap little or no economic reward for their service. But it is a fact that such devoted leadership exists, and that selfishness in the masses is not entirely unrestrained. These facts therefore indicate that there is something wrong with the theory that man is basically and essentially selfish and that all interest is self-interest.

If we examine this proposition, that all interest is self-interest, we find that it has a subtle ambiguity which hides a semantic fallacy. In one sense it is a truism; in another sense it is a falsehood. It is a truism if it means that every interest is an interest _of_ a self. Only selves have interests; and the satisfaction of an interest brings satisfaction to the self. But it is false if it means that every interest is an interest _in_ the self. Most of our interests are extroverted.

The direct pursuit of happiness is therefore a delusion and a snare. The Greeks long ago discovered the paradox that "to get pleasure we must forget it." To become an egoist is a personal tragedy. To be saved from this tragedy we need to develop interests in objects outside us, objective interests that are strong enough to absorb us. We need to find objectives that really grip us, lift us out of ourselves, call forth the full measure of thought and energy of which we are capable, and hold us throughout the years by opening up continuously ever new opportunities for constructive activity, with new problems calling for our devoted attention. Then life is full of satisfaction because it is full of interested activity. Happiness and satisfaction are ours without our pursuing them, because we have forgotten them in the pursuit of something more important.

Where shall we find an objective of such strong and lasting interest? The answer is really not difficult. Human beings are the most interesting of all objects. Science, art and other objects acquire most of their interest from their relation to human beings. And in so far as we take an interest in human beings it is normally in their well-being, rather than their ill-being, that we find satisfaction. Anger and hatred are exceptional attitudes usually due to fear and frustration; and the sadistic enjoyment of other people's suffering is a relatively rare mental abnormality. Most of man's inhumanity to man is not the expression of a direct extroverted interest but the incidental result of an introverted interest in the power, prestige, and feeling-states of the self. Extroverted interest in human beings therefore normally takes the form of an interest in human welfare. And this is the kind of interest which, if it plays the dominant part in the life of the individual, works most powerfully to maintain genuine integrity of personality and create the basic conditions of true happiness.

The philosophy of human motivation on which Fascism, Communism, and laissez-faire Liberalism alike rest is therefore profoundly mistaken. It rests on a semantic fallacy and on a failure to analyze accurately the real ends in which human beings find satisfaction. So far as the predominant attitudes of life are concerned there is no incompatibility between the duty to self and the duty to society. It sounds like a paradox, but the paradox is profoundly true. Its truth is attested by the personality studies of modern psychology. But it was discerned long ago by the insight of philosophers and religious teachers. It is stated in the "hedonistic paradox" of the Greeks which we have already quoted: "To get pleasure we must forget it." It is also expressed in two of the most piquant sayings of Jesus: "Seek ye first the kingdom of God and all these things shall be added unto you." "Whosoever will save his life shall lose it, but whosoever will lose his life for my sake shall find it." We find ourselves, and reap the fruit of happiness, when we lose ourselves in interest in human welfare.

This means that there is hope for progressive attainment and expansion of the conditions of a free social order by drawing men out of themselves to take a wider interest in their fellows. It means that it should not be impossible to find leaders with devotion to the cause of humanity beyond the claims of any selfish interest. But it does not mean that the duty to society and to self--to one's own inner integrity--will never involve self-sacrifice. The path of high devotion is definitely not the same as that envisaged in the doctrine of "enlightened self-interest." The prophet still is sometimes stoned or crucified. But if we are to cultivate the kind of personality that can realize the strength and joy of devotion to human welfare, we must be prepared to go through with it when the going gets tough. The sort of leader who can help society in solution of its present problems must be the sort of man or woman who, with singleness of purpose, can take the rough with the smooth, working for the common good, finding satisfaction in that work itself, and not be diverted from it by any thought of personal prestige or easy private happiness.

APPENDIXES

I. Suggested Supplementary Reading
II. About the Authors

APPENDIX I

SUGGESTED SUPPLEMENTARY READING

SCIENCE IS EVERYBODY'S BUSINESS

Atomic Energy Act of 1946. 79th U.S. Congress, 2nd Session, Public Law 585. Washington, U.S. Government Printing Office.
Atomic Energy Commission. Semiannual Reports. Washington, U.S. Government Printing Office.
J. P. Baxter. Scientists Against Time. Boston, Little, Brown, 1952.
W. I. B. Beveridge. The Art of Scientific Investigation. New York, W. W. Norton, 1950.
Bulletin of the Atomic Scientists. Chicago, Atomic Scientists of Chicago.
H. Butterfield. Origins of Modern Science. New York, Macmillan, 1951.
I. B. Cohen. Science, Servant of Man. Boston, Little, Brown, 1948.
J. B. Conant. Science and Common Sense. New Haven, Yale University Press, 1951.
Walter Gellhorn. Security, Loyalty, and Science. Ithaca, Cornell University Press, 1950.
Selig Hecht. Explaining the Atom. New York, The Viking Press, 1947.
Ralph Lapp. The New Force. New York, Harper and Bros., 1953.
The National Science Foundation Act. 81st Congress, 2nd Session, Public Law 507. Washington, U.S. Government Printing Office.

NATIONS IN TURMOIL

T. A. Bailey. America Faces Russia. Ithaca, Cornell University Press, 1950.
J. F. Dulles, War or Peace. New York, Macmillan, 1950.
C. V. Easum. Half-Century of Conflict. New York, Harper, 1952.
R. N. C. Hunt. The Theory and Practice of Communism. New York, Macmillan, 1951.
S. Mikolajczyk. The Pattern of Soviet Domination. London, S. Low, Marston, 1948.

Fairfield Osborn. Our Plundered Planet. Boston, Little, Brown, 1948.
L. K. Rosinger. The State of Asia. New York, Knopf, 1951.
W. B. Smith. My Three Years in Moscow. Philadelphia, Lippincott, 1950.
E. A. Speiser. The United States and the Near East. Cambridge, Harvard University Press, 1950.
Gustav Stolper. German Realities. New York, Reynal and Hitchcock, 1948.

OUR WORLD COMMUNITY

Everyman's United Nations. 2nd Edition. New York, United Nations. 1950.
E. P. Chase. The United Nations in Action. New York, McGraw-Hill, 1950.
W. O. Douglas. Strange Lands and Friendly People. New York, Harper, 1951.
L. L. Leonard. International Organization. New York, McGraw-Hill, 1951.
The United Nations Bulletin. (Published by the U.N. Department of Public Information every two weeks.)

WHAT THE UNITED STATES CAN DO

Carskadon and Modley. U.S.A., Measure of a Nation. New York, Macmillan, 1949.
The Constitution of the United States.
W. R. Espy. Bold New Program. New York, Harper, 1950.
Editors of Fortune. U.S.A., the Permanent Revolution. New York, Prentice-Hall, 1951.
E. P. Herring. The Politics of Democracy. New York, W. W. Norton, 1940.
Gerald Johnson. This American People. New York, Harper, 1951.
David Lilienthal. This I Do Believe. New York, Harper, 1949.
Theodore Morgan. Introduction to Economics. New York, Prentice-Hall, 1950.
S. H. Slichter. The American Economy. New York, Knopf, 1949.
U.S. President; Annual Economic Report. Washington, U.S. Government Printing Office.
B. L. Smith, H. D. Lasswell, R. D. Casey. Propaganda, Communication and Public Opinion. Princeton, Princeton University Press, 1946.

APPENDIX II

ABOUT THE AUTHORS

Eugene P. Boardman (Chapter 16, "Asia Emerges")

Associate professor of history, Dr. Boardman obtained a Ph.D. degree in the field of his specialty, Far Eastern history, from Harvard University. He taught at the American University of Beirut in Lebanon from 1932 to 1935. His knowledge of the Chinese and Japanese languages enabled him to serve as Marine Japanese Language Officer in the Pacific War Theater between 1941 and 1946. He spent part of 1951 in Hongkong as a Fulbright Fellow, shortly after the Chinese Communist government had gained control of the Chinese mainland.

Marshall Clagett (Chapter 4, "Science Has a Long History")

Associate professor of the history of science, Dr. Clagett received his Ph.D. degree in history and the history of science at Columbia University, where he taught the history of science before joining the faculty of the University of Wisconsin. His research interests are in the history of physics and of ancient and medieval science, and he has written several books on these subjects. He was a Guggenheim fellow in 1946 and again in 1950-51. He is on the editorial board of the journal Isis.

Noble Clark (Chapter 11, "Mouths to Feed")

Associate Director of the Agricultural Experiment Station of the University of Wisconsin, Mr. Clark has devoted his career to harnessing science to the task of increasing the quantity, improving the quality and lessening the cost of crops and livestock. In 1947 he headed an international mission to Poland to work out methods to increase food production, and in 1948 he was deputy director-general of the United Nations Food and Agriculture Organization.

ABOUT THE AUTHORS

James F. Crow (Chapter 12, "Mouths to Feed")

Associate professor of zoology and genetics, Dr. Crow received his Ph.D. degree from the University of Texas. He taught at Dartmouth College before joining the faculty of the University of Wisconsin. His specialty is the genetics of the fruit fly, Drosophila. He is associate editor of the journal, Genetics.

Farrington Daniels (Chapters on scientific research and atomic energy)

Professor of Chemistry, Dr. Daniels received his Ph.D. degree at Harvard in 1914 and has taught at the University of Wisconsin since 1920. During 1945-46 he was Director of the "Metallurgical Laboratory," the war-time atomic energy headquarters in Chicago, and when the Argonne National Laboratory replaced the Metallurgical Laboratory in peacetime, he was Chairman of the Board from 1946 to 1948. He is author of four books in the field of physical chemistry. Among his research interests are chemical kinetics, photosynthesis, atomic power, solar energy, and geochemistry of uranium. He was elected President of the American Chemical Society for 1953.

Chester V. Easum (Chapter 15, "Trouble in Europe")

A professor of history, Dr. Easum saw Europe as a Rhodes Scholar and as an infantry officer between 1916 and 1920 and as a Research Fellow of the Oberlaender Trust in 1936-1937. He received his Ph.D. degree from the University of Wisconsin in 1928. Books written by him include The Americanization of Carl Schurz; Carl Schurz, vom deutschen Einwanderer sum americanischen Staatsmann; Prince Henry of Prussia, Brother of Frederick the Great. He has recently written a chapter on Germany in the symposium Contemporary Europe. His latest work is Half-Century of Conflict. In 1954 he will be engaged as Research Fellow of the Guggenheim Memorial Foundation on a study of the Hohenzollern Empire.

ABOUT THE AUTHORS

A. Campbell Garnett (Chapter 28, "Life, Liberty, and the Pursuit of Happiness")

Professor of Philosophy Garnett received his education in his native Australia and in England. He came to the University of Wisconsin in 1937 and in 1949 was appointed chairman of the Department of Philosophy. He is the author of seven books, the last of which, The Moral Nature of Man, was published in 1952.

Fred Harvey Harrington (Chapter 24, "Our Foreign Policy; Toward a Better World")

Professor of history, Dr. Harrington took his Ph.D. degree at New York University and has specialized in American diplomatic history. He was a Guggenheim Fellow in 1943-44 and has written God, Mammon and the Japanese, a book on Korean-American relations, and Fighting Politician: Maj.-Gen. N. P. Banks.

Charles W. M. Hart (Chapter 17, "Colonial Peoples in Transition")

Associate Professor Hart joined the Department of Anthropology and Sociology at the University of Wisconsin in 1948. He received his education and anthropological training in Australia, the land of his birth, at the University of Sydney, in the United States at the University of Chicago, and in England at the London School of Economics. He spent several years in social research work in the Pacific area before assuming teaching duties at the University of Toronto, Canada, in 1932.

Richard Hartshorne (Chapter 12, "World Patterns in Politics and Geography")

A professor of geography and, in 1949, president of the Association of American Geographers, Dr. Hartshorne received his Ph.D. degree from the University of Chicago in 1924. From 1941-45 he served in the Office of Strategic Services as Chief of the Geography Division and Assistant

Chief of the Research and Analysis Branch. In 1949 he was a visiting professor at the National War College. He is author of The Nature of Geography and of numerous articles on political geography.

Ralph K. Huitt (Chapter 25, "Making Sense out of Politics and Pressure Groups")

Ralph K. Huitt is a native of Texas. He received his Ph.D. at the University of Texas in 1949. His fields of teaching and research include politics, public opinion, and legislation. He is now an assistant professor of political science at the University of Wisconsin. He is a contributor to the American Political Science Review.

C. Leonard Huskins (Chapter 9, "Controlling Science in Russia")

Late professor of botany and cytology at the University of Wisconsin, Dr. Huskins received his preliminary education in Canada and then returned to England, his birthplace, to obtain the Ph.D. and D.Sc. degrees in Botany at the University of London. While in England he worked with Karpetchenko and other Russian botanists and geneticists between 1925 and 1930. He visited Russia in 1926, at their invitation, and corresponded on scientific matters with Russian scientists until the Iron Curtain was drawn after World War II. His recent researches were concerned with linking descriptive cytology and cytogenetics with biophysics and biochemistry. In 1951 he was elected president of the Biology and Medicine Section of the Royal Society of Canada. He passed away in July, 1953.

Mark H. Ingraham (Chapter 27, "Intellectual Freedom-Its Social Use")

Dr. Ingraham has long been professionally concerned with the subject of his chapter. In 1938-39 he was president of the American Association of University Professors, and since 1942 he has been Dean of the College of Letters and Science at the University of Wisconsin. As Dean, he deals with broad educational policies, control of the academic programs of students in his college, with personnel and budget matters, --and, of course, with problems of intel-

ABOUT THE AUTHORS

lectual and academic freedom. His special field is mathematics in which he took his Ph.D. from the University of Chicago in 1924.

Theodore Morgan (Chapters 20-23 on domestic and international economics)

An associate professor of economics, Dr. Morgan received his Ph.D. degree from Harvard University in 1941. He spent the years 1932-34 and 1936-38 in Hawaii, travelling to the Orient in 1934 and to Europe in 1935. A specialist in business cycles, he served as Deputy Governor of the Central Bank of Ceylon from mid-1951 to mid-1953. He is author of: Introduction to Economics, Income and Employment; and Hawaii, A Century of Economic Change - 1778-1876.

Ralph O. Nafziger (Chapter 26, "Making Sense out of Propaganda")

Professor Nafziger is Director of the School of Journalism at the University of Wisconsin. A former newspaperman, he became a teacher after several years of graduate study. He obtained his Ph.D. degree at the University of Wisconsin in 1936. During World War II he served for a time as Chief of the Media Division, Office of War Information.

Michael B. Petrovich (Chapter 13, "Russia and the Communist Way of Life")

A native of Cleveland, Ohio, Dr. Petrovich is an historian who spent the war years, 1943-46, as a research analyst for the Balkan Section of the Office of Strategic Services. From 1946 to 1948 he was a Rockefeller Fellow in Russian and Balkan Studies and was in Eastern Europe when the Russians began to close the Iron Curtain. As assistant professor of the University of Wisconsin, he will spend two years of research in Greece.

ABOUT THE AUTHORS

Llewellyn E. Pfankuchen (Chapter 14, "The Way We Think in the Democratic West," and Chapters 18 and 19 on collective security and world government)

A professor of political science, Dr. Pfankuchen received his Ph.D. degree from Harvard in 1931. He is a specialist in international law, is the author of a documentary textbook on this subject, and was a member of the International Secretariat at the San Francisco Conference which framed the charter for the U.N. Organization.

William B. Sarles (Chapter 8, "Controlling Science in the United States")

Dr. Sarles received his Ph.D. degree from the same University that enjoys his services as a professor of bacteriology. During World War II he served in the Navy and since the war has been a consultant to the Research and Development Board of the Department of Defense.

Thomas M. Smith (Co-editor)

Mr. Smith has been assistant in the course on Contemporary Trends for four years. He will take his Ph.D. in the History of Science at the University of Wisconsin and has accepted an assistant professorship at the California Institute of Technology where he will devote part of his time to the history of aviation.

Abbott Payson Usher (Chapter 10, "Man Molds the World")

An economic historian, Dr. Usher was a visiting professor at the University of Wisconsin from 1949 to 1951 after retiring from Harvard, where he received his Ph.D. in 1910. He has given special attention to the history of modern technology and has published several books including, *An Introduction to the Industrial History of England*, *A History of Mechanical Inventions* (scheduled to be republished in revised and extended form in 1954), and *The Early History of Deposit Banking in Mediterranean Europe*. He has co-authored with Professors Bowden and Karpovich *An Economic History of Europe Since 1750*.

INDEX

Academic freedom, 322, 329
    abuses, 330
Academic tenure, 330
Academies of science, 36
Acheson-Lilienthal report, 67
Acton, 91
Africa, 136, 137
Agricultural changes,
    transportation, 111
    improvements, 118, 120
Agriculture and industrialization, 122, 277
Air warfare routes, 145
Alpha particles, 11
American Assoc'n University Professors, 321, 329
American
    companies abroad, 292
    cultural influence, 290
    democracy vs. communism, 290
    government, checks and balances, 303
    political system, 303
    and Russian histories, 149
    strength in democracy, 159
Antiexpansion attitudes in U.S., 287
Appendices, 347
Aristotle, 31, 32
Army administrators in former colonies, 214
Asia, 138, 140, 145, 147, 188, 196, 197, 199
Astronomy, history, 30
Atlantic nations, 138, 144, 147
Atom, 9, 14, 17
Atomic age beginning, 7
Atomic bomb, 21, 27
    civilian defense, 62
    control, 59
    conversion to electricity, 69
    tests, 59, 60
Atomic Energy Act, 65, 349
Atomic Energy Commission, 21, 23, 65, 66, 349
Atomic energy control by UN, 67, 68, 233, 234
    secrecy, 66
    world gov't. for, 68

Atomic pile, 7, 22
Atomic power, 24, 25, 26, 27
Atomic scientists, 64
Atomic warfare, 67, 69, 157, 223, 230
Australia, 142, 143
Austria, 179

B

Bailey, 349
Balance of power, 164
Baruch, 67
Baxter, 349
Becquerel, 10
Bell report, 213
Berlin, 184, 186
Beta particles, 11
Beveridge, 349
Bipartisan foreign policy, 296
Birth rates, 119, 124, 126
Bismark, 179, 180
Boardman, 188, 351
Bohr, 12, 17
Bonn, 186
Boxer uprising, 193
Brandeis, 329
Brazil, 137
Breeder piles, 25
British parliament, 303
Bulletin of the Atomic Scientists, 64, 349
Bush, 74, 93
Butterfield, 349

C

Can the world feed its people?, 125
Canada, 130
Capitalism, 165, 172
Carskadon, 350
Casey, 350
Censorship, a creeping paralysis, 319
Chadwick, 13
Chang Kai-Shek, 182, 194
Chase, 350
China, 139, 146, 193, 221, 222, 226

Chinese power in Asia, 195,
Clagett, 28, 351
Clark, 116, 351
Civilian Defense, 62, 63, 64
Civil liberties, 296
Cohen, 349
Cold war, 222
Collective security, 217
Colombo plan, 279
Colonial administrations, 209
Colonies,
    education, 202, 203
    freedom, 210, 211
    indirect rule, 201
    pattern, 200, 201, 202
    peoples in transition, 199
    problems, no middle class, 202
    revolution, 199, 200, 205
Communism, 117, 140, 153, 154, 172, 185, 285
    and the Far East, 157
    fear of, 160
    in China, 194, 195
    objections, 332
    a perilous challenge, 149
    weakness in, 161
Communist
    ambitions, 158
    friction, 157
    opportunity in poverty areas, 213
Compartmentalization of research, 75, 76
Compton, 20
Conant, 349
Congress
    and foreign affairs, 295
    and president, 303
Constitution, U.S., 350
Contemporary trends, iii
Controlling science in Russia, 81
Controlling science in the U.S., 71
Controls in science, 47
Cooperation, 336
Cuba, 209
Culture enrichment, 328
Curie, 11
Critical size, 22, 26
Crow, 116, 352

D

Dangers in opposing free discussion, 316
Daniels, iii, 1, 9, 17, 39, 49, 59, 352
Decentralization, cities, 63
Declaration, human rights, 336
Democracy, 84, 169, 170, 171
Democratic west, 163
Depression, 165, 273
    and inflation, 259
Devaluation, 246, 262
Devoted leadership, 343, 344
Dialectical materialism, 85, 96
Dicoumarol, 51
Disarmament, 223
Diversification policy, 277, 278
Dollar scarcity, 245, 246, 247
Douglas, 350
Dulles, 349
DuPont Company, 20, 53
Duty, 335, 344

E

Easum, 178, 349, 352
Economic
    ambitions, 275, 276
    attitudes, influence of the past, 274
    changes, tensions, 113
    conditions abroad, 280, 292
    depression, 259, 262, 263, 264
        banking system, 270
        causes of, 267, 269, 270, 271
        fallacious explanations, 267, 268, 269
        foreign policies, 270
        interest rates, 260, 261
        public spending, 263, 267, 270, 271
        recovery, 265, 266
        speculation, 269, 270
    development, gov't. aid, 276
    difficulties, postwar Europe, 280
        specialized agriculture, 277
    effects, gov't. spending, 261
        political decisions, 274

INDEX

history since 1930, 273
post war predictions, 266
"pump priming", 263, 264
recovery, 265, 266
specialization, 111, 276, 277
Education
  natives, 208
  world farmers, 122
Einstein, 15, 18
Eisenhower, 183
Electron, 10
Element, 9
Energy requirements, 3
Energy resources, 105, 113
English gov't., 303
Enlightened self-interest, 342, 343
Equality of political rights, 340
Errors, 41
Espy, 350
Europe, 132, 133, 134, 144
  economy, competition, 112
  importance, 115
  trouble in, 178
European Recovery Program, 279, 281, 282
European struggle, 147
European wars, 134
Everyman's UN, 350
Exchange rates, 246
Exploding the atom, 17
Exploring the atom, 9
Exports from U.S., 268

F

Federal union, 231
Fermi, 15, 18
Financial aid to needy Countries, 278, 279
Fiscal policy, 261
Fission, 1, 6, 16, 17, 19
Food
  economy, 103, 104
  production, increase, 120, 121
  requirements, 2
  transportation, 116
Foreign policy in American politics, 295
Fortune editors, 350
Free discussion, 296
Freedom, 322, 327, 328, 329, 339

Freedom (continued)
  intellectual, 321, 322
  to marry, 339
  of religion, 339
  of speech, 329, 339
  of teachers, 330
Freight movements, 109
Fulbright program, 293
Fusion, 1, 8

G

Galileo, 35
Gamma rays, 11
Garnett, 335, 353
Geiger counter, 11
Gellhorn, 349
Genetics, 82, 84
Geographical political patterns, 128
Geographical realms, 128
Germany, 178, 180, 184
  political importance, 221
  power vacuum, 185, 187
  Western, 186
Gold standard, 262, 270
Greece, 224
Greek science, 31, 32
Groves, 18
Guns or butter, 264, 265

H

Hahn, 16
Half-century of conflict, 178
Half-life, 13
Hanford, 20
Harrington, 285, 297, 353
Hart, 199, 353
Hartshorne, 128, 353
Hawaii, 143
Health through science, 324
Hecht, 349
Helping the world, 175
Heredity and environment, 86, 87, 88, 89
Herring, 350
High death rate, 124
Hiroshima, 18, 59
History of science, 28
Hitler, 133, 181
Hobbes, 342
Holmes, 329
Hoover, 262
Huitt, 301, 354

INDEX

Human rights, 225, 339, 340, 341
    and obligations, 335, 336, 337
Human welfare, 344
Hunt, 349
Huskins, 81, 354
Hybrid corn, 49

I

Ideologies, Soviet Union and West, 163
Impoverished areas, 251
Incentives, industrial development, 57
Incomes, contrast in, 251, 252
India, 140, 141, 206, 207
Indochina, 140, 197
Indonesia, 196, 198, 211, 212, 224
Industrial development, 55, 57
Industrial research, 53
Industrialization trends, 276
Inflation, 259, 267, 271, 272
Influencing politicians, 306,307
Information channels, 319
Information on public affairs, 312
Ingraham, iv, 321, 354
Inside of research, 39
Intellectual freedom, 321, 322, 323, 325, 326
Interest groups, politics, 305
International bank, 279
International Court of Justice, 220
International organizations, 175
Iron consumption, 106
Iron curtain, 134
Isolationist views, 287
Isotopes, 13, 19, 23, 24
Italian colonies and UN, 224

J

Japan, 139, 183, 194
    economic difficulties, 190
    post war reform, 189, 190
Java, 142
Johnson, 350

K

Kaiser, William II, 180, 181
Kapista, 97
Keynes, 166, 167, 168, 263, 273
Kipling, 201
Korea, 140, 190, 191, 192, 226, 227
Kuomintang, 193

L

Laissez-faire policy, 166, 167, 168, 172, 342
Lamarck, 87
Land routes, 146
Lapp, 349
Lasswell, 301, 350
Leaders in underdeveloped countries needed, 208
Leadership, 311, 345
League of Nations, 218, 226, 230
Legal, orderly procedure, 332, 333
Lenin, 82, 97, 98
Liberalism, 341, 342
Lie, Trygve, 225
Life, Liberty and pursuit of happiness, 335
Lilienthal, 350
Link, 51
Lippman, 83
Litvinov, 181
Lobbying, 305, 306
    attempts to regulate, 308
Logic, 31, 32
Los Alamos, 21
Loyalty check, 76, 78, 79
Luxembourg Declaration, 235, 236
Lysenko, 82, 84, 86, 89, 91, 95

M

Malthus, 117
Majority and minority rights, 169, 170, 171
Majority rule, 331, 332
Manchu monarchy, 193
Manhattan District, 18
Man molds the world, 103

INDEX

Manufacturing, encouragement, 276
Mao Tse-Tung, 196
Maritime fringe, 111, 112
Marshall plan, 185, 279, 281, 282, 288, 291
Marx, 95, 98, 153, 167, 173, 184
Marxian socialism, obsolete, 113
Mediterranian, 135
Meitner, 16, 17
Mendeleev, 12
Mexico, 131
Middle class, importance, 213
Middle east, 136
Mikolajczyck, 349
Mineral eoonomy, 103, 107
Missionaries, 204
Modley, 350
Mohammedan area, 135
Monetary policy, 260
Monopoly, a public trust, 58
Monroe doctrine, 131
Moral purpose, 333
Morgan, 242, 251, 259, 275, 350, 355
Mouths to feed, 116
Muller, 85, 98

N

Nafziger, 310, 355
National Science Foundation, 73, 349
Nations in turmoil, 101, 102
Natural resources, 257
Nehru, 199
New ideas, 326, 327
Newton, 13, 14, 19, 35
Neutrons, 20
Nitrogen fixation, 51, 52
North American realm, 130
Nuclear chain, 7, 19
Nuclear reactors, 22, 24
Nucleus, 12

O

Oak Ridge, 19
Office of European Economic Co-operation, 282
Oppenheimer, 21
Osborn, 349
Our foreign policy, 285
Our world community, 215

Overcrowding, 205
Overpopulation, 127, 204, 257, 258
Oversimplification, problems, 286

P

Pakistan, 141
Palestine, 224
Paris conference for European recovery program, 281, 282
Patents, 57, 58
Peace of Westphalia, 179
Penicillin, 50
Petroleum of middle east, 136
Petrovich, 148, 355
Pfankuchen, 163, 217, 230, 356
Philippines, 141, 142, 197, 213
Photosynthesis, 3
Pilot plant, 56
Plant growth, 23
Plutonium, 20, 25
Point four program, 125, 126, 212, 213, 225, 279, 282, 291, 292
Poland, partition, 182
Political
  discussion, foreign policies, 296
  independence, 213, 225
  influence, home district, 305, 306
  parties, function, 303
Politics, indispensible, 302
Politics and social decisions, 301
Polymerization, 54
Population control, 127, 258
Population increase, 116, 123
Population types, 119
Poverty formerly taken for granted, 275
President, 303, 304, 350
Pressure groups, 301, 306, 313
Preventive war fallacy, 158
Price controls, 271, 272
Private vs. public interest, 341
Production, high rate necessary, 273
Production, social cost, 244
Productivity of land, 107

Propaganda, 306, 310, 313, 315
  and the "big lie", 315
  critical evaluation, 318
  freedom for, 317
  good and bad, 313
  in social decisions, 310
  sources, made public, 320
  suppression dangerous, 317
Prosperity, resources needed, 253
Prosperity in U.S., 252, 253, 254, 255, 256
Proton, 13
Public health, 251, 252
Public influence, 308
Public opinion vital, 311
Public ownership, 173
Purchasing power in U.S. largely domestic, 268
Pursuit of happiness, 343

R

Race barriers, 201
Radiation sickness research, 42, 43
Radioactive carbon, 13, 23
Radioactivity, 15, 20
Radium, 11
Railroad transportation, 108, 110, 111
Rationing, 271
Reconstruction Finance Corporation, 261, 262
Research, 45, 46, 71, 73, 255
Research
  in agriculture, 121
  control, 73, 74
  in social sciences, 47
  support, 55
Resources, political importance, 115
Roentgen, 10
Role of gov't., 165, 166
Roosevelt, 18, 262
Rosinger, 350
Rudeness toward public servants, 330, 331
Russia, 134, 135
  and the Allies, 156
  and the communist way of life, 148
  and the west, 99
  in World War II, 182

Russian-American
  civilizations, 152
  conflict, 207, 208
  early friendship, 151
  economies, 152
  history, 149, 150
  political differences, 151
Russian
  economic recovery, 282
  geneticists, 89, 90, 91
  philosophy, 96, 98, 99
  revolution, 150
Russo-Japanese war, 191
Rutherford, 11, 14

S

Sabotage, 316
Samoa, 206
San Francisco, 230
Sarles, 71, 356
Science, 29, 38, 40, 41
  can't be stopped, 324
  everybody's business, ix
  fundamental and applied, 92, 93
  history, 29, 33, 35, 36, 37
  influence, 37
  laboratories, 37
  pure and applied, 30
  put to work, 49
  requires freedom, 326
  trends in Russia, 96, 97
Sciences, difference in the, 41, 42
Scientific method, 35, 39, 47, 81, 85
Scientific research, techniques, 44
Scientists, 46
Scientists' freedom, 79, 80
Seaborg, 20
Secrecy, 18, 66, 75, 76, 77
Security
  against violence, 336
  from false defamation, 337
  of livelihood, 337
  of property, 338
  from want, 338
Self-gov't., when ready, 206, 207
Shatter zone, 133, 136
Siberia, 140, 146
Sino-Soviet pact, 195

Slichter, 350
Smith, 165, 350
Smith, T. M., 356
Social behavior improving, 325
Social progress lagging behind technology, 325
Socialism, 167, 172, 173, 174
Soil conservation, 121
Sokolovsky, 186
Solar engine, 6
South America, 130, 131, 132, 137, 211
Soviet Union policy, mistakes in, 160
Soviet Union's agreement with Hitler, 155
Soviet Union and atomic Control, 157
Soviet Union,
  changing foreign policy, 154, 155, 156
  dissatisfaction, 160
  geographical importance, 133
  in world economy, 115
Speiser, 350
Stalin, 181, 182, 183, 184
Stimson, 64
Stolper, 350
Strassman, 16
Streit, 231
Sunlight, 1
Sun Yat-sen, 193
Supplementary reading, 349
Syria, 224
Szilard, 18

T

Tariffs, 225, 243, 247
Third world war, 297
Thirty years war, 179
Thomas, 332
Thompson, 10
Tito, 160, 184
de Toqueville, 92
Trade,
  implies specialization, 242, 243
  makes world more productive, 242
  restrictions, 243, 244, 245
    fallacies in, 244
    for infant industry, 245

Trade restrictions (cont'd.)
  from war, 244, 245
Transition, food economy to fuel economy, 105
Transportation, 107, 108, 110, 111
Treaty of Versailles, 180, 287
Truman, 18, 126
Truman doctrine, 185

U

Undernourishment, 116
Unemployment, 261, 265
United Nations, 62, 67, 68, 175, 176, 177, 217, 219, 221, 222, 225, 226, 227, 230, 279
  administrative units, 218
  atomic energy, 223, 233
  Bulletin, 350
  charter, 218
  collective security, 228, 229
  disarmament, 223
  evaluation, 222, 223, 224, 225, 226, 229
  failures, 222
  General Assembly, 218, 219, 228
  handicaps, 221, 222
  and Korean war, 227, 228
  importance, 297
  increasing strength, 229
  organization chart, 219
  peace settlements, 220
  police force, 223
  secretary general, 222
  Security Council, 218, 220, 222, 226
  successes, 224
  technical assistance, 225
  test in Korea, 192
  Trusteeship Council, 218, 219, 225
  veto power, 223, 227, 228, 239
United States,
  attitudes, World gov't., 237, 238, 239
  commercial expansion, 286
  congressional difficulties, 305
  cooperating countries, 292
  debt, 264, 266

United States, (cont'd.)
   economic depression, 260
   expanding nation, 286
   feeding world, 125
   financial aid given, 279, 283
   financial strength abroad, 291
   foreign investments, 286
   foreign policies, 289, 293, 294
   foreign responsibilities, 288
   geographical importance, 130, 131
   human rights, 340
   increasing productivity, 246
   influence abroad, 144, 286, 290, 291, 293
   military responsibilities abroad, 288, 289
   moral leadership, 161, 162
   passages to Europe, 144, 145
   policy in southeast Asia, 198
   political parties, loose federations, 304
   post war difficulties, 148
   productive giant, 251
   prosperity,
      reasons for, 251, 252, 253, 354, 255
   special foreign ties, 294
   technical assistance abroad, 283
   tied to world economy, 288
   two political parties, 304
   and United Nations, 294, 295, 297
   westward expansion, 286
Universities' responsibility for discoveries, 58
UNRRA, 279
Uranium, 19, 25, 27
   splitting, 6
Uranium-235, 19, 25
Urey, 19
Usher, 103, 356

V

Victorian liberalism, obsolete, 113

Vietnam, 197
Voice of America, 290, 314, 315

W

Ward, 167
Water transportation, freight, 108, 110
Weed killer research, 46
Western civilization, 138, 148
Western economies, 175
Western society, consent of governed, 176, 177
Western way of life, 164
What the United States can do, 249
What we can do, 299

Whitman, 318
Why trade?, 242
Wigner, 18
Wisconsin Alumni Research Foundation, 58
Workers' skill, improvements, 256
World before 1914, 164
World constitution, 236
World economy, instability, 114
World federal gov't., 235, 236, 237
World gov't., 230, 231, 232
   analogy with U.S., 239
   by agreement, 233
   in atomic energy, 68, 175, 231, 235, 240, 241
   development slow, 240
   proposals and U.S. opinion, 237, 238, 239, 241
   representation in, 238
World patterns, 128
World phase in American history, 297
World poverty, 251, 252
World War I, 180, 183

X

X-rays, 10

Z

Zhukov, 186